Religions of India : A Multidimentional Study

Religions of India : A Multidimentional Study

U.S. Shaji

CYBER TECH PUBLICATIONS
4264/3, Ansari Road, Daryaganj, New Delhi-110002 (India)
Ph.: 011-23244078, 011-43559448 Fax: 011-23280028
E-Mail: cyberpublicationsdelhi@yahoo.com
Website: www.cybertechpublications.com

RELIGIONS OF INDIA : A MULTIDIMENTIONAL STUDY

U S Shaji

First Edition 2010

Published by : Asian Offset Printers

G.S. Rawat for **Cyber Tech Publications**
4264/3, Ansari Road, Daryaganj, New Delhi-110002 (India)
Ph.: 011-23244078, 011-43559448 Fax: 011-23280028
E-Mail: cyberpublicationsdelhi@yahoo.com
Website: www.cybertechpublications.com

Preface

India, the land of spirituality and philosophy considers religion as an integral part of its entire tradition. The worship of various religions and its rituals play a significant role in every aspect of human life in the country.

India is the birthplace of two great religions of the world, namely, Hinduism and Buddhism. It is also the birthplace of one of the oldest religions of the world, Zoroastrianism, and home to an ancient religion, Jainism. Sikhism is another very recognizable religion which began here bringing together the best aspects of Hinduism and Islam.

Followers of religions originated in other countries such as Islam, Christianity, Bahaism and Judaism also form a part of the population of secular nation, India. Hinduism accounts for 80% of the population of India. The second largest religion is Islam, at about thirteen percent of the population. Stating the hospitality of Hinduism towards all other religions, John Hardon writes, "However, the most significant feature of current Hinduism is its creation of a non-Hindu State, in which all religions are equal;..."

Other native Indian religions are Buddhism, Jainism, Sikhism. Ancient India had two philosophical streams of thought, the Shramana religions and the Vedic religion, parallel traditions that have existed side by side for thousands of years.

Both Buddhism and Jainism are continuations of Shramana traditions, while modern Hinduism is a continuation of the Vedic tradition. These co-existing traditions have been mutually influential. About two percent of Indians adhere to Christianity. Zoroastrianism and Judaism have an ancient history in India and each has several thousand Indian adherents.

Though inter-religious marriage is not widely practiced, Indians are generally tolerant of other religions and retain a secular outlook. Inter-community clashes have never found widespread support in the social mainstream, and it is generally perceived that the causes of religious conflicts are political rather than ideological in nature. India's religious diversity extends to the highest levels of government. The Constitution of India declares the nation to be a secular republic that must uphold the right of citizens to freely worship and propagate any religion or faith (with activities subject to reasonable restrictions for the sake of morality, law and order, etc).

— *Author*

CONTENTS

1

INTRODUCTION

India known as the land of spirituality and philosophy, was the birthplace of some religions, which even exist today in the world. The most dominant religion in India today is Hinduism. About 80% of Indians are Hindus. Hinduism is a colorful religion with a vast gallery of Gods and Goddesses. Hinduism is one of the ancient religions in the world. It is supposed to have developed about 5000 years ago. Later on in ancient period other religions developed in India.

Around 500 BC two other religions developed in India, namely, Buddhism and Jainism. Today only about 0.5% of Indians are Jains and about 0.7% are Buddhist. In ancient times Jainism and specially Buddhism were very popular in India. Indians who accepted Buddhist philosophy spread it not only within the Indian sub-continent but also to kingdoms east and south of India. These three ancient religions, Hinduism, Buddhism and Jainism, are seen as the molders of the India philosophy. In 'modern' period new religions were also established in India.

One comparatively new religion in India is Sikhism and it was established in the 15th century. About 2% of Indians are Sikhs. There were other attempts to create new religions in India but they did not always succeed. For example, a Moghul emperor, Akbar, who reigned between 1556-1605, tried to establish a new religion, Din-E-Elahi, but it did not survive. There are other religious philosophies whose believers see themselves as a separate religion, but they do not always get this recognition. For example Lingayat of south India see themselves as a different religion, while others see them as a sect of Hinduism. There are also some tribal communities who demand to be recognized as separate religion from Hinduism. In the 19th century some Hindu reformers tried to remodel Hinduism to adjust it to modern period.

Along with the religions that developed in India, there are followers of non-Indian religions. The largest non-Indian religion is Islam. They are about 12% of India's population. Christians are more then 2% of India's population. There are also Zoroastrians who even though make less then 0.01% of India's population, are known around India. There are also a few thousand Jews in India. Judaism and Christianity might have arrived in India before they arrived in Europe.

In the conventional narrative, Indian history begins with the birth of the Indus Valley Civilization in such sites as Mohenjo-Daro, Harappa, and Lothal, followed by the coming of the Aryans. These two phases are usually described as the pre-Vedic and Vedic periods. It is in the Vedic period that Hinduism first arose, though some elements of Hinduism are clearly drawn from the Indus Valley civilization. In the fourth century BCE, large parts of India were united under the emperor Ashoka; he also converted to Buddhism, and it is in his reign that Buddhism first spread to other parts of Asia. It is during the time of the Mauryas that Hinduism first began to take the shape that fundamentally informs the religion down to the present day, though popular or Puranic Hindism is generally dated to around the beginning of the Christian Era. Successor states were more fragmented. Islam first came to India in the eighth century, and by the eleventh century had firmly established itself in India as a political force; the North Indian dynasties of the Lodhis, Tughlaqs, and numerous others, whose remains are visible in Delhi and scattered elsewhere around North India, were finally succeeded by the Mughal empire, under which India once again achieved a large measure of political unity. These are certainly the generally accepted contours of Indian history before the advent of colonialism, though specialists are all inclined to write this history with particular emphases and accents.

The European presence in India dates to the sixteenth century, and it is in the very early part of the eighteenth century that the Mughal empire began to disintegrate, paving the way for regional states. In the contest for supremacy, the English emerged victors, their rule marked by the conquests at the battlefields of Plassey and Buxar. The Rebellion of 1857-58, which sought to restore Indian supremacy, was crushed; and with the subsequent crowning of Victoria as Empress of India, the incorporation of India into the empire was complete. By the early part of the twentieth century, a nationalist movement had emerged; and by 1919-20, Mohandas Karamchand ('Mahatma') Gandhi had emerged as, if not the virtually undisputed leader of this movement, certainly its most well-known and formidable architect. Successive campaigns had the effect of driving the British out of India in 1947, but not before they had partitioned it, and carved out the Muslim-majority state of Pakistan -- later itself dismembered into Pakistan and Bangladesh.

Since at least the eighteenth century, India has been associated in the European imagination as preeminently a land of religion. By the late nineteenth century, Europeans (and increasingly Americans) were coming to India as a landthat promised spiritual release from the weariness of the material life. In the twentieth century, this reputation appeared to be solidified. The struggle for independence came to be waged under the leadership of Gandhi, whose unflinching advocacy of non-violence endeared him to admirers as a man of religion and peace; and in the 1960s, when the enduring image of India was as a land suffused spirituality, Westerners flocked to India to avail themselves of the spiritual advice and teachings of countless number of Indian gurus. This image has taken something of a battering in recent years, and today Westerners, when they think at all of India, think of the country as engulfed by religious 'wars' and hatred, as ensnared by perpetual Hindu-Muslim conflict; meanwhile, the gross materialism of middle-class Indians, given naked encouragement by the state, indigenous and foreign corporate interests, the culture of modernity, and international finance organizations such as the

IMF and the World Bank, has all but eroded the image as a land of sublime spirituality.

What is indubitably unique about India as a 'land of religions' is that it is the birthplace of several major world religions. Three-fourths of the people describe themselves as adherents of Hinduism, the oldest continuous faith in the world. Though today Hinduism has spread to all parts of the world, taken there by Indian migrants, Hinduism has, and will continue to have, an indelible association with India; and perhaps in no other case is the association between a faith and a land so close as it is with Hinduism. This religion produced a vast corpus of texts: preeminent among them have been the Rig Veda, the Upanishads, the Bhagavad Gita, the Ramayana, and the Bhagvata Purana; and the commentaries of Shankaracharya; modern-day classics include the Gospel of Sri Ramakrishna, the Gita-Rahasya of Tilak, and Conversations with Sri Ramana Maharishi.

India is equally a land of other faiths: the world's second largest population of Muslims, nearly 130 million in number, is to be found in India, and there are also some 25 million Christians. Indian Islam has enjoyed a relationship that is at once syncretistic and agonistic with Hinduism, and the fruits of this encounter have been many, extending from the more obvious vocal and classical music of India, Mughlai cuisine, and Indo-Mughal architecture, to the lived practices common to adherents of both these great faiths. In antiquity, Buddhism flourished in India, and it is in Bodh Gaya that the Buddha gained enlightenment; his great contemporary, Mahavira, is the founder of Jainism, also uniquely Indian.

Today Jains are among India's most distinguished trading and business communities; and the legacy of Jain art and culture is just as profound. Sikhism, another Indian faith, is often imagined as the Protestantism of Hinduism: today there are nearly 15 million Sikhs in India, and perhaps as many as 2 million outside India, whose practices and precepts may well change the nature of the faith in India. India also has the largest community of Zoroastrians, also known as Parsees, and though in recent years the once-thriving and very old Jewish community of Cochin has all but disappeared, the small Jewish community of Bombay still makes its presence felt in the public realm.

But all these are only the institutionalized forms of religious worship in India, and a bewildering array of other religious practices, both outside the faiths and within the faiths, are encountered all over India. Various devotional poets, religious mendicants, renowned men and women of spirituality, and local holy men and women wear no religious tags, and their teachings and lives continue to be an example to the common realm of humanity.

From the 9th century to the 16th century, from the Deccan to the north, and from Bengal in the east to modern-day Gujarat and Maharashtra in the West, India was swept by the fervor of bhakti, or devotion.

The songs, lyrics, and religious compositions of the bhakti poets — Nammalvar, Jnaneshvar, Kabir, Tulsidas, Surdas, Tukaram, Vidyapati, Chandidasa, Mirabai, among others — are still sung to popular and classical music alike, and scarcely any kind of literature resonates more with Indians than do their compositions. Similarly, though the institutionalized religions are associated with great architectural monuments, such as the Hindu temple cities of South India (Kanchipuram, Rameswaram, Chidambaram, and many others), the Mughal splendors of Delhi, Agra, and Fatehpur Sikri, or the Golden Temple at Amritsar, the roadside monuments and shrines are even more indicative of the manner in which these faiths interweave with the lives of their adherents.

THE VEDAS AND POLYTHEISM

Hinduism in India traces its source to the Vedas, ancient hymns composed and recited in Punjab as early as 1500 B.C. Three main collections of the Vedas--the Rig, Sama, and Yajur--consist of chants that were originally recited by priests while offering plant and animal sacrifices in sacred fires. A fourth collection, the Atharva Veda, contains a number of formulas for requirements as varied as medical cures and love magic.

The majority of modern Hindus revere these hymns as sacred sounds passed down to humanity from the greatest antiquity and as the source of Hindu tradition.

The vast majority of Vedic hymns are addressed to a pantheon of deities who are attracted, generated, and nourished by the offerings into the sacred flames and the precisely chanted mantras (mystical formulas of invocation) based on the hymns. Each of these deities may appear to be the supreme god in his or her own hymns, but some gods stand out as most significant. Indra, god of the firmament and lord of the weather, is the supreme deity of the Vedas. Indra also is a god of war who, accompanied by a host of storm gods, uses thunderbolts as weapons to slay the serpent demon Vritra (the name means storm cloud), thus releasing the rains for the earth. Agni, the god of fire, accepts the sacrificial offerings and transmits them to all the gods. Varuna passes judgment, lays down the law, and protects the cosmic order. Yama, the god of death, sends earthly dwellers signs of old age, sickness, and approaching mortality as exhortations to lead a moral life. Surya is the sun god, Chandra the moon god, Vayu the wind god, and Usha the dawn goddess.

Some of the later hymns of the Rig Veda contain speculations that form the basis for much of Indian religious and philosophical thought. From one perspective, the universe originates through the evolution of an impersonal force manifested as male and female principles. Other hymns describe a personal creator, Prajapati, the Lord of creatures, from whom came the heavens and the earth and all the other gods. One hymn describes the universe as emerging from the sacrifice of a cosmic man (purusha) who was the source of all things but who was in turn offered into the fire by gods. Within the Vedic accounts of the origin of things, there is a tension between visions of the highest reality as an impersonal force, or as a creator god, or as a group of gods with different jobs to do in the universe. Much of Hinduism tends to accept all these visions simultaneously, claiming that they are all valid as different facets of a single truth, or ranks them as explanations with different levels of sophistication. It is possible, however, to follow only one of these explanations, such as believing in a single personal god while rejecting all others, and still claim to be following the Vedas. In sum, Hinduism does not exist as a single belief system with one textual explanation of the origin of the universe or the nature of God, and a wide range of philosophies and practices can trace their beginnings somewhere in the hymns of the Vedas.

By the sixth century B.C., the Vedic gods were in decline among the people, and few people care much for Indra, Agni, or Varuna in contemporary India. These gods might appear as background characters in myths and stories about more important deities, such as Shiva or Vishnu; in some Hindu temples, there also are small statues of Vedic deities. Sacrificial fire, which once accompanied major political activities, such as the crowning of kings or the conquest of territory, still forms the heart of household rituals for many Hindus, and some Brahman families pass down the skill of memorizing the hymns and make a living as professional reciters of the Vedas. One of the main legacies of Brahmanical sacrifice, seen even among traditions that later denied its usefulness, was a concentration on precise ritual actions and a belief in sacred sound as a powerful tool for manifesting the sacred in daily life.

KARMA AND LIBERATION

The Upanishads, originating as commentaries on the Vedas between about 800 and 200 B.C., contain speculations on the meaning of existence that have greatly influenced Indian religious traditions. Most important is the concept of atman (the human soul), which is an individual manifestation of brahman. Atman is of the same nature as brahman , characterized either as an impersonal force or as God, and has as its goal the recognition of identity with brahman . This fusion is not possible, however, as long as the individual remains bound to the world of the flesh and desires. In fact, the deathless atman that is so bound will not join with brahman after the death of the body but will experience continuous rebirth. This fundamental concept of the transmigration of atman , or reincarnation after death, lies at the heart of the religions emerging from India. Indian religious tradition sees karma as the source of the problem of transmigration. While associated with physical form, for example, in a human body, beings experience the universe through their senses and their minds and attach themselves to the people and things around them and constantly lose sight of their true existence as atman , which is of the same nature as brahman . As the time comes for the dropping of the body, the fruits of good and evil actions in the past remain with atman , clinging to it, causing a tendency to continue experience in other existences after death. Good deeds in this life may lead to a happy rebirth in a better life, and evil deeds may lead to a lower existence, but eventually the consequences of past deeds will be worked out, and the individual will seek more experiences in a physical world. In this manner, the bound or ignorant atman wanders from life to life, in heavens and hells and in many different bodies. The universe may expand and be destroyed numerous times, but the bound atman will not achieve release.

The true goal of atman is liberation, or release (moksha), from the limited world of experience and realization of oneness with God or the cosmos. In order to achieve release, the individual must pursue a kind of discipline (yoga, a "tying," related to the English word yoke) that is appropriate to one's abilities and station in life. For most people, this goal means a course of action that keeps them rather closely tied to the world and its ways, including the enjoyment of love (kama), the attainment of wealth and power (artha), and the following of socially acceptable ethical principles. From this perspective, even manuals on sexual love, such as the Kama Sutra (Book of Love), or collections of ideas on politics and governance, such as the Arthashastra (Science of Material Gain), are part of a religious tradition that values action in the world as long as it is performed with understanding, a karma-yoga or selfless discipline of action in which every action is offered as a sacrifice to God. Some people, however, may be interested in breaking the cycle of rebirth in this life or soon thereafter. For them, a wide range of techniques has evolved over the thousands of years that gives Indian religion its great diversity. The discipline that involves physical positioning of the body (hatha-yoga), which is most commonly equated with yoga outside of India, sees the human body as a series of spiritual centers that can be awakened through meditation and exercise, leading eventually to a oneness with the universe. Tantrism is the belief in the Tantra (from the Sanskrit, context or continuum), a collection of texts that stress the usefulness of rituals, carried out with a strict discipline, as a means for attaining understanding and spiritual awakening. These rituals include chanting powerful mantras; meditating on complicated or auspicious diagrams (mandalas); and, for one school of advanced practitioners, deliberately violating social norms on food, drink, and sexual relations.

A central aspect of all religious discipline, regardless of its emphasis, is the importance of the guru, or teacher. Indian religion may accept the sacredness of specific texts and rituals but stresses interpretation by a living practitioner who has personal experience of liberation and can pass down successful techniques to devoted followers. In fact, since Vedic times, it has never been possible, and has rarely been desired, to unite all people in India under one concept of orthodoxy with a single authority that could be presented to everyone. Instead, there has been a tendency to accept religious innovation and diversity as the natural result of personal experience by successive generations of gurus, who have tailored their messages to particular times, places, and peoples, and then passed down their knowledge to lines of disciples and social groups. As a result, Indian religion is a mass of ancient and modern traditions, some always preserved and some constantly changing, and the individual is relatively free to stress in his or her life the beliefs and religious behaviors that seem most effective on the path to deliverance.

Four main religion were born in India while the others came with invaders, travellers and missionaries from abroad. Despite the multitude of faiths prevalent in India, the country has by and large, been free of any internecine strife. Hindus constitute an overwhelming majority in the country and it is a creed which is renowned for its catholicity of outlook. For

Hindus, religion is a tool to achieve a one-to-one communication between god and man. However, Hinduism became too ritualistic; and in the 6th century B.C., a great social churning took place in the country – out of which emerged Jainism and Buddhism.

Jains place self-conquest above all else – it is one of the most ascetic of faiths, with its votaries living in the most spartan manner imaginable.

Buddhism, on the other hand was exported to the Far East, although its philosophy was almost snuffed out in the land of its origin. An iconoclastic faith like Buddhism could not compete with ritualistic Brahminism that cleverly co-opted Buddha into their 'holy pantheon of gods'.

By the 12th century, India began to get coloured with a distinctly Islamic flavour as wave after wave of Islamic hordes descended on the country. Drawing sustenance from the Koran and the Sunnah (sayings of Prophet Mohammad), their missionary zeal was unmatched.

Although Islam (which has two main sects – the Shias and the Sunnis) is as distinct from Hinduism as chalk from cheese, the two faiths learnt to coexist with each other, cheek by jowl. and the confluence of the two religions produced a cultural syncretism, which is exemplified by the Urdu language – an amalgam of Persian and Hindi. and out of the fusion of the two cultures arose new religious denominations – uniquely Indian, which characterised the Hindu-Islamic interface.

The best example of that synthesis are the Ahmediyas – a sect that abides by the Holy Koran and the Prophet, yet practises idolatry which is a decidedly Hindu custom. Christianity and if you think that Christianity came to India with the Europeans – you would be off the mark by 1500 years.

For St. Thomas came to India in 50 A.D. and brought the teachings of Jesus along with him – even before the Messiah was adopted by Europe. But the Europeans did bring with them a scientific temper and the Indian Renaissance of the 19th century, was largely due to their influence.

As Albert Einstein said "religion without science is mere superstition" and men like Raja Ram Mohan Roy and Swami Vivekananda strove to inculcate a rational outlook among their countrymen.

Vivekananda put it eloquently when he said that "I do not believe that a god, who cannot provide me food to eat on earth will ever give me paradise in heaven".

INDIA USED RELIGION IN POSITIVE MANNER

Suffice to say in the end that we could actually work miracles if we used religion in a positive manner. India is a land which has always been tolerant of people belonging to different races and religions. After all the Jews who have been persecuted the world over, have never been discriminated against in India. and the Zoroastrians fled Iran in the eighth century and sought sanctuary in India, when they suffered maltreatment in the former country. Small wonder then that most major religions have made their presence felt in India.

2

HINDUISM

Hinduism is a religion with various gods and goddesses. According to Hinduism, three Lords rule the world. Brahma: the creator; Vishnu: the preserver and Shiva: the destroyer. Lord Vishnu did his job of preserving the world by incarnating himself in different forms at times of crisis.

The three Lords that rule the world have consorts and they are goddesses. Consort of Brahma is Sarasvati; goddess of learning. Vishnu's consort is Lakshmi; goddess of wealth and prosperity. Shiva's consort is Parvati who is worshipped as Kali or Durga.

Along them there are a number of other gods and goddesses. To name a few of them, there is Ganesh, who has an elephant's head and he is also a son of Shiva and Parvati. Hanuman, who is an ape. Surya, Lord of sun. Ganga Ma, goddess of river Ganges. Samundra, Lord of the sea. Indra, king of the gods (but he isn't an important god). Prithvi, goddess of earth. Shakti, goddess of power. The Hindus call their goddesses 'Ma' meaning mother.

Some gods have more than one name. Shiva is also known as Shankar, Mahadev, Natraj, Mahesh and many other names. Ganesh is also called Ganpati. God Vishnu incarnated 9 times to do his job and in his every appearance he had a different form which are also worshipped as gods. Among his appearances, he appeared as Rama, Krishna, Narsimha, Parsuram and Buddha. Krishna also has different names, Gopal; Kishan; Shyam and other names. He also has other titles with meanings like 'Basuri Wala' which means the flute musician and 'Makhan Chor' which means the butter stealer. There are also gods who can change their forms, for example: Parvati can change into Kali or Durga.

Not all of these gods are worshiped by all Hindus. Some Hindus worship only Vishnu. Others worship only Shiva. Others worship only the goddesses and call these goddesses collectively as Shakti meaning power. Many of these goddess worshipers worship Parvati in her images as Kali or Durga. People who worship Shiva or Vishnu also worship characters and images connected with these gods. Vishnu worshipers (Vaishnaites) also worship his appearances. Shiva's worshipers (Shaivites) also worship images of bull called Nandi, who was Shiva's carrier and a unique stone design connected to Shiva.

There are also Hindus who worship all the gods. There are some gods who are worshiped all over India like Rama and Krishna and other gods who are worshiped more in one region than the other like Ganesh who is worshiped mainly in west India. Hindus also worship gods according to their personal needs. People who engage in wrestling, body building and other physical sports worship Hanuman, who in Hindu legends was an ape with lot of physical strength. Businessmen worship Lakshmi, goddess of wealth.

Though Hindus worship different idols, many Hindus believe in one God and perceive in these different gods and goddesses as different faces of the same one God. Others believe that idolatry is the wrong interpretation of Hinduism.

Hindus believe in reincarnation. The basic belief is that a person's fate is determined according to his deeds. These deeds in Hinduism are called 'Karma'. A soul who does good Karma in this life will be awarded with a better life in the next incarnation. Souls who do bad Karma will be punished for their sins, if not in this incarnation then in the next incarnation and will continue to be born in this world again and again. The good souls will be liberated from the circle of rebirth and get redemption which is called 'Moksha' meaning freedom. Hindus normally cremate their dead ones, so that the soul of the dead would go to heaven, except in a few cases of Hindu saints, who are believed to have attained 'Moksha'.

The main Hindu books are the four Vedas. They are Rig Veda, Sama Veda, Yajur Veda and Atharva Veda. The concluding portions of the Vedas are called Upanisads. There are also other holy books like Puranas, Ramayana, Mahabharta etc. The different gods and goddesses in the Hindu mythology are derived from these books. Ramayana and Mahabharta are the most popular Hindu books.

The main story of Ramayana is the story of Lord Rama. Rama was born in a royal family and was suppose to be the king, but because of his step-mother, he was forced to exile from his kingdom for fourteen years. During this period his consort Sita was kidnapped by a demon called Ravan, who was king of Lanka. Rama with the help of his brother, Lakshman, and an army of monkeys under the leadership of Hanuman, rescued Sita. Many Indians believe that the present day Sri Lanka was then the kingdom of Lanka.

Mahabharta is a family epic. In this epic the Pandva family and the Kaurav family who are cousins fight with each other for the control over a kingdom. Kaurav family, which consisted of 100 brothers rule an empire. The five Pandva brothers ask for a small kingdom which belongs to them. The Kauravs refuse to give the Pandvas the kingdom so there is a war between the Pandvas and the Kauravs in which it is believed that all the kingdoms of that period in India took part. In this war the Pandvas, with the help of Lord Krishna win the war. Before the commencement of the war, while the two armies are facing each other, one of the Pandva brothers Arjun gets depressed. Arjun is depressed because he has to fight against people whom he knows, loves and respects. At this point Krishna, (who was also a king of a kingdom, and participated in this war only as the chariot driver for Arjun) convinces Arjun to fight. Krishna lectures Arjun about life, human beings and their religious duties. He explains to Arjun that he belongs to a warrior caste and he has to fight for that's his destination in this incarnation. Those chapters in the Mahabharta which are Krishna's discourses on religious philosophy are called Bhagvad Gita. Because of it's importance the Bhagvad Gita is considered as a separate holy book. Another Hindu holy book that deals with religious duties is 'Law of Manu' or the 'Dharma Shastra'.

In the wars that occur in the holy books, as in Mahabharta, the different sides had different war weapons which had characters similar to modern day war weapons. In some stories the traveling vehicles were normally birds and animals. But these animals and birds had features similar to modern day aircrafts.

There were even aircrafts with over velocity of light. The main war weapons were bows and arrows. But these arrows were more like modern missiles than simple arrows. These arrows were capable of carrying bombs with destructive power similar to modern day chemical, biological or even atom bombs. Other arrows could be targeted on specific human beings. There were even arrows capable of neutralizing other arrows, similar to modern day anti-missiles.

Hindus have many holy places. Badrinath, Puri, Dwarkha and Rameshwaram are four holiest places for the Hindus. Other holy places are Varanasi, Rishikesh, Nasik, Pushkar, Ujjain and other places. Some rivers are also holy to them. Among them are Godavri, Yamuna and above all Ganges which the Indians call Ganga. Another holy river is Sarasvati and it is invisible. Hindus also worship and respect some animals and birds like cobra, apes, peacocks and cow. Hindus also respect some trees and bush trees. The famous and the most respected bush tree is Tulsi.

Some of the Hindu customs, which exist or existed, do not have their bearing in Hindu scriptures but became part of Hinduism in different ways and fashion. For example, the Hindus see in cow a sacred animal. Religiously there is no reason to see cow as sacred and it is believed that cows were made 'sacred' to prevent their slaughter during periods of droughts and hunger. Cobra worship also is not found in Hindu scripts. This custom became part of Hinduism when some Indian tribes who use to worship cobra adopted Hinduism.

Burning of the widow on the dead husband's pyre also has no religious justification.

This custom, outlawed in 1829, was probably brought to India by the Scythians invaders of India. Among the Scythians it was a custom to bury the dead king with his mistresses or wives, servants and other things so that they could continue to serve him in the next world. When these Scythians arrived in India, they adopted the Indian system of funeral, which was cremating the dead. And so instead of burying their kings and his servers they started cremating their dead with his surviving lovers. The Scythians were warrior tribes and they were given a status of warrior castes in Hindu religious hierarchy. The different castes who claimed warrior status or higher also adopted this custom.

There are four castes in Hindu religion arranged in a hierarchy. The highest caste is Brahman, and they are the priest caste of Hinduism. After them are the Kshatria, who are the warrior castes. After them are the Vaishya caste, who are business people. And after them are the Sudra, who are the common peasants and workers. Below these four castes there are casteless, the untouchables. The four castes were not allowed to have any physical contact with the untouchables.

Each caste is divided into many sub-castes. The religious word for caste is Varna and for sub-caste Jat or Jati. But sometimes in English the term caste is used in both cases. Religiously, people are born in a caste and it cannot be changed. Each caste has some compulsory duties, which its members must do. Each caste has professional limits which decides what profession each caste can follow. Each caste members can have social relations only with its caste members. Religiously this includes marraige and even eating only with caste members. Please note that socially the caste system is different from the religious form of caste system.

How did Hinduism originated is a difficult question. The accepted theory is that Hinduism was evolved after the historical meeting between the Aryans and Dravidians. Some claim that Hinduism is mainly an Aryan culture whereas the others claim that it is mainly a Dravidian culture. Religiously the Vedas were given by Brahma.

Before Hinduism there existed another religion in India called Brahmanism and its followers were called Brahmans. The Brahmans were the spiritual and moral guides of the Indian society. The members of this religion were a close sect and others could not join it.

The Brahmans slowly started accepting others into their religion and so was created Hinduism which included in it the customs which were not part of the Vedas. One of the reasons the Brahmans accepted others to their religion was the fear to loose their status as moral guides to priests of a new religion that started in India, namely Buddhism. The Brahmans even accepted Buddha as an incarnation of Lord Vishnu and part of his teachings and philosophy like non-violence into their religion.

HINDUISM—THE ESSENCE OF INDIA

Hindu Customs in Buddhism, Jainism, and Sikhism

Socio-cultural Interchange between Religious Communities in India : India is the birthplace of many religions, Hinduism, Buddhism, Jainism and Sikhism are all progeny of this part of our globe. But they are not the only religions that exist here. Adherents of Christianity, Islam, Zoroastrainism and Judaism also to be found in India. Over countless generations there has been significant exchange of customs, traditions, beliefs, rituals, etc., between these different religions Such an exchange is not peculiar to India and has been occuring the world over throughout the past.

In India though, the existence of many religions in the same social environment created a situation favourable for such an interchange of customs and rituals. The other fact that some religions existing in India are offspring of the amalgam of beliefs that co-existed under the heading Hinduism. This has also led to the presence of many features of the parent religion in the offspring religions. At times this has blurred the line dividing Hinduism from the offspring religions leading occasionally to tension of the offspring religions with their parent. One instance of this is the ire against the constitution of India wherein the term 'Hindu' includes Buddhists, Jains and Sikhs.

But interchange of customs and rituals has taken place even between religions originating in India and those brought into India from other parts of our globe. This interchange has also been a massive one for the reason that that apart from the fusion of customs as a result of co-existence of different forms of worship, the adherents of religions originating in other parts of the globe like Christianity and Islam are largely converts from Hinduism. This does not apply in the case of Zoroastrianism and Judaism as these two religions have tended to be insular and have jealously guarded against the entry of members of other faiths by way of conversion. But even then they display many traits which they have absorbed from other religions especially Hinduism.

Although this interchange has been quite substantial, it has not succeeded in bringing about identity in many important respects. Communal riots are still not a thinq of the past, sectarian feelings are still very much with as and there normally run counter to the spirit of nationalism and secularism. The result of this is perhaps India's having the dubious distinction of being a Secular society without a common civil code. For an appraisal of contemporary Indian society to be complete we ought to examine the nature and genesis of the different religions that exist around us, and also the extent to which they have influenced each other. To obtain an insisght into every religion, we shall briefly state the history of every religion since its inception, what it has borrowed from other faiths and what it has lent to it.

We start with the religion which is not only professed by a vast majority in India, but has also been the birthplace for many customs found in other religious communities in India.

A student of Hinduism can be compared with one of those blind-folded wise men who set about to examine an elephant by touching it and came up with totally different ideas about what the elephant looked like, none of which were factual.

Hinduism is like a multifarious ocean of beliefs and modes of worship with an indeterminate origin. It comprises within itself the most sublime philosophies and gross fetishism of all kinds of objects which are worshipped.

This is one religion with a history stretching from around the second millennium B.C.E. upto the present.

The Pantheism of Hinduism

A contemporary author has observed, "As a matter of fact orthodox Hindus have believed in every kind of theism, polytheism, and pantheism. They have worshipped any object which they prefer, or practically none. They followed any standard of morality or almost none. Yet they have been recognised as Hindus in good and regular standing as long as they have not flagrantly violated the rules of caste or for that offence been out-casted". Educated Hindus though have rejected the primitive features and have developed a refined religion which they follow alongwith the cruder versions that resemble primitive animism followed by their rural and tribal brethren.

Throughout its long history there have been many reform movements in Hinduism, the best known of which were Buddhism and Jainism in around the 6th century B.C.E. and Sikhism in the 16th century C.E. The recent reform movements such as the Brahmo Samaj, the Arya Samaj Prarthana Samaj, have been protests against ritualism and idolatory, but their membership is very small. In other primitive religions, when a great reformer has come, the entire primitive religion has become uniform, and unified and has consequently become cohesive and monotheistic as in the case of Zoroastrianism and Islam. But in India the followers of a reformer have always been a separate sect and the old Hindu religion has continued to be the religion of a vast majority.

As Hinduism has always been an eclectic religion it becomes difficult to identify all features which are universally recognised in this religion. The objects of veneration and worship in Hindu temples are very startling to those not familiar with the history of this hoary religion (One has to remember that the term religion is very loosely applied to Hinduism. It is more a collection of attitudes and forms of worship). It is widely recognised that most elements of present day Hinduism descended from the amalgam of the religious beliefs of the Aryans who are said to have come into India (West Punjab) around 1750 B.C.E. and those of the earlier peoples who reportedly were the founders of the Indus valley civilization.

Many scholars refute the Aryan invasion theory and also the date stated here for the entry of the Aryans into India. These scholars propound that India was the original home of the Aryans and it was from India that they spread to other parts of the globe. These scholars say that it was the Aryans themselves who founded the Indus (or Saraswati) valley civilization.

> *This is one point of view and the dating these scholars propound is supported by the star patterns mentioned in the Vedas, and the epics. Deciphering of the Indus Valley script as to be, in fact, Sanskrit also supports the point of view that the founders of the Indus-Saraswati-valley civilization were also Sanskrit speakers and hence Aryans (and not pre-Aryans). However, the author of this web page cannot claim any authority to either support or refute either theory. But then this debate is not relevant to our discussion as here we are not concerned with the fact whether the Aryans came into India from other parts of our globe or left India to go to other parts of our globe. That the Aryans existed in history is enough for our discussion. We are concerned with their modes of worship.*

The earliest objects of worship were the forces of nature and the religion was in essence polytheistic. Later on came the personified Gods like Brahma, Vishnu and Shiva while the polytheistic nature remained unchanged.

Partial Amalgamation through the Concept of Incarnation (Avatara)

With a view to having a unifying medium, in this mushrooming pantheon, was propagated the monotheistic philosophy that there is one God, one supreme reality (Brahman) and the various personified Gods, Goddesses and animistic objects of worship are incarnations (Avataras) of God. While God himself was indestructible, the various incarnations in which he descended to Earth in the form (Rupa) of an ordinary mortal had to go through the cycle of birth and death. The incarnation idea helped to partially unify the plethora of deities as different manifestations of a single divine entity. It also facilitated the absorption of deites from other religions and tribal cults which had been outside the pale of Hinduism.

Assimilation, acculturation, amalgamation have been the hallmarks of the development and growth of the Hindu religion.

Many deities are themselves a result of amalgamation of two or more deities. For instance we have Hari-hara who is an amalgam of Hari (Krishan who is an incarnation of Vishnu) and Hara (Shiva).

This amalgamation of the two recognised principal deities Vishnu and Shiva was undertaken to ease out the dualism in the Hindu religion due to the existence of the two principal sects Vaishnavism (worshippers of Vishnu) and Shaivism (worshippers of Shiva) who were frequently at loggerheads with each other. There are innumerable other sects though. Another deity who is also amalgam of Vishnu and Shiva is variously known as Sashta and Ayyappa. He has a famous shrine devoted to him at Sabarimala in Kerala.

The Ayyappa Mythology

The mythology behind Sastha, artfully explains this amalgam of Vishnu and Shiva. Briefly it is as follows:

After a long drawn strife between Gods and demons, they mutually agreed to temporarily sink their differences and with their combined efforts churn the ocean and draw out nectar (amrita) that existed at the bottom of the oceans. Both the Gods and demons stood on opposite sides and started the churning process with the help of Seshnaga (the celestial cobra) as a rope. The churning went on for and many beautiful and powerful things issued forth from the ocean. All these things were distributed equally between the Gods and demons. At last came the coveted nectar, but as soon I came up, the demons snatched it and ran away leaving the Gods high and dry. The Gods then prayed to lord Vishnu to retrieve their share.

To do this Vishnu struck upon an idea to deceive the demons. He took on the form of an enchanting maiden as Mohini known as the Mohini-Avatara of Vishnu. Mohini approached the demons who were having a loud argument as to how to distribute the stolen nectar amongst themselves. Taking advantage of this confusion Vishnu in the guise of Mohini offerred to distribute the nectar on condition that the nectar also be distributed amongst the Gods. Under the captivating influence of Mohini, the demons agreed and Mohini went about distributing the nectar, first among the Gods. Very deceptively she had made the Gods and demons sit in different rows, such that when the nectar was distributed to the last God sitting there, no nectar would be left for the demons.

Now unknowing to Mohini, her seductive form had captured Shiva's imagination and later he requested Vishnu to reappear as Monini before him. Despite being warned by Vishnu that Mohini was irresistible and that Shiva would fall prey to her charms, Shiva insisted that she appear before him confident as he was of his self-control. But lust being the weakest link in the chain of instincts, on seeing the inviting forn of Mohini Shiva's self-control gave way and out of the union of Shiva and Vishnu (as Mohini) was born Sastha who is a repository of all what Shiva and Vishnu stand for.

The External Symbols of being a Hindu

But among the Hindus, whatever the object of worship it was personified in the form of an idol. One cannot find a Hindu temple without a idol. Propitiation of the Gods takes place through the chanting of Mantras (hymns). This is done by the officiating priest.

Considerable importance is attached to purification which is done by sprinkling water on an object to be purified and to the ritual washing of hands and feet before performing a prayer.

Bathing in sacred rivers (notably the Ganga *i.e.* Ganges), is looked upon as an act of devotion that secures for a person a place in heaven. Fire plays a pivotal role in consecrating religious ceremonies, marriages, etc. The importance of fire originates in its being one of the forces of nature worshipped by the Aryans The vermilion mark on the forehead (Tilaka) alongwith the tuft of hair as the Pigtail (Shikha or Choti or Shendi) and the sacred thread (Yagnopavit or Janeu) are the external symbols that proclaim a Person's adherence to Hinduism. All these Practices are now on the wane and in urban areas they have nearly vanished.

The saffron colour is looked upon as and is to be found on flags atop temples and in the clothes worn by ascetics (Sadhus and Sanyasis). The traditional form of greeting among Hindus is the joining of hands called Namaskara.

The Four Ashramas (Stages of life)

Traditionally, life of a person was divided into four stages *viz.* Brahmacharya (childhood and celibate youth), Grithasta (householder) Vanaprastha (householder devoted to spiritual pursuits) and Sanyasa (ascetic). Sanyasa has been extolled as the culmination of an ideal life. The external signs of a person on becoming a Sanyasi were the unshorn hair and beard, the growth of fingernails, the forsaking of normal ablutions.

A Sanyasi was supposed to rise above the requirements of normal material life and devoted himself to the seeking of truth Society among the Hindus has been divided into four Varnas Brahmin (clergy), Kshatriya (nobility), Vaishya (traders and cultivators) and Shudra (menials). This division is a social issue that was given religious sanctity. Belief in rebirth (Punarjanma) and release from the cycle of birth and re-birth (Moksha) have been central to Hindu morality.

Another tradition that has been nurtured in Hinduism is that of the Guru. A Guru is supposed to play the role of a tutor and mentor. But among the Hindus, the Guru, has traditionally been considered to be more than just a tutor. Surprisingly in one Vedic hymn even Gods are referred to as Guru. (Gurur Brahma, Gurur Vishnuhu, Gururu Devoho, Maheshwaraha:

Guru Sakshat Para Brahma, Tasmayee Shri Gurveh Namaha.) Education, in India has been traditionally imparted through Gurukulas (homestead of a, Guru). A student (Shishya) had to spend his early years at a Gurukula where he was taught all the known disciplines of knowledge. But the term Guru has also had the connotations of a spiritual guide. The term Shishya could be taken to mean both student and disciple. It has not been uncommon for a person with a spiritual bent of mind to go in search of a Guru.

All spiritual personalities among the Hindus such as Swami Vivekananda, Swami Dayananda Saraswati, Swami Ramkrishna Paramhansa, etc., who attained the status of Gurus were once shishyas of some Guru. The Guru-Shishya tradition has had manifestations in innumerable Babas, Swamis and Gurus that are a part of our society, so much so that eight out of ten Indians would be followers of one Guru or another

Throughout our history, spiritual leaders and social reforms be looked upon as Gurus. In the absence of a founding father for Hinduism, these Gurus have played the role of guiding this conglomorate of beliefs (Hinduism) through the ages of history. In this context the role of Adi Shankaracharya has to be recalled.

ADI SHANKARACHARYA'S REFORM OF HINDUISM

Adi Shankaracharya can be considered as the only Hindu spiritual leader who was almost universally accepted in this religion. His philosophical standpoints of Vedanta were effective in overshadowing Buddhism on the philosophical and intellectual level. Shankaracharya came from a Brahmin family from Kalady in Central Kerala (South India). He is sald to have lived around the 8th century C.E. In the traditional manner he seems to have had his basic education in a Gurukula (traditional monastery where education was imparted in ancient times). From his early days he displayed a passion for philosophical speculation endless debates. Completion of primary education in the Gurukula did not satisfy his thirst for knowledge. While still in his teens he set out to explore the various centers of learning. His quest took him to north India where in one of the innumerable Buddhist monasteries, the philosophy of that religion caught his fancy and he spoke about this idea amongst his disciples and friends. One of Shankaracharya's disciples expressed readiness to enroll as a student in the Nalanda University, which in those days was the leading senter for Buddhist philosophical speculation.

But being a Brahmin by birth, Shakaracharya's disciple was refused admission. Undaunted by this the young monk upon a bold idea to gain entry into the Buddhist cloister. He shaved off the tuft of hair and pigtail, cast aside his sacred thread, wiped the ash (Bhasma) on his forehead, and dressed as a Buddhist monk he approached the Nalanda University again to be enrolled in a philosophy that had fired his imagination. Having secured admission this way, he stayed on for a few years and mastered Buddhist philosophy.

Steeled as he was in the rival Hindu schools of philosophy, he beset his tutors with incisive questions many of which exposed the weaker side of Buddhist philosophy. And day-by-day the master-philosophers at Nalanda began to grow suspicious of this curious student and henceforth they never let go an opportunity to cross-examine him. During one such grueling session Shankaracharya's disciple inadvertently slipped up and that cost him his identity (as a Buddhist monk) and very nearly his life.

The infuriated Buddhist Bhikkus (monks) caught hold of this imposter and threw him out of a window. Unfortunately for Shankaracharya's disciple, this meeting was in progress in one of the top floors of the multi-storied buildinqs of the Nalanda University. Realizing the peril he was in, whi1e falling to the ground, the disciple invoked the Vedas and cried out "If the Vedas are true not a single hair of mine will be hurt".

He fortunately survived the fall but one eye of his was brutally injured and gave him a severe pain. Knowing that with this event his life as a Buddhist monk has ended, he decided to return to his Guru Adi Shankaracharya. After he returned to his Gurukula, he asked Shankaracharya one question that had been bothering him lately. He wondered why his eye had been injured when he had invoked the Vedas.

Shankaracharya explained this anomaly by telling him that he had said "If the Vedas are true not a single hair of mine will be hurt.", thereby he had not expressed confidence in the power of the Vedas to protect him but had expressed a hope which entertained doubts as to the power of the Vedas. Shankaracharya told him that had he said, "The Vedas are true and they will protect me", he would have come out unhurt.

The Halebid temple complexat Halebid in Karnataka has been built by the Hoysalas in the 12th century.The architecture here represents the finesseof craftsmanship in granite.

Shankaracharya continued his studies and discourses for which he travelled far and wide throughout India. He is reported to have gone far north to Badrinath and Srinagar (in Kashmir). One thing for which he is remembered is his attempt to institutionalize Hinduism through the establishment of monasteries (Mutts or Mathas) under the charge of bishops (Jagadgurus). He established four such Mutts in different parts of the country. Although these institutions could not institutionalize Hinduism on the scale of other religions like Christianity or Buddhism, they left a lasting mark on the Hindu ecclesiastical organisation.

Sects within Hinduism made up this "Religion"

But in spite of this reform by Adi Shankaracharya, the centrifugal looseness inherent in Hinduism left no check on the innumerable sects with various objects and forms of worship that kept on mushrooming. What held the various sects together was the inclusion the principal deities like Brahma, Vishnu, Shiva, and the mother Goddess (Shakti) in the various sects, albeit in varying forms and the mutual recognition between the different sects of the validity of each other's patron deities (Ishta-devata). Thus worshippers of Vishnu did not generally castigate the deities Shiva and Shakti as non-Hindu nor did the worshippers of Shiva look upon Vishnu as alien deity.

Some Sects broke off from Hinduism

But at times some of the sects withdrew this recognition given to the deities of other sects and acquired an exclusionist character. Jainism, Buddhism and Sikhism are surviving examples of such sects. But on the whole the main body of beliefs that are brought under the heading Hinduism continued to be supple. On many occasions when it came into contact with alien forms of worship, it tried to incorporate them within itself.

One of the offspring sects, Sikhism originated as a fusion of elements of Hinduism and Islam. During the 18tb century the formation of the Bramho Samaj in Bengal under Raja Rammohan Roy aimed at combining the best elements of Western Christianity and Hinduism. Despite the picture of ultra-orthodoxy that Hinduism normally presents, distinctly non-Hindu concepts were absorbed into it. One of these is the concept of 'Niraakar Ishwar' the formless God* it found its reflection in some Hindu sects notably the Arya Samaj which is looked upon as a revivalist movement. The Arya Samaj upholds Vedic ritualism and disowns idol worship. The influence of Islamic ideas of God (Allah) being an abstract power, on some strains of Hindu thought cannot be ruled out.

Even in day-to-day life, Hindus adhere to many practices which originate in other religions. For instance the practice among Hindus, especially among women, of covering their head while offering prayers is a result of Mohammedan influence and is an adaptation of the Mohammedan practices of wearing Burkha, Chador and observing Purdah. So is the practice of burning incense sticks (Agarbattis and Dhoop) in temples which comes form the (originally Zoroastrian) Muslim practice of burning Loban. In ancient times women in India did not follow the custom of wearing a veil.

Thus Hinduism which is the religion of the majority in India has imbibed many concepts and beliefs from the religions it came into contact with. This is more relevant in the context of Hinduism and Hindu culture being regarded largely, exclusively and distinctly Indian. What we know as the Hindu religion has been born and bred in India. Not surprisingly are the terms Indian and Hindu considered as synonymous. It is a widely held opinion that Hinduism is the heart and soul of the Indian nation. Remove Hinduism and India loses its identity.

All this while being generally true, leads to notions that everything associated with Hinduism originated in India, which is, strictly speaking, incorrect. Hinduism has borrowed significantly from other religions although this has not been a one way affair.

We shall see below how Hinduism has much more significantly lent to other religions than it has borrowed from them. To understand the fusion of customs and beliefs of different religions we shall review the history of these religions in the folowing chapters. We first turn our attention to the second great religion that emerged from ancient India-Buddhism. This religion was also the first to institutionalize missionary activity and to reach global dimensions in the ancient period circa 300 B.C.E.

VEDANTA, SANKHYA, LOKAYATA

Hindu Philosophical Schools: In the history of religious beliefs in **ancient India**, philosophical and speculative thought played a very important role. There existed various philosophical schools of which Vedanta, Sankhya and Lokayata could be considered as representative of the three major schools of thought.

Vedanta's Theism, Sankhya's Materialism and Lokayata's Rationalism: While the Vedanta school was theistic (believing in the existence of God), the Lokayata school was **materialistic** and atheistic (believing in the existence of only those things whose existence could be seen, heard, felt, tasted and smelt). The Sankhya school was compromise between the other two schools. While these philosophical schools played all important role in influencing the development of Indian religions, these philosophical schools themselves did not evolve into separate religions. They could not so evolve as they were intellectual traditions without any mass following.

The lack of mass following had a positive effect as it kept the spirit of quest alive and disallowed the emergence of rigid commitment to certain ideas which prevented them from taking on the form of religion. Philosophical schools whether theistic or materialist remained distinct from religions proper. We shall explain in brief the nature of these different philosophical traditions.

Vedanta

Vedanta is the only philosophical tradition that remains alive today. The reason is that unlike any other philosophical school. Vedanta has been fully integrated into the Hindu religion. Vedanta literally means 'end of the Vedas' but it is interpreted as 'culmination of the Vedas'. The founder of Vedanta tradition is said to be the Vedic Seer Vyasa, but its most well known exponent was Adi Shankaracharya. There were others too like Sayanacharya, Madhavacharya and many others.

The Vedanta system virtually represents Shankaracharya's interpretation of the Sutras. The Sutras are a collection of rituals and practices that have been sanctioned in Vedic literature.

The essence of Vedanta philosophy is that all human beings have souls (Atman). And although physically all beings have a separate existence, their souls are actually not separate. They are merged into one supreme soul (Param-Atmah) or the absolute soul (Brahman).

This unity of different souls is called Advaita or non-dualism (also called Monism). The doctrine of Advaita is central to Vedanta philosophy. The visible and palpable universe around us is considered to be unreal (Mithya) which is but an illusion *i.e.* Maya), while that which is tbe supreme reality the absolute soul (Brahman) cannot be perceived by our normal senses of sight, smell, hearing or touch.

(The Vedanta philosophy continues to be very popular among Hindu philosophers and is a subject at many discourses at temples. There are many contemporary names associated with this philosophy. It is not possible to recollect all, but some of those who have based their principles on Vedanta Philosophy include A. Parthasarthy, Swami Chinmayananda, Maharshi Mahesh Yogi, among many others.)

Sankhya

The Sankhya school is relatively materialistic as compared to Vedanta. The founder of the Sankhya school is considered to be a philosopher named Kapila. The term Sankhya could be derived from Sankhyaa meaning 'numbers'. This could be so as Sankhya philosophy divides the universe into 25 principles (tattvas). The first 8 tattvas comprise of the material universe and are termed as Prakriti. One tattva (principle) is the motive power of the universe which is looked upon as the soul or spirit and is termed Purusha. The remaining 16 tattvas are the result of Purusha acting upon Prakriti and they constitute the material universe with all its movements of rotation, revolution, gravitation.

Thus everything begins with matter (Prakriti) but this matter in itself is inert or dead, it is activated by the stimulus provided to it by the motive power(Purusha) and the result of this is the active universe with its twinkling stars and rotating planets of which we are a part. The Sankhya system of ideas is thus not entirely theistic as it assumes the existence of both matter and motive power to begin with. The universe is not looked upon as the creation of a supreme creator. But the Sankhya doctrine is neither entirely materialistic. According to Sankhya, matter (Prakriti) which exists without any creator having created it, but is inert until it is activated by the motive power (Purusha).

Evidently the Sankhya doctrine tried to explain the existence (or creation) of the universe by extending the idea of sexual procreation to the entire universe. Incidentally, Purusha literally means "man" or male and Prakriti is one of the names of the Mother-Goddess.

Unlike Vedanta, the Sankhya doctrine was not incorporated into any religion. It never obtained wide acceptability among Hindu philosophers as did Vedanta. The most popular philosopher who is said to have propounded the Sankhya philosophy was Kapila. From the name it is uncertain whether this philosopher was a man or a woman. *(Modern Indian philosophers like Rahul Sankrutyan and Devi Prasad Chattopadhyay have referred to the specualtions of Kapila.)*

But Buddhism seems to have borrowed ideas from the Sankhya School. Thus this school appears to be of considerable antiquity and must have existed since before the 6th century B.C.E. when Gautama Buddha lived. But the Sankhya doctrine displays a dual character which arises from the attempts made to reconcile materialistic logic with the gaps in knowledge (perception) about the nature of the universe. In this sense the Sankhya doctrine proves inadequate as an intellectual doctrine as compared to another philosophical tradition or doctrine which was known as Lokayata (Derived from "Loka" meaning lay people) and which was thoroughly materialistic.

Lokayata

The Lokayata doctrine tried to explain the nature of the universe without the intervention of either God or devil.

"Truth" for the exponents of this tradition was that which could be perceived by human senses of sight, hearing, smell, taste or touch. This kind of a down-to-earth approach necessitated recognition of the limits to human knowledge and capacity. But it also tethered the exponents of Lokayata to a realistic and convincing approach. Nothing was accepted as a matter of faith and the quest to know more about the unknown was the driving force of this school.

According to the Lokayata doctrine, the universe was made up of active physical forces (like gravitation) which activated and stimulated each other. But these physical forces although active were not alive as they did not move about consciously towards any set purpose. This is where the Lokayata School differed from other philosophies which interpreted the "active" quality of these forces as proof of their being "alive".

The idea that the active powers of the physical universe like thunder, lightning, rain and storms were alive and moved about consciously to achieve a set purpose was the foundation of most philosophies. The exponents of Lokayata did not believe in concepts such as life after death or rebirth. A charge that was made against adherents of this philosophy was that they emphasized only the material aspects while disregarding spiritual ones. But this was natural in a school which looked upon only the perceptible as real. Lokayata looked upon Man and his psyche a result of the material conditions around him. In this respect this school came close to modern interpretations which look upon man to be ultimately a result of physical evolution of the universe, and religion together with all aspects of the human psyche a result of Man's intellectual and emotional evolution.

Thus the Lokayata philosophy which seems closest to the modern Rationalism, seems to have been popular at some stage in history in ancient India. The term Lokayata itself can be translated as 'widespread among the people'. Its principle exponent is considered to be a philosopher named Charavaka who is said to be a contemporary of Sri Krishna and if legend is to be believed, he was burned at the orders of Yudhisthira after the Mahabharat war. His crime was apostasy in declaring that the Vedas are not the ultimate in human knowledge.

Modern philosophers who have propounded this philosophy include like Dharmanand Kosambi, Rahul Sankrutyan and Devi Prasad Chattopadhyay. There existed other philosophical schools like Nyaya, Vaisheshika, Yoga and Mimansa, but the three schools discussed here represented the major under-currents of Indian philosophical thought. As mentioned earlier, philosophies interacted closely with religions and Hinduism, Buddhism, Jainism all show traces of ideas borrowed from the different philosophical schools which strictly speaking were part of no religion.

All the religions and philosophies we have so far discussed originated in ancient times, but among the religions that originated in India there is a mediaeval one without the mention of which our discussion would be incomplete. This religion is that of the Gurus of Punjab-Sikhism.

3

ISLAM

The Muslims are about 12% of India's population. But their influence on the Indian society was much stronger. The main reason was that there were many Muslims rulers in different parts of India. Most of the Muslim rulers of India were invaders from the west (see India in the past). Islam was established in Saudi Arabia. But most of Islam's spreaders in India arrived from non-Arab countries (It must be noted that Arab traders and travellers had arrived into India even before Islam was established in Arabia. These Arabs probably had their own places of worship, later on transformed into mosques.).

The first spreaders of Islam in India were individuals who saw in spreading Islam a holy precept. They began coming to India from the 11th century. They arrived in India from Bukhara, Turkey, Iran, Yemen and Afghanistan. The most famous preacher of Islam in India was Khwaja Chishti, who arrived from Iran and his sect is called Sufism. But the accepted assumption in India is that most of India's Muslims were converted to Islam through the sword. Meaning the Indians were given an option between death or adopting Islam. The third option was getting examined in Islam religion along with heavy taxes-Jeziya (poll tax) and Kharaj (property tax).

The process of converting Indians to Islam began in the 8th century, when the Arabs began invading north India and present day Pakistan. After the Arabs other Muslims invaded India. These invasions by Muslims in India were not continuous and not all Muslim invaders were Islamic fanatics. One of the Moghul emperors, Akbar, was very liberal and he even established a new religion, Din E Elahi, which included in it, beliefs from different religions. In some of the monuments built by Akbar symbols of different religions are visible. In contrast with Akbar his great grand son, Aurangazeb, was a fanatic Muslim and during his term the non-Muslims suffered a lot. Many worshipping sites of different religions were destroyed and transformed into mosques.

Most of the Indian Muslims converted to Islam were belonged to the lower classes of the Indian society. Besides these Muslims there are also Muslims who belonged to the ruling families of the different Indian kingdoms. Some of these rulers were Hindus who actually belonged to the warrior castes of the Hindu society and adopted Islam. Others are descendants of Muslim rulers who invaded India. The different Muslim rulers of India also brought to their kingdoms Muslim mercenaries, businessmen and slaves from different parts of the world like Russia; Afghanistan; Turkey; Arab countries and Africa. These people remained in India, married local Indians and converted them to Islam. Because of the different origins as stated and because of other reasons the Muslims of India refer to themselves not only as Muslims but also with other titles.

In general the Muslims of India like the Muslim world is divided into two main sects, Sunni and Shia. And just like in the whole Muslim world there is tension between these two sects. Each sect has many different schools. There are also Muslims who claim to be the descendants from the daughter of Prophet Muhammad and the men in this community add the title Syed before their names. Other claim to be the descendants from the first Muslims and add the title Sheik. Along with these Muslim world divisions, the Indian Muslims also have other divisions.

Different communities who adopted Islam in different ways have different community names. In west India the Bohra and Khoja are Muslim communities who adopted Islam influenced by different Muslim preachers. The Khojas also split into different communities. The leader of the Khoja (Nizari) community is Aga Khan. The Nawait are descendants of Arab and Persian immigrants. In south India in the state of Kerala, the Mophilla community is descendants from Arab merchants. A well known Indian Muslim community is Pathan. The Pathan are Muslims who arrived from Afghanistan. They normally have their surname as Khan. The Pathan have an image of being brave, honest and righteous. Many Indians who adopted Islam adopted the surname Khan and they claim that they are Pathans, which is not always true. The original Pathans claim that they originate from the Tribes of Israel.

In the beginning of the 20th century, some reformist Muslims organizations evolved in India who wanted to adjust Islamic philosophy to the modern world. These organizations wanted to cancel polygamy and were in favor of women education.

Came first Seemingly as a Message of Universal Brotherhood and Later as an Aggressor to Blanket India in a Dark Age for 700 years

A discussion on the above topic is bound to be a sensitive one for many of our countrymen. This is so as it brings into focus, issues like cultural identity, patriotism and extra-territorial loyalties. An objective discussion is all the more difficult as an emotional under-current is not ruled out altogether, whosoever the participants.

The varying opinions that Indians hold on an issue like cultural identity is highlighted when we talk of our country's ancient past before religions like Islam and Christianity were introduced into India or rather before these religions came into being in the country of their birth. A Muslim or a Christian would be indifferent if not hostile to India's past before his religion came on the scene.

The history and heritage of a nation belongs to all its inhabitants because their forefathers had made it. Subsequent conversion of some of the inhabitants to a religion originating in another country need not deprive them of this heritage. Had this been so, the Greeks after their conversion to Christianity should have disowned the Acropolis, the Olympia and looked with contempt and hatred on Athena, Zeus or Herakles who were deities of the ancient Greek religion and are still fresh in the memory of the Greeks. Similarly, the Egyptians should have disowned the pyramids, the Sphinx and erased the memory of the Pharoahs. This has not happened. But most Indians have varying ideas of their ancient heritage. The reason being that they adhere to different religions.

While the Hindus find it natural to be justly proud of the country' s heritage, the case is not so simple for those who have converted to religions imported into India from other countries. While a Muslim or Christian would feel lost when he moves into that period of Indian history when his religion was yet to come on the scene, a Hindu would not. Going 1500 to 2000 years back in the history of his country, a Muslim or a Christian would find himself surrounded by a religion, whose followers today claim has been the original religion of this country.

Would a Muslim or a Christian, like to associate with that period of his country's history which is alien to his cultural identity?

The answer may not always be "YES". This ambivalence on their part arises from the fact that there exists in India, a large majority of people who have maintained; an unbroken link with the country's past, through the medium of the Hindu religion. But what would have been the attitude of the people of India, had all of them been converted to either Islam or Christianity?The country's pre-Islamic or pre-Christian heritage, would still have been there. And the people of India, whatever be their religion, would have had to be proud, of the achievements of their forefathers who nevertheless had conformed to a different religion. Had they not been proud of these achievements, there would have been no one else who would have been.

But today this is not so and those Indians who have embraced another religion normally look upon with scorn on the country's ancient heritage before their religion came into the picture. The reason being that there is a large majority of Indians who due to their non-conversion to any other religion, look upon the whole of India's history and heritage as their own. The past of India is a common heritage of all Indians though it is unfortunate that lt has to he upheld largely by the Hindus.

Due to this complex and seemingly contradictory situation, it is imperative for an Indian to be familiar with the religions of external origin followed by his compatriots not only if we are to know each other better but to appreciate that cultural inheritance which belongs to all of us irrespective of religion.

To do this we would have to move away from Indian history and begin with the origin of the religions in the country of their birth. The first part of our discussion would take us to a desert town, which owes its existence to a place of pilgrimage. Here probably thousands of years before a religion was born, countless people trekked to pay homage to a meteor having the shape of a cube. Being a meteor, its flaming rush through the heavens would have been enough to make it an object with divine associations. Though the date of its descent is unrecorded, the event seems to have occurred deep in antiquity.

Diodorus Siculus, the Greek historian has referred to it nearly 700 years before the birth of Mohammed. (*i.e.* in around the 1st century C.E.) Arabian folklore has an explanation to offer as to the origin of the Kaaba (meaning 'the Cube').

The ancient patriarch Abraham (or Ibrahim) had two wives Sarah and Hagar. Hagar had borne Abraham a son, named Ishmael who was the object of jealously of the other wife Sarah who forced Abraham to banish Hagar and her son Ishmael into the desert. Hagar and Ishmael wandered far into the desert until they came to the valley of Baca (Mecca), where they were perishing from thirst. But the lords guardian angel revealed to them the spring Zem Zem. As she and her son lay by the spring, the Black Stone fell from the heaven at Ishmael's feet and he was promised that his children would become more powerful than those of Issac the son who was born to Sarah, Abraham' second wife. According to tradition Abraham himself joined Ishmael to build a sacred structure around the Kaaba.

(Mecca is referred to as Baca in the Old Testament, Psalm lxxxiv., quoted by C.F. Potter in The Story of Religion, George G. Harrap & Co. London, P. 279)

But whatever be the origin of the Kaaba, it was a popular place of pilgrimage in the 6th Century A.D. when Mohammed was born. In that period Arabia had many religious cults and the worship of the Kaaba was one of them. The worship of sacred spirits, stones, trees and mountains had buiit up a conception of guardian spirits incharge of every holy spot. These guardian spirits were looked upon as Gods and Goddesses. The term Allah some scholars think is of pre-Islamic origin and was the name of a specific deity worshipped at Mecca. In pre-Islamic Mecca, three goddesses were worshipped, they were Allat, Aluzza, and Mannat. They were called daughters of Allah.

The term 'Allah' is also supposed to be a contraction of Al-ilah which means "the God" In Muslim usage Allah is a proper noun which leads credence to the belief that originally Allah was the name of a specific diety. Such was the nature of religion when Mohammed was born. Mohammed is supposed to have been in 570 C.E. in a family of merchants, Mohammed was brought up by his foster-mother Halima as both his parents died when he was still a child. Mohammed grew to manhood with his uncle whom he accompanied on long camel caravan journeys across the desert. While still in his twenties he married a rich widow named Khadijah, who was then forty years of age.

During those days the Byzantine and Persian empires to the north of Arabia were at their zenith. They along with religions like Judaism and Christianity seemed to have made a profound impact on the young Mohammed.

He received his first public acceptance when during a dispute as to who would repair the Kaaba, he co-incidently walked into the assemblage after it had been decided to hand over the task to the person who walked in first after the decision was taken. The Kaaba had then been damaged by a flood. He did not know that by this co-incidence, he would not just get a chance to initiate the repairs to the Kaaba but also would become one who would change the map of the world and the religion of continents.

From then onwards Mohammed's mind turned more towards religion and he began neglecting his business. He was increasingly missed in the market place as he frequented solitary cave in the foothills of Mount Hira near Mecca.

One night, we are told, a voice broke into his meditations and ordered him to repeat to men the following words :

> *Recite in the name of thy Lord, who hath created all things; who hath created man of congealed blood.*

This revelation became the Sura 96 (Chapter 96) of the Koran. But Mohammed did not start preaching at once, he confided his experiences to his wife Khadija who in turn consulted a family friend named Waraka, who was considered to be wise in religious matters, Waraka thought that Mohammed's experiences were genuine, and thus began to grow Mohammed's admirers and followers, among whom were his slave Zeid and his cousin Ali (who was later to become the cause of the split of Islam into the Sunni and Shia sects). Under this initial stimuli he developed his message of universal brotherhood which he summed up in one phrase.

There is no God but Allah and Mohammed is his Prophet In this the influence of the Mosaic commandment of Judaism seems to have been clearly reflected. Moses was said to have proclaimed "Thou shalt have no other Gods before me".

> *Had Mohammed stopped at saying "There is no God" instead of saying, "There is no God but Allah and Mohammed is his Prophet", he could have become the greatest and most successful rationalist. Had he taught his followers to be humane, after militarily defeating their adversaries from India to France, he would have also become the most successful humanist.*

Into the then idolatrous nature-worshippers of Mecca his message cut like a sword. He pointed out that idols were nothing. The only reality was Allah, the only duty submission to Allah. The Arabic word for submission was "Islam" and Mohammed so drilled that word into the minds of his hearers that the whole religion he founded was named 'Islam'.

But Mohammed's denouncement of idol worship was not taken kindly by the people of Mecca whose prosperity depended upon the large number of pilgrims visiting the Kaaba and Mohammed's denouncement was in direct conflict with their interests. In retaliation the Meccans expelled Mohammed who then fled to Medina.

Here he was able to win a considerable number of converts. In due course he raised an army of his followers and victoriously marched on to Mecca in the year 630 C.E. This was one the first victories of Islam which was to spread to over three continents in only a few years from then.

But Mohammed had made concessions to the Meccans. The practice of Kaaba worship which he had earlier denounced. The practice of throwing stones at a pillar symbolizing the Devil was also carried along into the new faith. This came close to idolatory *i.e.* personifying the devil as a pillar. These pre-Islamic practices were now made part of the new religion along with the annual pilgrimage to Mecca (Haj) and even the kissing of the Kaaba and quaffing of the brackish waters of the Zem Zem.

We are told that after this, Mohammed returned to Medina and shortly afterwards contracted a disease caused by the eating of goat flesh poisoned by an enemy. After being in bed for a few days he passed away in the arms of his favourite young wife Ayesha.

Islam in India in the Lifetime of Prophet Mohammed

The story of Islam does not end here, within decades of Mohammed's death it spread from the borders of India to France.

Many of us do not know that Islam first came into India in the province of Kerala during the lifetime of Prophet Mohammed itself. Prophet Mohammed is said to have sent messengers to the Roman (Byzantine) Emperor Heraclius, the **Sassanian (Persian)** Emperors Chosroes (Khushrau Parvez) and Yazdgard, and to the Kings of China and Kerala (in South India). While the Sassanian and Roman Emperors rejected the Prophet's messengers and insulted them; the Kings of China and Kerala are said to have received the messengers with great courtesy.

King Cheraman of Kerala Voluntarily Converts to Islam in the 7th Century

This King from Kerala was Cheraman from the Chera dynasty of Kerala. He gave a patient hearing to the discourses of the Messengers of Islam. On hearing them, he was favourably impressed by their message of universal brotherhood which is enshrined in Islamic theology and is recommended to be practiced within the Muslim community.

(Ironically this concept is limited to the Muslim community alone, while towards the unbelievers what is advocated is relentless hatred. And in practice even within the Muslim community, in real life, the general attitude is of fanaticism and violence when the energy of the Muslims is not directed towards battling the non-Muslims).

But King Cheraman was favourably impressed with what he was told and he is said to expressed interest in Islam. Local legend says that King Cheraman visited Mecca and converted to Islam in the 7th century. This happened before Islam had become a military force and started off rampaging on its global Jihad. King Cheraman also built a Mosque in Kerala and many local people converted to Islam along with him.

The Peoples of Lakshadweep and Calicut Voluntarily Accept Islam

The people of Lakshadweep are converts from those days. As also are the Moplas (Mapillais) from the Calicut province of Kerala. In this phase of history of Islam, it was still a missionary religion. The Jihad started off a few decades later. (Incidentally, we may also recollect here that the people of Kerala had their second introduction to Islam in the 18th century, when Tipu Sultan, the usurper of the Mysore Principality marched into Kerala attacked the Zamorin (Samudrin) Raja of Calicut and set off converting the people of central Kerala to Islam.

Tipu Sultan's method was so unlike that of the Islamic Missionaries who had visited King Cheraman during the lifetime of Prophet Mohammed, Tipu went about with a Koran in one hand and a sword in the other giving the subject people of

Kerala a choice of accepting Islam or death. Doing this, he marched from Calicut up to Alwaye from where he was forced to retreat due to stiff resistance.)

The Jihad Starts Off — Making Evident the Intolerant Nature of Islam

But once the Jihad started off and the army of Islam secured victory after victory over all the prominent empires of those days-the Byzantine (Roman) and the Sassanian (Persian) Empires-Islam spread from France (Poitiers) up to India (Sindh). It was during these spectacular military successes, that the nature of Islam became evident as being intolerant of everything non-Islamic (*i.e.* non-Arabic). The aim of the victorious Islamic Armies was to wipe off everything pre-Islamic in the countries they overran in a few decades after the passing away of Prophet Mohammed. Thus began a process of Arabization of all the countries the Arabs overran in their Jihad.

Islam is basically a medium of Arab Imperialism-Military, Political, Economic and Cultural

Anwar Sheikh, a scholar of Islam writes the following in his essay entitled ISLAM-The Arab National Movement, about how and why Islam is basically a medium of Arab Imperialism-Military, Political, Economic and Cultural.

In the words of Anwar Sheikh:

1. The Prophet declared that he was the best individual of all humans; the Koresh, his tribe were the best of all Arabian tribes and Arabs were the best of all nations.
2. For this purpose, he used the oldest Semitic device of revelation to declare himself a prophet, who is supposed to have no axe of his own to grind but does what he is told by God.
3. As the Jews had a national God called "Yahwe," the Prophet chose Allah, the Lord of Kaaba, an idol of his own tribe, and raised it to the dignity of the one supreme God.
4. The Prophet made Kaaba, the sacred shrine of the Arabs as the holiest place of Islam so that whoever

believes in Islam must also acknowledge the greatness of Arabia and its people.

5. The Prophet Mohammed made Haj, *i.e.* pilgrimage to the Kaaba, an old pre-lslamic Arab rite, a basic tenet of his religion to impress upon foreign (non-Arab) Muslims the sanctity of Arabia, and create an everlasting source of income for the Arabs.
6. He insisted that God's covenant was not with Abraham and Isaac but with Abraham and Ishmael. It is universally known that Ishmael was the direct ancestor of the Arabs. Thus, one can clearly see that the purpose of Islam is glorification of the Arab nationalism.
7. The Kaaba serves a much greater national purpose of the Arabs than that which Jerusalem renders to the Jews or Rome to the Christians (Catholics). It is guardian of the Arab nationalism at the expense of the national conscience of the non-Arab Muslims who believe that they have no individual nationality of their own, and prefer to be called Muslims. Thus the Arabs have achieved the status of a nucleus whereas the non-Arab Muslims have gladly become their satellites in the hope of gaining paradise. It ought to be remembered that the Prophet shall not open the gates of paradise to those Moslems who are not friendly with the Arabs.

The Prophet said:

a. "May Allah humiliate those who seek to humiliate the Quresh (his tribe)." Sahih Tirmzi Vol. 2 p.335)
b. The Prophet said to Sulaiman Farsee (the Persian Convert), "If you bear odium against the Arabs, you bear odium against me." (Sahih Tirmzi Vol.2. p.840)
c. The Prophet said: "I will not intercede for those or love them who are not fair with the Arabs." (Sahih Tirmzi Vol. 2 p.840) Of course, there is a difference of opinion about the degree of accuracy about these Hadiths *i.e.* the Prophet's sayings, yet they are there. If they were inappropriate they would have been expunged. They are correct because they correspond with the Arabic ethos of Islam.

8. The Prophet built the structure of Islam around the sanctity of his own person by declaring himself:
   a. the Intercessor,
   b. the blessing for the mankind, and
   c. the model of actions for all faithful.
9. Since Muhammad preferred Arabs to other nations, love of the Arabs becomes a prerequisite of Islam.
10. Since faith means belief in both Allah and Muhammad, the Islamic God represents duality as the Christian doctrine of Trinity represents Three-in-one. Not only Muhammad was an Arab, Allah, the Lord of the Kaaba, was also an Arab statue. Thus Islam is there to serve the Arab cause.
11. The Koran is an Arabic document. It is primarily a book for the understanding and guidance of the Arabs. Calling it a universal message is just an innovation for subjugating the non-Arab Muslims to the national hegemony of the Arabs.

Islamic Jihad is a Perpetual Declaration of War on Non-Muslims

Islam, in fact, is a perpetual declaration of war against all those, who do not believe in Muhammad. This war is not confined to words but it is really brutish, barbaric and bewildering. It makes society a hot bed of mutual hatred based on discrimination of Momin (Muslim) and Kafir (non-Muslim). Thus, it ignites the flame of eternal conflict far more dangerous, debilitating and devastating than Karl-Marx could ever visualize: "They (unbelievers) are Satan's party they are the losers.... Those (the Muslims) are God's party....they are the prosperers." (LVIII The Disputer: 20)

What the Koran says about Jihad

The Muslims are commanded to wage an everlasting war against the unbelievers and are assured victory in the struggle. Surely, the Marxist social philosophy is an extension of the Koranic doctrine. To realize the significance of this statement, one ought to read the following:

1. On unbelievers is the curse of Allah. (The Cow: 161)
2. Allah is an enemy to unbelievers. (The Cow: 15)
3. The worst of beasts in Allah's sight are the ungrateful, who will not believe. (Spoils of War: 55)
4. Oh ye who believe! the non-Muslims are unclean. (Repentance:17)
5. Oh ye who believe! Murder those of the disbelievers and let them find harshness in you. (Repentance: 123)
6. Oh believers, do not treat your fathers and mothers as your friends, if they prefer unbelief to belief, whosoever of you takes them for friends, they are evil-doers. (Repentance: 20) 7. Humiliate the non-Muslims to such an extent that they surrender and pay tribute. (Repentance: 29)

Through the doctrine of hatred, Islam incites Muslims against non-Muslims and proposes Jihad as the solution to make Islam the dominant faith. What is Jihad? It is the battle against unbelievers such as the Hindus, the Christians, the Jews, the atheists-in fact, unbelievers of all sorts.

Jihad is nothing but an Inducement to Murder and Plunder non-Muslims for their Sheer Crime of Not Believing in Muhammad.

Since humans do not like harming innocent people, Jihad is nothing but an inducement to murder and plunder non-Muslims for the sheer crime of not believing in Muhammad. It is called a "holy war." Those who return home victoriously, come laden with booty, which includes wealth and non-Muslim women for concubinage and free seduction but those "crusaders" who are killed "in the way of Allah" go straight to paradise where ever-young virgins of exquisite beauty and pretty boys anxiously wait to serve them! Even more stunning is the fact that while every code of moral conduct treats murder, rape, plunder, lechery as sins, Islam counts them as acts of piety.

For more on this refer to Islamic Culture by Anwar Sheikh.

Illegitimate Sex Amongst Muslims is Haram, but for a Mujahid Taking Up Non-Muslim Women as Concubines in a Jihad is Legitimate.

Carnal gratification, man's greatest desire, is the first temptation that the concept of Jihad carries. A Mujahid *i.e.* the Islamic warrior, who at that time suffered pangs of sexual starvation in the torrid land of Arabia, was promised plenty of sensual enjoyment as a reward for participating in the carnage whether or not he survived the rigors of the battlefield.

If he (a Mujahid-Islamic warrior) got killed, he was assured that the houris waited for his glorious company in Jannnat *i.e.* paradise, and if he survived, he had a share in the plunder, which included women of the infidels. Islam has prescribed flogging, and death-by-stoning for sexual offenses such as fornication and adultery because it holds such acts as unlawful when committed out of wedlock but when a Muslim "fights in the way of Allah" to murder the infidels and plunder their property, then the Koran relaxes this rule:

"And anyone of you who has not the affluence to be able to marry believing free women in wedlock, let him take believing handmaids that your right hand owns......So marry them, with their people's leave, and give them their wages honorably as women in wedlock, not as in license or taking lovers." (Women, IV: 25) These verses demonstrate beyond a shadow of doubt that amongst Muslims, the Koran forbids sexual intercourse outside wedlock: marriage is a must for the fulfillment of sensual desires, but this law is blown off by the wind of change when it comes to a Mujahid (the Holy warrior):

During the battle of Autas, the Muslims captured some women along with their husbands. Though earlier, a Muslim had been forbidden sexual intercourse with an unbelieving married woman, at this occasion, it was revealed to the Prophet that Allah had relaxed this restriction and permitted copulation to the warrior if she had fallen to his lot in the battle and thus became his property. (TIRMZI, vol. one, P 417)

In the Islamic Jihad, sex was a big bait to attract followers, and eventually, make them sincere devotees. After the people of Taif-the last major Arab City to resist Islam-surrendered in February, 631 C.E., to escape horrors of the siege, Muhammad was presented with three beautiful women; he gave one of them "to Ali, another to Usman and the third to Omar." To realize the significance of this episode, one ought to remember that both Ali and Usman were his sons-in-law and Omar was his father-in-law.

The holy warriors of Islam have been given an unusual privilege of sexual merriment. If they survive the battle, they secure concubines but if they fall, they are sure to enter paradise full of houris (beautiful maidens to be turned into concubines), living in the most luxurious environment.

"For them (the Muslims) is reserved a definite provision, fruit and a great honor in the Gardens of bliss reclining upon couches arranged face to face, a cup from a fountain being passed round to them, while, a pleasure to the drinkers..... and with them wide eyed maidens flexing their glances as if they were slightly concealed pearls. (The Rangers, 40-45)

"Surely for the God-fearing awaits a place of security gardens and vineyards and maidens with swelling bosoms." (The Tidings: 30)

The houris are ever-young women who have wide eyes, flexing glances and swelling bosoms. Fancy the modesty of Allah and holiness of His manners. Can anyone honestly say that it is not a lure to attract followers?

The Motivation for Plunder, Loot and Booty in the Koran

The Koran also legitimizes booty and loot secured from non-Muslims during a religious war-Jihad:

"Eat of what you have taken as booty, such is lawful and good. " (The Spoils, VIII: 70)

To make his followers, the merciless looters, he thoroughly drilled them in hatred of non-Muslims, the potential victims:

1. "Surely the worst of beasts in God's sight are the unbelievers." (The Spoils: VIII: 55)
2. " Certainly, God is an enemy to the unbelievers. " (The Cow: II: 90)
3. "Oh ye who believe! fight those of the unbelievers and let them find in you harshness." (Repentance: IX: 123)

4. "Humiliate the non-Muslims to such an extent that they surrender and pay tribute." (Repentance IX: 29)

Since it was plunder that paved the way to spread Islam, even those things that the Prophet himself had declared sacred, lost their sanctity when they proved inconvenient. For example, the Koran says:

"Then, when the sacred months are drawn away, slay the idolaters (The non-Muslims) wherever you find them, and take them, and confine them, and lie in wait for them at every place of ambush" (Repentance, IX: 5)

One must also note that, as fame of the Prophet's arms rang throughout Arabia, the Arab pagan tribes turned to him in hordes. All this happened to secure protection against any surprise Islamic raid, which had become the destiny of the infidels for not accepting Islam. An element of surprise, marvel and curiosity also formed a part of this submission. Arabia had not seen a man of Muhammad's stature before.

However, this all took place during the last few years of the Prophet's life. Thus, the new converts had no experiential loyalty for the new religion. Possibly, the greater factor of their disappointment was the fact that the chances of further booty were practically nil because almost entire Arabia had come under the grip of Islam. What proved even more devastating was the fact that now the Muslims had to pay religious taxes such as Zukaat (the tithe). Thus, it is not surprising that, at the death of the Prophet, there was a terrible explosion against Islam, which curbed human freedom through restraints of faith and rituals. Most tribes of the Arabian desert rebelled against Islam to display their apostasy.

Abu Bakr, The First Caliph of Islam, following example of the Prophet, made plunder the pillar of his foreign policy and unleashed the Arabian booty-hunters on Egypt and Iran. This is how the Arab Empire was founded, leading to the spread of Islam.

During the 20th century, Islam has lost its luster as the projected ambassador of peace, compassion and humanity in the face of the rising tide of human rights and the instinctive demand of justice for all. It has caused a lot of embarrassment to the Muslim propagandists. Therefore, to pull wool over the eyes of the non-Muslims, some Muslim scholars say that the Islamic Jihad is a defensive war against the aggressors.

The Prophet has said:

*"Acting as Allah's soldier for one night in a battlefield is superior to saying prayers at home for **1000** years." (Ibne Majah, vol. 2, P 166)*

Now, one can see for one's self the violent nature of Islam, its purpose and the methods of securing it.

For more on this refer to Islamic Jihad by Anwar Sheikh.

Islamic Way of Life v/s a Civilized Way of Life

This intolerant aspect of Islam imposed the outlook of desert tribal nomads (the Bedouin Arabs) on all those who were converted to Islam. The victorious Muslims converted people in the lands they overran at the point of the sword. ***"Accept Islam or Die"***, this was the general attitude of the truculent Muslim armies the world over. Such intolerance of everything non-Islamic has been typecast with Islam till today.

Hence in many non-Muslim eyes Islam came to represent intolerance, persecution and all that goes against a decent and civilized outlook. And Muslims generally came to be looked upon as those misguided humans whose outlook was limited to a lower level of human consciousness.

The track record of slash-smash-burn-destroy-slaughter of the victorious Islamists represented a choice for all non-Islamic peoples between being civilized or being Islamic. A choice to be made in favour of Islam on the pain of death. Hence, in the eyes of many citizens of the world for the past 14 centuries, the phrase "Islamic Civilization" is a contradiction in terms. You can either be Islamic or be civilized.

Whatever Islamic principles in the Koran may say about co-existence of Islam with Non-Islamic people, at the practical level, past history of the 14 centuries of Islam bears evidence to the fact that Muslims have never reconciled to having non-Islamic people anywhere in the globe. And as Islam does not accept co-existence of non-Islamic people anywhere on the globe, it is logical to foresee either a victory of the non-Islamic forces over Islam or vice versa. A victory over Islam would have to be such that it would once and for all put an end to the threat of an Islamic victory the world over. The second logical scenario is to foresee a victory for the Islamic Jihad over all non-Islamic people across the globe.

In this scenario, the ultimate saviour of humanity would have to come forth from within Islam itself. A saviour who would repudiate Islam and re-establish a civilized way of life. Needless to add here that although Islam is the most bloodthirsty and cruel face of sectarianism, all religions have had their role in dividing humanity. And in the final analysis all of them would have to become extinct so that Humankind can march towards a World State where there would be complete freedom for every citizen of the world to choose how to co-relate with what is beyond human knowledge. Freedom to consider that what is beyond human knowledge as a supernatural power which has to be won over by praying before it; OR to treat the unknown as a frontier of human knowledge and to push this frontier so as to bring an increasing part of phenomenon that makes up the universe within the bounds of human knowledge.

Islam Comes to India as a Military Force

Islam came into India as a Military force in the year 715 C.E.., in the Province of Sindh, but it made inroads into the country proper between 1020 and 1194 after which Mohammedan power was established in north India and a century later also in the Deccan and continued to be the dominant power till its formal end in 1857.

Conversion to Islam

In the 700 years that Islam has existed in this country as a military power, there has been tremendous interaction between Hindus and Muslims. This interaction has had its negative and non-negative aspects. Muslims came into India as invaders as they had in almost all countries where they are present today.

Most Muslim rulers were fanatical proselytizers of their religion. Under the rulership of Delhi Sultans the public worship at Hindu temples was generally forbidden, Hindus were not allowed to build new temples or repair old ones. Some rulers like Allah-ud-din Khilji and Feroz Shah Tughlak would desecrate temples upon the conquest of new territory as a symbol of victory of Islam. One some occasions a particularly fanatical Muslim king like Sikander Lodi would a fit of paranoia desecrate or destroy temples even in peaceful times.

*"In **1669** Aurangzeb issued a general order for the destruction of Hindu temples." As per rough estimates about **3000** (Three Thousand) temples were destroyed and converted into Mosques in the **750** years of Muslim rule in India. But let bygones be bygones. The fact is mentioned here only to set the record straight. In my personal view all such controversial structures should be taken possession of by an educational trust and be converted into schools to preach the unity of Humankind. And eventually not just such controversial structures, but all places of religious worship should cease to be prayer houses and should be used to house schools for humanist and rationalist education. (This obviously is the author's personal view)*

"During the sultanate and later under Aurangzeb, many hundreds of thousands of Hindus were forcibly converted to Islam. Shah Jahan appointed a superintendent of converts charged with the special responsibility for making converts. The sentences of criminals and prisoners of war were readily remitted and the individuals were granted daily allowances upon embracing Islam. The conversion of Muslims to Hinduism, on the other hand, constituted the crime of apostasy and was punished by death. The Jaziya, a special tax levied on all non-Muslims, was both a heavy financial-burden and a badge of inferiority borne by the Hindu; it also stimulated conversions to Islam.

Thus, during the 7 centuries of Mohammedan rule a significant portion of our countrymen had to change their religion by force of circumstances. And in 4 erstwhile Indian Provinces viz. West Punjab, Sindh, East Bengal and NWFP the Muslim converts came to constitute a majority by the present century. The multi-religious character of India is largely an ugly litter of intolerance, persecution, penal taxes, conversion of faith at the point of the sword, discriminatory civil and criminal laws, defilement and conversion of places of worship from that of one faith to another, all of which the country witnessed during the seven centuries of Muslim rule.

With the coming of British rule, the position of Muslims changed from that of rulers to that of subjects. This position was acceptable as along as the rulers were Britishers, but with the possibility of independence coming closer the Muslims, or at least their leaders could not reconcile to being ruled, in a democracy, where the Hindus were in a majority. The bloody surgery of partition and its aftermath are now a part of history and need not be recalled here.

But despite partition and the creation of a homeland for the Muslims from India, they continue to comprise the largest minority in this country. Hindus and Muslims continue to live side-by-side through communal riots and the interaction of day-to-day life.

This the sketch of historic interaction between Hindus and Muslims. But though the two communities came in touch with each other as a result of a conflict and remained in a state of hostility towards each other, the interaction over many centuries has also helped in an exchange of ideas. One reason for this was the enlightened policy of Emperor Akbar which marked the beginning of a Hindu-Muslim rapproachment. Though this policy was reversed by Aurangzeb, the strains of rapproachment, amidst conflict, have filtered down till today.

Hindu Customs Among the Muslim Community in India (and Pakistan)

But the more significant reason for a socio-cultural interaction between the two communities was the fact the overwhelmingly large proportion of Muslims are converts from

Hinduism and their ancestors time or the other been Hindus. Though their conversion in almost all cases had been at the point of the sword or through some other compulsion like penal taxes, discrimination in the eyes of the law under Muslim rule, the converts consciously and sub-consciously carried with them the strains of their pre-Muslim past. This is not to say that Islam did not influence Hinduism, it did as we have seen earlier in the section on Hinduism. The influence of Hinduism on Muslims is more pronounced on communities like the Bohras, Kutchi Memons and Khojas who embraced Islam relatively recently, *i.e.* about 200 years back.

Similarity in Surnames/Family Names amongst Indian (and Pakistani) Muslims

To gauge the influence of Hinduism one only needs to ask a Khoja or Bohra his name. Names like Allibhai Premji, Abdul Hashim Premji, etc. occur frequently among the Bohras and Khojas. Hindu Surnames occur more frequently among Muslims in general for instance, Chowdhury, Khatri, Patel, Dalwai, Parkar, Munshi, etc.

(These names are being quoted only as proper nouns, any resemblance with actual names of individuals is accidental and not intentional.)

Khoja social functions reveal the surprising presence of Hindu customs. For instance during a Khoja wedding a coconut is used as an auspicious fruit. In Maharashtra, Muslim women from the Konkan region even wear the Mangal Sutra after wedding. The wearing of flowers, (forbidden in Islam) by Muslim women is a common Hindu custom carried on by the converts.

Idolatary amongst Indian (and Pakistani) Muslims

Islam denounces idolatory, but in India we have cults like Saibaba in Maharashtra where Muslims worship a personified saint alongwith the Hindus. This apart the more common practice of flocking to pilgrimages to Mazhars, (tombs) of saints like Salim Chisti exists generally among Indian Muslims only. Worship at personal tombs is but one step behind worshipping personified deities. Flowers are offered at these Mazhars the pilgrims shower Flowers, a custom which smack of borrowings from Hindu customs. Even the custom of spreading a sheet (chaddar) of flowers is an Indian adaptation of an Islamic custom. In other Islamic countries such sheets are made of silk and satin (like the one spread over the Kaaba), only in India are flowers used.

FAKIRS, SUFIS, PIRS—THE MUSLIM SANYASIS

The Muslim practice of Sufism embodied in the many Pirs, Sufis and Fakirs emphasizes on universal brotherhood. Although Sufism seems to have originated in Iran, Sufism in India has an unmistakable influence of the Hindu practices of Yoga, Pranayam and the concept of Sanayasa with its Sanyasis, Sadhus and Rishis. Interestingly the Sufis and Fakirs undertake exercises derived from the Hindu discipline of Yoga. In fact all through the middle ages up to the present age their have been many Babas (saints) who are Muslims, but attract both Hindu and Muslim disciples.

The Sufi movement seems to to have originated in Iran. It does not seem to have any presence in Arabia and other Arab states. The Sufi tradition seems to borrow a lot from the pantheistic mysticism of pre-Islamic Zoroastrianism and Manichaeism (a pre-Islamic religious sect in Persia). The earliest Sufi saint-poet in India is considered to be Amir Khusro who lived in Delhi in the 13th century. Dara Shikoh the eldest of son of the Mughal ruler Shah Jehan seems to have been deeply influenced by Sufism. He is accredited with having undertaken a translation of the Upanishads from Sanskrit to Persian. (He incidentally was killed by his younger brother Aurangzeb in the battle of succession to the Mughal throne.)

The Sufis in India have represented a contrast to the general Islamic attitude of Jihad. The Sufi tradition stands out as a stark exception to the general Muslim temperament of either converting or killing the non-Muslims (Kafirs), imposing penal taxes and generally tyrannizing the non-muslim people. Had the Sufi tradition been dominat in mainstream Islam, the history of the world of the past 14 centuries would have been different-but this is only a hypothetical possibility.

The Sufis have borrowed extensively from the Rishi Parampara of India, the discipline of Yoga, Pranayam (breath control) and Hasya Rasa (the Sufi tradition of performing the dance of Joy). The Sufi tradition in India also seems to have been influenced by the Guru-Shishya parampara (Master-disciple tradition) of India which dates from the days of the Vedic Rishis, through Gautama Buddha, Mahavir, Guru Nanak Dev Ji, and the various saints of the Bhakti Movement-all of whom decried the practices of caste discrimination and preached the message of universal brotherhood of man with social justice for all. The Sufi tradition has borrowed from and strengthened this stream of priniciples of universal love and brotherhood of man that have been a part of the Sanatana Parampara of India for the last 4000 years. The Sufis incidentally also celebrate the Indian festival of Basant.

The Sufi tradition along with the other similar traditions like that of the Druze, Bahais (founded by Bahaullah in Iran), Ahmediyas (Quadianis), etc., represent an attempt to assert the universal brotherhood aspect of Islam. But as they do not characterize mainstream Islam it was necessary for them to shift away from the mainstream of Islam (*i.e.* the Shariah as interpreted by the Mullahs-clergy). In most cases the followers of such sects have been declared non-Muslims and there have been fatwas issued against them for blasphemy.

The blasphemy excuse has been used against all those who have tried to digress from the accepted principles of Islam (the Shariah as interpreted by the Mullahs-clergy). Blasphemy is only for speaking about Islam. But ironically, in the last 14 centuries of Islam, Muslims have with impunity gone about destroying the places of worship belonging to those of other faiths, smashing idols and converting non-islamic people at the pain of death.

The Bohras, Khojas and Kutchi Memons

It is noteworthy that a small segment of the Bohras and Khojas come close to the Sufi outlook of pantheist mysticism. Some of them even continue to revere Hindu Gods especially Sri Krishna who some consider to be an earlier prophet of God,

Mohammed being the last one. This can be explained by the fact that in the state of Gujarat from where the Bohras and Khojas hail; Sri Krishna is a very popular deity. Thus in spite of their conversion the Khojas and Bohras have tried to incorporate their pre-Muslim beliefs into their new faith.

Dress Styles amongst Indian (and Pakistani) Muslims

Even at the purely social level there have been common elements in the dress-styles of Hindus and Muslims. Muslim women still largely wear the saree, especially so in the rural areas. Even in some Muslim communities the Dhoti is worn by the males. The Punjabi dress of Hindus of the north is borrowed from the Muslims (though it had earlier been brought into India by the pre-Islamic Shakas and Kushanas. The Ghagara worn by women in north India is a unique blend of Hindu and Muslim dress styles. The wearing of bangles, bracelets, ear and nose Rings is a custom borrowed by the Muslim women from their Hindu counterparts.

Hindu Mercantile Laws amongst the Bohras, Khojas and Kutchi Memons

Among the Bohra, Khojas and Memons the Hindu mercantile law is applied in trade and commerce. Hindustani Music and Kathak-An amalgam of Bharatamuni and Arabic-Persian Dance Styles Even the Moghal rulers patronized the intermixing of Indian and mid-eastern dance styles. The Lucknavi Kathak is an admixture of the originally Indian Kathak (which is typified today by the style of the Jaipuri Gharanaa or Jaipuri School). While the Lucknavi Gharana has many elements of mid-eastern and central Asian dance styles. Music has been another area where a fusion has taken place under official patronage. Many Ragas (metres' and Swaras (tunes) of Hindustani classical music are a result of the amalgam of Hindu and mid-eastern musical traditions.

Caste amongst Indian (and Pakistani) Muslims

Even the Indian caste system has proved to be indelible to the Islamic touch. Indian Muslims still refer to themselves as Rajputs Jats, Gujjars, etc. and caste considerations are present during match-making. Thus we can see that though Islam was spread by the sword and it acted as an exorcist to redeem the newly won adherents from the influence of their original religions, quite a few traces of pre-Islamic culture did manage to seep into the lifestyle and consciousness of the Indian converts to Islam. (Note on ISLAM by the author: Here is it pertinent to note that some historians blame the Hindu-Muslim divide on the British policy of divide-and-rule of pitting Hindus against Muslims and vice versa. The British did follow a policy of divide-and-rule. But then the division which the British only exploited for their ends, was brought about by the 700 years of Muslim rule that went before the arrival of the British. The root of the Hindu-Muslim problem is that despite the usual tyrannical Islamic practices of conversion of the Kafirs or un-believers (of Islam), the conversion process (Jihad) in India achieved only 20% success; while 80% of the population remained non-Muslim. This is the reason for the partition and the recurring communal riots. Had the Hindus successfully checked the Muslim invaders at the Indus, or if the Muslims, after their conquest had converted all the non-Muslims to Islam, there would have been a uniform population and hence no partition and no communal riots. Wherever the conversion of the non-Muslim population to Islam was partial we have communal problems-in Bosnia, Cyprus, Lebanon, Philippines, apart from India. These countries along with the rest of the non-Muslim part of the world are *Dar-ul-Harb* (Zone of Kafirs or un-believers hostile to Islam) according to Islamic categorization of the world.

While in areas of *Dar-ul-Islam* (Islamic Zones) where the entire population has been converted to Islam, say like Egypt or Iran we do not have communal problems on the scale as they are in India. Egypt and Iran are two countries which had a rich pre-Islamic civilization, but are today completely Muslim. (Though the Muslims there sometimes wonder what they should make of the pre-Islamic past of their genetic ancestors. Not so in India, or Pakistan where the Muslims do not recognize their pre-Islamic past at all, or recognize it as "Haram"). To digress a bit, the socio-cultural-psychological reasons for the arbitrary tyrannical rule of the Muslim rulers across the globe is their temperament which they have imbibed along with their religion from the Arabs who display traits like fanaticism and short-temperedness in their extreme. The reasons why these traits should exist among those Arabs who originate from the Saudi Arabian Peninsula are to be found in their harsh natural environment. Saudi Arabia, the birth-place of Islam is devoid of fertile plains and river valleys which are congenial to the development of a settled civilized life. This was responsible for the atrophy of residents of the Arabian peninsula into barbarism, and their exclusion from civilization for a long time till the beginning of the 20th century and discovery of oil. The Arabs (In the interior of the Saudi peninsula the Arabs still live in a tribal society). The same cannot be said of the people of Mesopotamia, Assyria and Egypt who today consider themselves to be Arabs but were the founders of great riparian civilizations of the ancient world. The absence of a civilized way of life among the Arabs (from the Arabian peninsula) nourished the fanatical attitude which later became a characteristic of Islamic thought and way of life.

This attitude was transmitted to other people who were converted to Islam. Added to this was Islam's monotheistic character because of which Mohammedans tolerated no other religion. This singularistic and exclusive character of monotheistic Islam precluded any possibility of assimilation into itself of other deities or forms of worship. And whenever Islam had the support of the force of arms, its fanatical and intolerant nature found brutal expression in the annihilative repression it unleashed whenever it came in contact with another religion or culture.

This cultural lineage of the Muslim rulers made itself evident in the forcible conversion of peoples of other faiths to Islam at the point of the sword, destruction of places of worship belonging to other faiths, the imposition of Jazia tax on non-muslims and other policies whose objective was to stamp out all other religions and to Islamize the countries they overran in their Jihad. While saying all this we have to remember that we are talking against certain traits like religious fanaticism and violence which have been used by humans to impose their will on fellow humans since time immemorial. We should not forget that we are not talking against any nation or against people from any part of our globe.

All past human history with all its nobleness and wickedness is OUR history. That no human can deny! We as humans have to own up all of it. And, for the future, we have to learn to exterminate the wickedness and carry forward the nobleness. Whether the process of exterminating the wickedness, would require physical elimination of those who are steadfast in their wickedness or they can be reformed and be made to see reason is an open question. But by whatever means-reform or revolution-the wicked and their wickedness have to be eliminated for their own benefit and for the benefit of Humankind at large. So that ultimately we can bring an end to the pre-history of Man and begin our march into what can truly be called Human History. That phase of the history of our species where we can begin our journey towards a World State of Humankind, based on the philosophy of Rationalism and Humanism.

It also needs to be recalled here that humans have always fought one another to impose one's will on the other humans.

The Hindus have done it in a subtle way with their caste system within India; and their acculturation of the peoples of Indo-China and the far East-although it should be said that the Hindus did not invade other parts of the globe.

The Christians (Europeans) have done it in their crusades and more so in their colonization of the Americas where they wiped out the Incas, Aztecs, and other Red Indian people and their pre-colonial cultures; the colonization of Australia where the Christians marginalized the Maoris with the forced treaty of Whitanee; the European colonization of Africa, and South Asia (India, Pakistan, Bangladesh) for a planned economic plunder. In addition, Christian missionaries functioned during colonial times with the overt and covert support of the ruling colonial European Christian powers. Hence a large part of the post-colonial population of these countries is Christian.

4

CHRISTIANITY

About 2.5% of India's population are Christians. Christianity arrived in India almost about the same period as it arrived in Europe, meaning about 2000 years ago. Christianity originates in Israel. The first Christians were Jews and in the beginning Christianity was seen as a Jewish cult. Most of the Apostles of Christians acted in Europe to convert the Europeans to Christianity.

But one of the Apostles, St. Judas Thomas, arrived in India and converted Indians to Christianity. St. Thomas was a carpenter and a disciple of Jesus. He was brought to India by a merchant to build a temple. St. Thomas arrived in Kerala, in south India in 52 AD. He succeeded in converting local Indians to Christianity. His converts were called Syrian Christians. One assumption says that some of the Syrian Christians were actually Jews converted by St. Judas Thomas to Christianity. The disciples of Jesus at first intended to convince the Jews to adopt the philosophy of Jesus as new Judaism. Later on other Christian saints arrived to India as missioners. But most of the Indian were converted to Christianity by the missionaries who arrived in India with the European powers from 15th century.

The European powers arrived in India for commercial reasons, especially spices. But they also started converting local Indians to Christianity. Five European countries sent their representatives to India, Great Britain; France; Denmark; Netherlands and Portugal. Of the five European powers the Portuguese were most enthusiast to baptize Indians. The

Portuguese were the first European power to arrive in India. Their first ship, under the leadership of Vasco DaGama, arrived in south India in 1498 after it had circled the whole continent of Africa. The Portuguese inspired by the Pope's order to baptize people around the world not only fought wars against the local Indian rulers, but they even tried to enforced their Roman Catholic prayers on Syrian Christians.

After many wars the Portuguese were defeated by local rulers and they had only one big pocket of control in India, Goa. The Portuguese not only fought the Indian rulers, but they also fought against other European powers in India especially Dutch and English. Many Portuguese churches in Kerala were turned into English and Dutch churches after they were captured by these powers.

The English missionaries started acting in India at a much later period. The British, unlike the Portuguese, didn't allow the missionaries to enter their territory in the beginning. The British arrived in India in 1600 and they allowed the missionaries to enter their territory only from 1813. The British allowed different churches to establish missionaries in their territory. The missionaries didn't only spread Christianity, but they also did humanitarian deeds giving the needy basic necessities of life like food, clothes and shelter.

The missionaries also built schools in India and many of them even today have Christian or European originated name. The British church missionaries succeeded less than the Portuguese in converting Indians to Christianity, but unlike the Portuguese who tried to enforce Christianity, these Protestant converts were voluntary. The Portuguese were also aware of the Indian custom according to which the wife followed her husband's faith and therefore married their men to Indian women.

There are about 30 million Christians in India. The major centers of Christianity in India are Kerala, Tamil Nadu, Goa, Manipur and Mizoram. There is also a big community of Christians in Mumbai. The main division of Christians in India is like in the Christian world, Protestants and Catholic. There are also different denomination among them, Syrian Church, Armenian Church, Anglican Church and others. Most of the India Christians were converted by the Portuguese. There is also an Anglo-Indian community in India.

The second largest religious minority in India is that of the Christians. The Indian Christians consist of three main sects *viz.* the Syrian Christians, Roman Catholics and Protestants. Christianity was, we are told, first brought into India only a few decades after the passing away of Lord Christ.

But it was the apostle St. Thomas who is popularly believed to have introduced Christianity into India around the 1st century of our era. Thus Christianity seems to have come into India far before it had reached many European countries like Britain and Germany.

In talking of Christianity one generally loses sight of the fact that it was born in Asia and thus to begin with it is an oriental religion. Jesus Christ whose name the religion bears was born in Bethlehem in what is today the state of Israel.

"Among ancient legends there is one told of a little boy who once amused himself at play by modeling images of sparrows. As he was delighted with his creations. He clapped his hand whereupon the little birds took fright and flew away." This story of the child Jesus was one of the most popular of the many infancy narratives which the early Christians told about their leader.

Magis— Zoroastrian Priests

Like that of many other prophets the birth of Jesus was foretold through an angelic announcement. This announcement we are told brought forth three Zoroastrian priests from ancient Persia to pay their homage to the divine babe, as they interpreted the angelic announcement as heralding the birth of a Zoroastrian apostle. The three priests referred to as Magi (from Magian- a name for the ancient Zoroastrians) were also spoken of ' as three wise men or three kings from the east who brought gifts to the child Christ. But this angelic announcement that there is born Jesus 'king of the Jews' also eventually had repercussions when the news reached the tyrant Herod who was then the actual king of the Jews in Palestine.

The birth of another King' within his kingdom seems to have frightened him and in a effort to destroy this new 'King' he decreed that all babies in this kingdom should be killed. But, Jesus was saved as his parents whisked him away to Egypt outside Herod's kingdom. Most of Jesus' early childhood was spent in Nazareth. When he was still a young boy of around 12 years his parents *viz.*, his mother the Virgin Mary and his foster-father Joseph took him to Jerusalem for the spring time religious feast of the Passover. At the end of the first days journeying homewards they missed him. After searching for two days they found him in the Temple at Jerusalem, discussing theology with the learned doctors, impressing them with his wisdom and comprehension.

(Much has been said about Mary being referred to as a Virgin and Joseph as his foster father. The question is posed as to who was Jesus' real father. Such questions are also asked in the case of Kunti and her son Karna in the Mahabharata epic of the Hindus. For the devout the scriptural explanation of Virginity should suffice but for more critical students of history these questions call for an answer if human standards are applied to the scriptural accounts.)

Biographers of Jesus talk of the 18 silent years of his life, referring to the time between the incident in the temple when he was 12 years old and his baptism by John at the age of 30. To this important period of his life the Gospel sources devote but one sentence, Luke's statement that he increased in wisdom and stature and in favour with God and man. But this statement only says that he was a normal youth and young man."

Christ and Sri Krishna

But according to some scholars Jesus visited Kashmir in India in this period and during his stay conversed with Sages in India. It is also said on his death, his body was brought into Kashmir where it lies buried in a Shrine which bears the Arabic version of his name *i.e.* Isa. Some others even confound

Christ with Krishna and assert that both were one and the same person. As both were born in a pastoral setting, the birth of both was foretold by a divine announcement, the reigning king (Kansa in the case of Krishna) felt threatened with the birth of the God-Child, the reigning king made efforts to kill the child, the reigning king killed other children, the God-child was whisked away to safety across a water body, etc. And above all the name Isa (Jesus) Christ is a corruption of Esha (Lord) Krishna. But so far no conc1usive proof, has been found to support this far-fetched theory.

Coming back to Jesus, after his baptism he continued preaching his gospel in doing which he also acquired the role of a healer of diseases due to the sick people whom he cured in the course of his preachings. He had twelve select disciples one of whom was named Judas. As the teachings of Jesus gradually brought him into conflict with the Jewish religious establishment who contrived with the Roman an authorities to execute Jesus. In this they were helped by Jesus' own disciple Judas who betrayed him for the sake of a few silver coins. Jesus was thus held prisoner, he was tried by a Roman Court of law and sentenced to death. Before his execution he had his last meal (supper) with his disciples, at which he reiterated his preachings.

The last supper' is an incident popularly engraved into Christian psyche second only to the crucifixion. After Jesus was put to death on the cross, we are told, that after three days he was resurrected from his grave, after which he preached from some more days before passing into eternity.

Chrisianity's umbilical cord with Judaism

But Christianity and Christians were not a distinct religion different from Judaism. They were mainly Jews who looked upon Jesus as their leader but who had not detached themselves from Judaism. Even after the passing away of Jesus Christ, his teachings spread only in the Jewish quarters of cities outside Palestine. It was at Antioch in Syria where for the first time the Gentiles or Non-Jewish people were preached the teachings of Christ. In the liberal atmosphere of Antioch the teachings of Christ grew rapidly among the non-Jewish population. Now the question arose whether these non-Jewish followers of Jesus Christ should first be converted to Judaism-as Christ was himself till then looked upon as a Jewish Reformer of Judaism.

The answer to this question was decided upon at Antioch itself sometime in the 3rd century during at ecclesiastical conference. At this conference it was decided. that the followers of Jesus Christ were not a Jewish sect but constituted an international religion. It was also decided that the non-Jewish converts to the new faith need not adopt the Jewish faith, they need not practice circumcision, nor follow the law of Moses in toto. This made the disciples of Jesus Christ a new faith, distinct from its parent faith Judaism. The faith spread rapidly due to missionary activities amongst the laity in the Roman empire.

Incorporation of Christianity as the Roman State Religion

The next step was taken after the nominal conversion of the Roman Emperor Constantine to Christianity following the conversion of most of the Roman laity to the new religion. This process was not smooth, as his son, relapsed into the old Roman beliefs and was called the "Apostate" in Christian Chronicles. But Constantine's grandson was a devout Christian and was called the "Pious".

Roman Influences on Christianity

The result of this back and forth movement in matters of faith in the Roman royal family was that it eventually led to the abandonment of Hebrew and the acceptance of Latin as the ecclesiastical language and Rome as against Jerusalem as the ecclesiastical center where the papacy was founded and was based at Rome the heart and capital of the (Roman) empire as also the rewriting of the Bible as the New Testament different from the original Old Testament of the Jews. This completed the breach between the faith of Jesus and Judaism. But in driving this wedge the influence of the Roman empire should not be lost sight of as after the conversion of the Roman Royal family followed by the Roman nobility and finally the remaining Roman laity to Christianity. The occidental Roman empire was naturally interested in shearing away of the oriental roots of a faith which it had made its state Religion. From then onwards Christians and Christianity became synonymous with Europe and Europeans.

Christianity in India 40 years after Christ

But as mentioned earlier in this chapter, Christianity originally came to India before it reached many of the West European Christian countries of today. It is supposed to have reached India between the 1st and 3rd centuries of our era. But these early attempts to introduce Christianity into the country could make any major dent. Only small pockets in the South were converted and are today's Syrian Christians mainly from Kerala and some parts of Tamil Nadu.

These Christians mostly come from the Namboodri Brahmin caste of Kerala. They represent an interesting sociological entity. Devout Christians as they are, they are also stout-hearted nationalists with a strong Malayali identity which translates to a strong national (Indian) identity. Hypothetically speaking, if all Indians had been converted by the Apostle St. Thomas to Christianity all Indians might have been like (the prototype) Syrian Christian Community-Christian yet specifically national.

Portuguese Bring Christianity (as Catholicism) into Goa

Christianity (as Catholicism) into Goa came into our country in a large way only after the 15th century alongwith the Portuguese Colonists. The Portuguese were Roman Catholics and when they reached Indian shores were still under the influence of the crusades and. the inquisition. In the early centuries of their rule in Goa, Daman and Diu they did make the use of force to effect conversions of the native Hindus to Christianity.

A part of the early converts to Christianity were a result of the taking of Indian wives by the Portuguese officials. These converts were termed Mestizos (of mixed blood). To these were added the progeny of extra-marital relations between the colonial officials and the native womenfolk. The offspring of such relations were brought up as Roman Catholics. These facts have been recorded in the Portuguese records of the Colonial Period. The occurrence of aquiline features and fair skin in some Goan Christian families seems to be an inheritance of such relations.

In the early part of Portuguese rule, the Colonialists are also recorded to have forcibly converted temples into churches. As per local traditions in the villages around the Basilica of St. Francis Xavier near Panjim in Goa, There originally existed a Shiva temple on the site of the Basilica which was demolished by the colonial authorities to put up the Basilica.

After the Shiva temple was destroyed the local populace constructed a small Shiva-linga nearby in memory of their temple. Till today this Shiva-linga is being worshipped and the age old tale is told to visiting tourists. All this is not being said with a new to unearth long forgotten events, but to record facts of the means used by a colonial power to implant its faith on Indian Soil.

It is well known generally that the Portuguese apart from being ardent proselytizers also observed strict racial segregation and followed a policy of discrimination against all native Indians whether Hindus or Christians. The emigration of some families of Goan Christians to Mangalore in the 16th century was a result of discriminatory treatment by the Portuguese. Even today there exists a significant Konkani speaking Roman Catholic community around Mangalore.

The third segment of Indian Christians are the Protestants. They form a minority among the Christian community and are a result of the Protestant Missionaries. The British colonialists largely kept away from proselytizing activities. Conversions to Christianity during British rule were mostly due to the activities of missionaries. Indian Christians have generally not lived a barrack-like existence like the Muslims. There has been a significant social interaction between the Hindus and Christians and the feeling of animosity that exists vis-a-vis the Muslims has been absent in the case of the Christians. As almost all Indian Christians are converts from Hinduism they display many traces of their pre-conversion culture.

Hindu Customs Among the Christian Community in India

To begin with Indian Christians, especially the Protestants have still preserved the surnames of their pre-conversion days. In many cases they also have Hindu first names. This makes them completely identical with the Hindus, at least externally. The reason could partly lie in the fact that many converts to Protestant Christianity were voluntary one's and belonged to the upper echelons of Hindu society. The conversion of the Rev. Vaman Narayan Tilak is one example. These voluntary converts to Christianity turned to that religion consequent to philosophical speculation. It is natural for such converts to preserve a strong nationalistic identity in spite of the conversion.

Marriage Customs Among the Indian Christians

But among all segmpnts of Indian Christians the aspects of their social life, which has preserved their Indian roots as the manner of celebrating Christian festivals especially Christmas and their dress habits.

During Christmas and new Year festivities, it is common among Indian Christians to burst crackers, light lamps, exchange sweetmeats, draw designs with coloured powder outside their doorsteps, etc. All these practices have been a carryover from the Hindu festival of Diwali. If one goes to a Roman Catholic wedding one would see that a day before the wedding is to take place, the groom and his best man are given a special bath by the groom's relatives.

In this bath the groom and his best man are smeared with milk, eggs yolk and scents. This custom is no doubt borrowed from the Hinduism where the groom is given a bath with Sandal-wood paste and Turmeric powder, a day before the wedding.

The Christian practice of the best man pulling a chord to release a shower of tiny coloured thermocole balls on the bride and groom during the wedding festivities come very close to the Hindu custom of throwing vermillion coloured grains of rice on the couple during a traditional Hindu wedding. Even after the wedding, or after a death in the family, Christians in Goa follow the practice of mass feeding of beggars and poor people, this custom seems to be a carryover of the Hindu custom of feeding brahmins and poor people during any important social and religious function.

Caste among Indian Christians

Conversion to Christianity has not erased the caste system from the Christians. Christians still privately continue to refer to themselves by their caste affiliations like Prabhoos, Bamons, Kolis, Bhandaris, etc. and caste considerations are rarely absent during matchmaking especially among Christians in rural areas. Some Christian converts who were Brahmins originally still in some cases, wear the sacred thread though their number is less.

But Christians commonly wear the black thread around their wrist as a good luck charm as do the Hindus. The belief of an evil eye and other taboos persist among the Christians and the method of warding off the effect of the evil eye *i.e.* Drishta as it is known among Hindus (or Nazar as it is called among the Muslims) is by circling a pinch of salt and chilli powder around the person who is believed to have been affected.

Christian women often wear sarees like their Hindu counterparts and some of them even wear bangles and apply the Hindu caste mark, Kum Kum or tilaka on their foreheads. The wearing of the Mangalsutra necklace among Protestant Christian women is obligatory after marriage, as it is among the Hindus.

Some Christian families have continued their pre-conversion Practice of praying and asking for boons before Hindu deities during annual Festivals-though this is frowned upon by the Christian clergy.

The traditional Christian form of greeting each other by saying 'Peace be with you' is accompanied by the joining of hands which is an adaptation of the Hindu practice of Namaste. Even when praying Indian Christian carry flowers, and garlands to church. The practice of garlanding the cross and icons is a carryover of the Hindu practice of garlanding idols. In the west this practice is absent where only candles are lit before the

Cross. But like the Muslims, the Christians in India also bear a mark imprinted by History. It is the past association of both these faiths with conquerors who tyrannized a large part of the Indian population.

The cultural tensions involving the Christian community derive from a widespread feeling in India that Christianity is a Western Religion which was brought into this country as a result of colonial rule and is today a living relic of our colonial past. In the minds of many Indians, Christianity and Christians are associated with the support of western imperialist rule.

A contemporary historian says, "It must also be stated that, with some notable exceptions, Christians tended to remain aloof from the Indian nationalist movement. A sense of identification with their Portuguese and British co-religionists is far from the entire explanation, although undoubtedly this is the most important factor."

This kind of relationship exists even today between the Muslim and Christian communities and the countries from where these religions came into India. As in the case of the Muslims, the policies of Pakistan and the Arab states towards India have an effect on the position of Muslims vis-a-vis the country, in a similar way though to a far lesser degree, the foreign policies of the U.S.A., U.K., Portugal, etc., have a bearing on the position of the Indian Christians vis-a-vis the country and consequently vis-a-vis the Hindu community.

Thus, the Niyogi Report submitted to the Govt. of India some years back saw a direct and sinster relationship between the objectives of the Indian churches and American foreign policy objectives in the cold war".... The loyalty which the Indian Christians extend to the Vatican was interpreted as an objectionable from of extra-territoriality'

5

SIKHISM

About 2% of India's population are Sikhs. Even so, the Sikhs, because of their unique appearance sometimes stand for India. Traditionally the men keep their hair and do not shave their beard or moustache. They gather their head hair in a turban. Sikhism is comparatively a new religion in India. This religion was established by Guru Nanak. Nanak was born into a Hindu family in 1469 in the Punjab region. Since childhood he loved to travel, learn and preach humanity. In those days people who taught and preached were titled Guru meaning teacher, his followers became to be known as Sikhs meaning learners. And so Guru Nanak developed a new religion and it also included beliefs from the two dominant religions in the Punjab region, Hinduism and Islam.

Some claim that Guru Nanak tried to developed a new religion and included in it what he thought were the good beliefs of these two religions. Like in Islam the belief in the existence of one invisible God. Like in Hinduism the belief in Karma and reincarnation, meaning your actions in this life will decide your fate in the next incarnation. The Sikhs also cremate their dead ones as is done in Hinduism.

The creators of Sikhism tried to abolish some of the Indian customs such as the caste system and Sati-burning of the widow. In Sikhism everyone has equal rights irrespective of caste, creed, colour, race, sex or religion. Sikhism rejects pilgrimage, fasting, superstitions and other such rituals. Sikhism does not have a clergy class as it considers this as a gateway to corruption. However they have readers and singers in their temples. A Sikh place of worship is called Gurdwara. Sikhism does not support pilgrimage to holy sites because according to Sikhism, God is everywhere and not in any certain place. But Sikhism has a few important sites, of which, the Hari Mandir, also known as the 'Golden Temple' in Amritsar in Punjab is the most important site and is considered the holiest shrine of Sikhism.

Sikhism emphasis community services and helping the needy. One of the distinct features of Sikhism is the common kitchen called Langar. In every Gurdwara there is a Langar. Every Sikh is supposed to contribute in preparing the meals in the free kitchen. The meals are served to all and are eaten sitting on the floor and this is to emphasis the point that all are equals. Sikhism does not believe in holding fasts for body is God's present to human being and therefore humans must foster, maintain and preserve it in good sound condition, unless fasting is done to foster the human body like healthy diets.

Guru Nanak who established Sikhism was its first Guru. After him there were nine more Gurus who were the highest religious authority. The last Guru, Guru Gobind Singh, proclaimed that after him the Guru of the Sikhs would be the holy book of Sikhism, Guru Granth Sahib.

Guru Granth Sahib is written in Gurumukhi script. It includes the writings of the Sikh Gurus and the writings of Hindu and Muslims saints. But out of humility Guru Gobind Singh did not include his own writings in the book he had proclaimed as the permanent Guru of the Sikhs. His writings appear in a separate book called Dasam Granth. Guru Gobind Singh is also the Guru behind the unique appearance of Sikh men.

During Guru Gobind's term as the Guru of the Sikhs and also before him, the ruling empire of Punjab region was the Moghul Empire. The Moghuls were Muslims. Some of the Moghul emperors, like Aurangazeb were fanatic Muslims who harassed the non-Muslims, including the Sikhs. Some of the Sikh Gurus were even executed by the Moghul emperors. In order to stop their persecutions, Guru Gobind decided to make his followers, the Sikhs (meaning learners), a community of fighters. He changed his surname to Singh, which means lion. His followers also changed their surname to Singh. Since then a ceremony of baptizing was established among the Sikhs in which the boys were given the title Singh and the girls were titled Kaur meaning princess. In those days "Singh" as a surname was very popular among a famous warrior caste of north India, the Rajputs. Some of the first Sikhs were also Rajputs.

In order to make it easier for his followers to recognize each other, Gobind Singh, chose five marks, some of which even today symbolize the Sikhs. The five signs were, uncut hair; comb; sword or dagger; bracelet on the right wrist and shorts. The religious Sikhs dress according to Guru Gobind Singh's order, carrying a sword. Most of the Sikhs even today have uncut hair and gather it in a turban. But some easygoing Sikhs cut their hair or they do not gather their uncut hair in a turban.

The emphasis on militant tradition and community service in Sikhism continues even today and many Sikhs serve in the Indian army or police. The Sikhs also have a reputation as experts in steering, from cars to airplanes.They were among the first communities in India who dared to drive vehicles specially lorries. India being a vast country needed drivers who could also travel at nights. But many Indians believed in superstitions like ghosts and haunted places, while the Sikhs rejected these kinds of beliefs and therefore traveled at nights, since then their reputation as steering masters of India.

Defended Our Self-Esteem and Re-asserted Our Original Humanist and Rationalist Outlook

From the 11th century onward North India was subject to invasions from the Afghans and Turks. Punjab which has been the gateway into India since ancient times, bore the brunt of the Islamic onslaught. The victory of the invaders meant not just a new ruler but a ruler who was committed to spread his religion among the conquered people-with all means, fair and foul.

Towards this end the Muslim conquerors imposed the Jazia tax on the conquered *i.e.* non-Muslim people, destroyed non-Muslim places of worship and converted people to Islam at the point of the sword.

On the other hand the existing religion, Hinduism with its unbending caste system and rigid ritualism had become long overdue for reform. Voices of dissent against orthodoxy and ritualism had begun to be heard even before the birth of Sikhism. Dyaneshwar and Namdeo in Maharashtra, Basaweshwara in the south were among those who preached the message of equality of all humans irrespective of their caste and creed. Such was the environment in which was born Nanak whom the Sikhs look upon as their first Guru.

The Life-Story of Guru Nanak Dev Ji

The life story of Nanak is eloquent as to the nature of the society that surrounded him as also of the mind of this simple yet noble person. Nanak was born in the year 1469 at a village near the present-day city of Lahore.

He was born in a **Kshatriya** family. His family is said to have belonged to the Bedi sub-caste. At his birth, we are told by the Adi Granth that 33 crores of Gods paid homage to the infant. His mother Tripta was noted for her piety and his father, Kalu was a merchant by profession.

Nanak was a brilliant boy since his early days and had mastered many of the Shastras while still young. We get an insight into the boy's mind when during his thread ceremony he riddled the officiating **Brahmin** priest, with questions as to how the mere placing of a thread around his body could initiate him into the religion.

As a young man Nanak was fond of visiting ascetics and hermits and brooding over the discussion he had with them. Troubled by Nanak's non-wordly attitude his father tried to settle him in business. But Nanak's mind was involved in something far beyond the ordinary affairs of life. Once having given a large sum of money to be paid to another merchant Nanak non-chalantly distributed the sum among a group of beggars and returned home empty-handed. After this his father gave up hope of rehabilitating his errant son in wordly affairs.

The God "Brahm" Appears before Nanak

Nanak continued to brood over issues dear to him. One day his brother-in-law who had come on a visit to Nanak's place decided to take Nanak with him and install him in Government service. In this assignment Nanak was fairly successful but his mind roamed elsewhere. Once when he had gone to have his morning bath, he disappeared into a nearby forest where it is said, God appeared before him and said "I am God, the primal Brahm" and you are the Guru. Three days after disappearing into the forest Nanak returned. But he did not wait long, he gave up his job, distributed among the needy whatever possessions he had and with one companion whose name was Mardana and who was a musician, Nanak set out to preach his gospel.

Nanak combined his preachings with devotional music and became a popular evangelist. Another technique of his to attract quick attention was his attire, which was a combination of the tradition of the Hindu and Muslim dress. This way he also emphasized the superfluous nature of tradition and in his preachings, emphasized that there was a religion greater than the one embodied in tradition and rituals. An important theme of his preachings was "There is no Hindu Muslim, all are the children of God". *'Na koi Hindu, na koi Turak, sab hai kudrat de bande'.*

Nanak's Ridicule of Hollow Ritualism

Spreading his gospel he visited many places of pilgrimage. Once while he was on a visit to Kashi (modern Varanasi) he saw people taking a purificatory bath in the Ganges and then throwing water in a particular direction so that it reached the heavens where their departed ancestors resided. On seeing this Nanak joined the devotees, but he started throwing water in the opposite direction.

When asked the reason for his anomalous behaviour, Nanak explained that he was watering his fields in Punjab which were about 500 miles from Kashi. On hearing his explanation he was made a laughing stock of the crowds but he turned the tables on his scornful audience by asking them how the water could reach the heavens if it could not reach his fields just 500 miles away. Though born a Hindu, Nanak was quite careless of the formal demands of Hinduism and openly attacked some of its practices.

Once during his travels he asked for food at a wayside house and was offered deer meat which he ate heartily. For this he was rebuked by Brahman priests. But Nanak felt no qualms for having violated convention and his caustic reply to the priest was that, it was foolish for a man who was born of flesh and who continually lived in flesh to abstain from eating it. In his sermons he frequently ridiculed rituals held sacred by the orthodoxy.

Once during a sermon he posed a question to his audience as to what was the point in going to snake pits and worshipping a snake as a God when they would kill the same snake without hesitation if it chanced to enter their homes. Nanak's views would have sounded heretical and sacrilegious to the devout, but during his lifetime itself Nanak had acquired a considerable following among the peasantry in Punjab.

Nanak's visit to Mecca and the Kaaba

In the course of his missionary activity Nanak often visited foreign countries. According to local folklore, he is said to have visited, Mecca in the guise of a Muslim devotee. But his ignorance of Mohammedan etiquette nearly cost him his life. On his first night at Mecca he slept with his feet towards the Kaaba. He was rudely awakened by an Arab clergyman who said, "Who is this sleeping Kaafir (infidel), who lies with his feet towards God?". To this Nanak replied "Turn my feet in the right direction where God is not". And when the clergyman turned Nanak's feet to the proper Mohammedan position, the sacred Kaaba itself turned round following Nanak's feet in their semi-circular revolution-or so, we are told, through Sikh folklore.

Hindu and Muslim disciples of Nanak

Nanak continued his missionary activities till the end of his days. When his end was near he had acquired a large following among the Hindus and also among some Muslims who had recently been converted to Islam at the point of the sword by the Sultans and Mughals who then were in power at Delhi. But when Nanak lay on his deathbed an unseemly quarrel broke out among his followers. The Hindus wanted to cremate the body of their Guru while the Muslims wanted to bury it.

We are told that to teach a lesson to his warring disciples Nanak asked each of the groups to place flowers at his dead body on either side and those whose flowers remained fresh throughout one night could have possession of his body. But after this was done, to everybody's surprise on the said morning when the shroud was lifted there was no body but only flowers and all of them were fresh. Thus even after his death as during his life Nanak taught the people the falsity of the barriers of religion.

Sikhism after Nanak

Nanak had appointed a disciple of his, named Angad, to succeed him as the next Guru. During Nanak's days there were many preachers who spread similar views among people. Dyaneshwara, Namdeo. Basaveshwara, Kabir, Tulsidas were a few among them. But it was only Nanak's tradition that lived on while that of the others withered away soon after the death of the founders. The reason why only Nanak's tradition survived the death of the founder could be found in the fact that Nanak did not present himself as belonging to any particular religion and his message was directed towards all.

Nanak wanted to propagate a message of universal brotherhood and did not limit himself with reforming the religion of his birth, although one of his objectives was to rid Hinduism, of casteism and ritualism. Another and more important reason could be the line of successive Gurus that followed Nanak and continued, to preach the message of universal brotherhood whose propagation he had initiated. After Nanak came 9 Gurus who succeeded each other in the following order:

Guru Nanak Dev Ji

Guru Angad Dev Ji

Guru Amardass Ji

Guru Ramdass Ji

Guru Arjan Dev Ji

Guru Hargobind Saheb Ji

Guru Har Rai Saheb Ji

Guru Har Kishen Saheb Ji

Guru Tegh Bahadur Saheb Ji

Guru Gobind Singh Ji

Guru Granth Saheb Ji

Sikhism under the Successive Gurus

Nanak did not present his teachings as though they were a separate religion but laid emphasis on the universal brotherhood among all humans irrespective of the religion they followed. But gradually the followers of Guru Nanak and of the, Gurus, who succeeded him acquired the status of a distinct religion which was one among the many others which had existed till then. To begin with no name was given to the followers of Guru Nanak but later on they acquired a name. The term 'Sikh' used to describe term means 'disciple' of the Guru and is derived from the term 'Shishya' which in Sanskrit means 'disciple'.

The Twentytwo Segments

Under every successive Guru, the position of the followers as a separate and organised religion was further crystallized. The third Guru Amardass divided the territory inhabited by his followers in twenty two segments and spiritual administrators were appointed for each of the segments. The fourth Guru Ramdass established a temple near Lahore which could be looked upon by the followers as the seat of spiritual and temporal authority of the Guru. This temple was called the Harimandir and later the Harmindar Saheb or the Darbar Saheb Gurudwara. A lake was dug around it for devotees to bathe before offering prayers. This lake was termed the Amrit-Sarovar (lake of nectar) from which the city that grew around it derived its name 'Amritsar'.

The fifth Guru Arjan Dev compiled the Sikh canon)the Adi Granth (later to be called Guru Granth Saheb Ji) which alongwith the Sukhmani and the Japjee compiled by Guru Nanak, forms part of the worship (Ardas) of the Sikhs.

Guru Arjan Dev instituted practices which were to have far-reaching impact on the making of the Sikh community. In this he was surpassed only by the last Guru, Gobind Singh.

'Piri' and 'Miri'

Guru Arjan Dev declared that it was the duty of every Sikh to give one tenth of his income to the communal treasury and he appointed collectors for each of the twenty two segments to implement this. Thus Sikhism became a theocracy and a state of which the Guru was virtually a king. He used to wear two swords one on each hip which came to known as the 'Piri' the Saint and 'Miri' the Administrator. Here we see the combination of the role of the Church and the State in the context of Sikhism.

Amibivalance towards Hinduism

Though Sikhism began as a message of universal brotherhood among followers of all religions, it was gradually itself transformed into a separate religion. Its relationship with Hinduism remained a problematical one. This was so although as the Gurus preached the message of universal brotherhood all the Gurus themselves and almost all of their followers were drawn from Hinduism. Added to this was the burden of oppression of the Mughal emperors who looked upon the Sikhs as a group of heretical Hindus who tried to sow confusion amongst the followers of Islam. Guru Arjan Dev Ji tried to resolve the status of Sikhism by stating that:

"I have broken with the Hindu and the Musalmaan.

I will not worship with the Hindu, nor like the Musalmaan go to Mecca,

I shall serve Him and no other,

I will not pray to idols, nor say the prayer of the Musalmaan

I shall put my heart at the feet of the one Supreme Being,
For we are neither Hindus nor Mussalmaans.

Martydom of Guru Arjan Dev

But in the eyes of the Mughal rulers, the followers of the Gurus were Hindus who tried to undermine Mughal sovereignty. For this the Sikhs were violently repressed. In the reign of the Mughal Emperor Jehangir, Guru Arjan Dev Ji was the first Guru to be martyred (at the hand of the Mughal oppressors). Jehangir sentenced Guruji to be beheaded after being tormented for days. Burning hot sand was poured on his bare body. After being subjected to such inhuman torture, Guruji we are told, expressed a desire as his last wish, to have a bath in the Ravi river before being beheaded. Guru Arjan Dev Ji who had suffered brutally at the hands of his Mughal tormentors, went into the river till his head disappeared into the swirling currents of the Ravi-never to return. Thus he became the first Sikh Guru to lay down his life due to Mughal oppression.

It was under the later Gurus that Sikhism came to appear as the militant wing of the Hindu community. The idea of Sikhs being defenders of Hinduism was strengthened during the tenure of the 9th and 10th Gurus. Guru Tegh Bahadur and Guru Gobind Singh. During the tenure of these two Gurus the nature of the Sikh religion underwent a fundamental change. And from being a sect with ascetic and pacifist ideals, the Sikhs were transformed into an aggressive military theocracy.

Militarization of the Sikhs due to Mughal Oppression

The changes brought about by Guru Gobind Singh were so fundamental that they represented a new phase in the history of Sikhism. It is worth recalling the circumstances that led to this change. Understanding this phase of Sikh history is all the more important as it led to the formation of Sikhism as we know it today.

This phase of the Sikh religion was a direct result of Mughal oppression. The Mughal rulers had no love for a sect that originated from among the Kafirs (Hindus) but had adapted

Islamic ideas like monotheism rejection of idol worship, military theocracy and who with the indigenous Hindu terminology of expression tried to secure a following also among the adherents of Islam. This was unbearable to the Mughals who looked upon the Sikhs as wanting to usurp the platform of Islam and stall the process of converting Hindus (in Punjab) to Islam.

Sikhism was in the Eyes of the Mughals-a Panic Reaction of the Hindus against Islam

For the Mughals, Sikhism represented a panic reaction from within the Hindu community to salvage its status as non-muslim by accepting the positive ideals of Islam like rejection of idol worship, casteism and ritualism of its Hindu parent religion and infusing militancy into the new Hindu converts to Sikhism. In the eyes of the Mughal rulers, the Sikh reform was detrimental to the conversion of the Hindus to Islam; and the militancy of the Sikhs was harmful to the security of the Mughal empire. Hence the bitter oppression of the Sikhs by the Mughals which was even more severe than the oppression of the Hindus in general.

During the reign of Aurangzeb the severest wave of oppression was unleashed on Non-Muslims with a view to Islamize the country. As the Mughal oppression found tough resistance from the Sikhs they were the favourite target for the Mughals. Here the story of Guru Tegh Bahadur and Guru Gobind Singh needs to be.

The Martyrdom of Guru Tegh Bahadur

During the reign of Aurangzeb Guru Tegh Bahadur who was the then Guru of the Sikhs was approached by a group of Hindu Pandits from Kashmir with a plea for protection from Mughal oppression. True to the spirit of his faith the Guru decided to approach the fanatical Mughal emperor Aurangzeb himself for a redress of the grievances. Unfortunately at the Mughal court he received abuses and threats. He was told to accept Islam on the pain of death. To prove his word the Mughal emperor Aurangzeb tourtured to death the members of the Guru's entourage one after the other. But Guru Tegh Bahadur did not lose his composure and calmly demanded a halt to the repressive policies. Wanting to teach a lesson to the obstinate Guru and to set an example to his followers the emperor ordered that the Guru to be beheaded. Thus after Guru Arjan Dev, Tegh Bahadur was the second Sikh Guru to meet a violent death at the hands of the Mughals. But after his execution some of his followers managed to sneak out the Guru's severed head from Delhi and carried it to Anandpur. At the place where the Gurus severed head was cremated, a Gurudwara was erected to commemorate this sacrifice undertaken in defence of the Dharma. This place is known to us today as the Anandpur Saheb Gurudwara.

The Khalsa Panth of Guru Gobind Singh Ji

When Guru Tegh Bahadur was martyred, his son Gobindrai, who later became Guru Gobind Singh) was still a boy, but the events which had overtaken his father, influenced him deeply and after succeeding his father as the next Guru, he was determined to carry out the struggle against Mughal oppression. Towards this end he undertook a radical transformation of the Sikh religion. This transformation was too fundamental to be termed as a reform and it virtually amounted to the establishment of a new religious order. And though he transformation differentiated the subsequent Sikhism (the Khalsa Panth from the earlier one; more in temporal and worldly aspects rather than in spiritual matters, it led to the first major split among the Sikhs.

The five Ks (Kakkars)

The transformation of Sikhism as the Khalsa Panth was formally launched by Guru Gobind Singh Ji on Baishakhi (New year) day in the year 1699. The new community was termed the Khalsa Panth or the 'Pure Sect' as its followers were required to be far more strict in observing the tenets of their reformed faith. The followers of the Khalsa were required to observe five visible symbols of membership. These signs as we know were: 1) Unshorn Hair (Kesha), 2) A curved dagger (Kirpan), 3) A comb (Kangva), 4) A steel bangle (Kada), 5) A pair of shorts (Kachha). All members of the Khalsa were required to suffix their name with the term 'Singh' meaning 'lion'. Guru Gobind

Singh's aim in forming the Khalsa Panth was to build up a militarized community which could resist Mughal oppression. An anecdote about his forming of the Khalsa army is worth recalling.

The Formation of the Khalsa Army

Once the Guru was delivering an inspiring speech before a group of Sikh youths on the necessity for every youth in the community to be ready to sacrifice everything he had including his life for the cause of his faith. The response of the youths was enthusiastic and many expressed their readiness to get enrolled in the Khalsa Panth. But the Guru' s standards of integrity were very high and he said that he would require the heads of those who wanted to join the Khalsa. The Guru pulled out his sword and beckoned the enthusiastic youths to come forward and lay down their lives there and then.

The youths were dumbfounded and for some moments nobody volunteered to sacrifice his life, while the Guru waited with his unsheathed sword in hand. Finally one of the youths turned up and offered his head to the Guru saying that his head already belonged to the Guru and the Guru may have it if he wanted. The Guru caught hold of the youth and led him inside the sacrificial tent that had been erected for the occasion. After sometime there was a piercing scream form the youth and the Guru emerged from the tent and in his hand was a blood-stained sword. The Guru now demanded another head.

His audience was benumbed at this evident gruesome scene and many devotees fled the place in disgust saying that the Guru had gone mad! But out of the few remaining youths another one offered his head to the Guru. After some time a few select youths had offered their heads to their Guru and has been "sacrificed" by the Guru, while many others had fled carrying with them the memory of a ghastly episode.

> *But those who fled were never to learn the secret of what happened to those brave youths, five in number, who had offered their heads to the Guru and who were the first Panj Pyaras. Contrary to the impression that he created, after leading every youth into the tent, the Guru*

embraced each of them and installed them as his select soldiers who were to form the Khalsa army. This army was the bravest that could be had as it was made up of men who had proved that they would lay down their lives to serve their Guru and the Panth in their struggle with the Mughal oppressors.

The Fierce Commitment to Overthrow Mughal Oppression

There is also a less known tradition which Guru Ji is said to have shared orally with the Panj Pyaras in the tent after they had offered him their heads. After baptising them as the first 5 members of the the Khalsa "Pure" Panth *Guru Ji decided to have the Panj Pyaras observe the 5 kakkars which included wearing a Kada (signifying a bangle)-as a sign of not yet having fulfilled a commitment of overthrowing the Mughal tormentors who then ruled Punjab(and the rest of India). The Kada was meant to instill a compelling sense of commitment in them to defeat their Mughal tormentors.*

This aspect of the kada signifying womanhood and shame was later not mentioned for obvious reasons and is not reflected in the Sikh legend. It was this act on part of Guru Ji that spurred on his followers to avenge their oppression by the Muslims and finally led to their successes under Maharaja Ranjit Singh in 1799. (This tradition of fighting Delhi was quoted again by the terrorists during the anti-Indian insurgency of the 1980s. But then the rulers of Delhi were different in 1980 from those in 1699!)

Sahejdharis and Keshadharis

Those members of the Sikh Panth (sect) who observed the five visible signs, and also used the suffix "Singh" (lion) with their names, imbibed the fighting spirit inculcated by Guru Gobind Singh. They came to be known as *Keshadharis* (wearers of unshorn hair) and those Sikhs (*i.e.* virtually all the remaining people of Punjab) who revered the Gurus but did not accept the 5 Kakkars laid down by Guru Gobind Singh Ji and did not use the suffix "Singh" were called *Sahejdharis* (casual devotees), or plainly speaking-Punjabis (*i.e.* Punjabi Hindus).

The Sahejdharis were also followers of the Gurus, though they did not belong to the Khalsa Panth. And despite this difference, there did not exist a feeling of belonging to different sects among the two sects of the followers of the Gurus till recent times.

Banda Bairagi

Banda Bairagi personifies the ethos of Punjab. His story signifies the oneness of the Sahjedharis and the Keshadharis. Banda Bairagi was born into a Sahejdhari family. He was a devout person from his childhood. Immense love for the Guru attracted him to Guru Govind Singh Ji. In his youth, Banda Bairagi became a Keshadhari and was baptised as Banda Singh Bahadur by Guru Ji. Banda Singh Bahadur carried on a relentless fight against the Muslims. After a stormy life, full of daring adventures, he died on the battlefield fighting the Mughal Oppressors. His name has become legendary in Punjabi folklore.

The Political History of the Sikhs

The later history of the Sikhs is more a political history rather than religious and centers around the establishment of a sovereign kingdom by Maharaja Ranjit Singh. Here let us digress into the politico-military situation in North India in the mid 18th century.

The Persian Invasion of 1740 by Nadir Shah

The immediate impetus for the establishment of the Sikh kingdom came from the invasion of North India by Ahmed Shah Durrani (Abdali) the ruler of Afghanistan in 1759/61. On his way to Delhi, Ahmed Shah burnt down the Harmindar Saheb Gurudwara at Amritsar.

Abdali stayed on in Delhi for 2 years and was planning to settle in India forever, when he was challenged by the Marathas. The Marathas who then were on their ascendancy in North India had since the first Persian-Afghan invasion by Nadir Shah, the king of Persia in 1740, established themselves as a dominant power in Northern India. The 20 years from 1740 to 1760 saw a see-saw battle between the Afghans and the Marathas for the domination of North India. With the defeat of Mohammed Shah, the Moghul Emperor in 1740 by Nadir Shah (in whose army Ahmed Shah Abdali was a general), the Mughal power steadily declined and its place was usurped by the Rohillas who were led by an ambitious and ruthless chieftain named Najib Khan. Najib's ambition was to supplant the Moghal Emperor and crown himself as the ruler of India by capturing Delhi.

The Rise of the Marathas in Punjab

But the growing power of the Marathas in their northward expansion, stood between Najib and his ambition. To overcome the Marathas, in 1755, Najib invited Ahmed Shah Abdali from Afghanistan to help him in defeating the Marathas and crown himself the ruler of India. In this, he was thwarted by the Marathas who decisively defeated the Rohillas and Afghans near Delhi in 1756. The defeat was so decisive that Najib Khan surrendered to the Marathas and became their prisoner.

The Maratha forces were led by Shrimant Raghunath Rao and Malhar Rao Holkar. After defeating the Afghan-Rohilla forces, the Marathas pursued the Afghans into the Punjab upto the Khyber pass. The last frontier of the Marathas was at Attock in today's NWFP (or Paktoonistan) on the Afghan border. Thus after nearly 800 after the last Punjabi King Tirlochan Pal Shahi had been defeated by Mahmud of Ghazi in 1020 C.E. did that part of India come under Indian rule in 1756 due to the liberation of Punjab by the Marathas.

Meanwhile with machinations and trickery, Najib Khan won over Malhar Rao Holkar and secured his release. On his release Najib started to undermine the Marathas once again and treacherously killed Dattaji Shinde (eldest brother of Mahadji Shinde). Najib continued to battle the Shindes in 1757-58 and with his newly found confidence again invited Ahmed Shah Abdali to invade India.

The 3rd Battle of Panipat-1761

Abdali's second invasion was launched in 1759. The **Marathas** who after their successes in 1756 had been hibernating in Maharashtra and Central India again woke up and in alliance with the Jat King Suraj Mal of Bharatpur formed an alliance. This alliance led by Shrimant Sadshiv Rao Bhau and Shrimant Vishwas Rao (the Peshwa Shrimant Balaji Baji Rao's son) won spectacular victories and captured Delhi and Kunjapura (where the Afghan treasury and armoury was located). Here the alliance developed cracks due to the Maratha insistence on not allowing the Jats to loot Delhi. This ultimately split the alliance and Suraj Mal withdrew from the alliance.

The Marathas consequently marched upto Panipat, but instead of continuing their attacks to completely defeat the partly defeated Abdali and Najib Khan, they stayed put at Panipat, blocking the way of the Afghans back to Afghanistan. Seeing their way back to their homeland blocked, the Afghans now became restless. They in turn, decided to block the way of the Marathas back into the Deccan. This stand-off continued for a few months, while the Afghans cut-off all supplies to the huge Maratha army. The Afghans with Najib Khan meanwhile recaptured Delhi and Kunjpura.

On the decisive day of 14th January 1761, the Marathas decided to break-through the Afghan blockade and re-enter Deccan. The disastrous battle saw about one hundred thousand Maratha troops being slaughtered in a matter of eight hours. But the Afghans too suffered heavy losses and decided enough was enough and went back to Afghanistan never to return to India.

The defeat of the Marathas and the withdrawal of the Afghans created a power vacuum in North India in the period 1761-1790. It was this vacuum that was filled up by the rising Sikh power under the dynamic leadership of Maharaja Shri Ranjit Singh Ji.

The Rise of the first Sikh Kingdom

When the history of Maratha-Afghan warfare was being enacted, the Sikhs in Punjab had formed themselves into Misls (Local Armed Battalions). Though they did not actively participate in helping the Marathas against the Afghans, they nursed a grievance against the Rohillas and Afghans.

On the departure of the Afghans, the Sikhs reasserted themselves in the Punjab and Maharaja Ranjit Singh Ji who was the leader of one of the most powerful Misl, formed a kingdom with its capital in today's West Punjab in Pakistan. His kingdom stretched beyond the Hindu Kush into Afghanistan. Able generals like Jussa Singh Ahluwalia, and Hari Singh Nallua helped in pushing the frontiers of the Sikh kingdom into Afghanistan.

It was a tradition in those days for the eldest son of every family from Punjab to join the army (of the Maharaja) by observing the 5 Kakkars. Brave generals like Jussa Singh Ahluwalia and Hari Singh Nallua took the Sikh armies deep into Afghanistan and they are reputed to have brought back the original Gates of the Somnath Temple which had been desecrated by Mahmud of Ghazni in the 11th century. The gates had been carried off by Mahmud to Afghanistan and had remained there ever since. Maharaja Ranjit Singh Ji retrieved them and brought them back to India.

Maharaja Ranjit Singh Ji's reign marked the consolidation of Indian sovereignty in Punjab after first Muslim invasions eight hundred years before in 1020. The Marathas had broken the continuous Muslim occupation of Punjab by liberating it in 1756 and Maharaja Ranjit Singh Ji consolidated Indian rule in Punjab a few years later. The kingdom established by Maharaja Ranjit Singh Ji successfully resisted the Afghans, and Rohillas and also out-matched the new imperialist power of the British successfully till Maharaja Ranjit Singh Ji was alive. At his death, the Maharaja had warned about the impending coming of the British.

> *On his death-bed he is said to have expressed a desire to offer his most precious possession to the Jagannath Puri temple at Orissa. He was asked by the chief Mahant (priest) of the Jagannath Puri temple as to what he considered most precious. In reply Maharaja Ranjit Singh Ji is said to have told the Mahant that as a Keshadhari follower of the Guru, his unshorn hair was most precious to him and he wanted to donate that to the temple along with umpteen gold and jewellery.*

It was during the reign of Maharaja Ranjit Singh Ji that the Harmindar Saheb Gurudwara at Amritsar which had been burnt down by Ahmed Shah Abdali in 1760, was repaired and was completely plated with gold and from then onwards it came to be known as the Golden Temple.

Such was Maharaja Ranjit Singh Ji who consolidated Indian rule in India's frontier state which had been earlier liberated by the Marathas. Unfortunately the Marathas could not retain their hold over the liberated areas, many of which were re-occupied by the Rohillas and Afghans after a few years. But the rise of the Sikh power ensured that a large part of the Maratha achievements of rolling back alien rule could be consolidated and expanded.

The Coming of the British

The Sikh kingdom survived for some years after the passing away of Ranjit Singh but in a few years after his death the British defeated the Sikh forces at Chillianwalla in 1856 and annexed the kingdom. Maharaja Ranjit Singh Ji's son, the teenaged son Duleep Singh was taken into custody by the British and sent to London for studies! Ironically it was the Indian Sepoys (troops) of the British East India Company who fought aginst their Sikh compatriots to bring about the downfall of the last independent Indian kingdom of the pre-British period.

Though the British annexed the Sikh kingdom, they recognised the fighting spirit and bravery of the Sikh soldiers and enrolled a large number of them into the British colonial army.

The Sikh troops again ironically, proved to be loyal supporters of the British crown especially by their role in quelling the Uprising of 1857 which was spearheaded by sepoys (troops) from Bihar and the United Provinces who had mutined against the British. It was these sepoys who had earlier helped in securing Punjab for the British Crown! For this reason after 1857, troops from UP and Bihar fell out of favour with the British, and Sikh troops were favoured by them for enrollment in the army and despite participation of many Sikhs in the freedom struggle, they continued to form the bulk of Indian troops in the British colonial army and even today form a significant proportion in the Indian Army.

Modern History of the Sikhs-The Arya Samaj and the Singh Sabha

In the 19th century many parts of India-under British rule-saw a religious and philosophical revival. The Brahmo Samaj in Bengal, the Prarthana Samaj in Maharashtra, the theosophical society in Madras, the Arya Samaj in Punjab were some of these many movements.

In Punjab, the Arya Samaj was led by illustrious leaders like Swami Dayananda Saraswati and Lala Lajpat Rai. Initially the Keshadharis were also a part of the Arya Samaj. The principles of the Arya Samajis like rejection of idol worship and of casteism and reduction of ritualism made it quite familiar with the principles of the Gurus. But the rigidity of the Arya Samaj principles subjected the teachings of the Gurus critically (and in the opinion of this writer also with an evident bias against the Gurus).

In "Satyarth Prakash", the mouthpiece of the Arya Samaj, the Gurus were severely criticised and on some trumpted up argument Guru Nanak Dev Ji was called a Dambhi (Hypocrite). This unjustified criticism of the Gurus due to a negatively revivalist (reactionary) streak in the Arya Samaj alienated the Keshadharis from the Arya Samaj. As a reaction to this, most of the Keshadhari followers of the Arya Samaj split from the Samaj and joined the Guru Singh Sabha which had been formed around roughly the same time as the Arya Samaj.

The Guru Singh Sabha was later to act as an ideological spearhead of the Keshadharis. This ideology was based on differentiating the Keshadharis (*i.e.* the Sikhs) from the Sahejdharis (*i.e.* Hindus). This dubious credit for creating this split between the Keshadharis and the Sahejdharis was evenly divided between the orthodoxy and revivalism of the Arya Samajis and also the teachings of some the Gurus *e.g.*, Guru Arjan Dev Ji's statement that we are "neither Hindus nor Musalmaans". But the Sahejdhari's led by the Punjabi Brahmin orthodoxy which had a strong presence in the Arya Samaj, made a rapproachment between the Keshadharis and the Sahejdharis increasingly remote. This set the stage for the Gurudwara Agitation of the 1920s.

The Gurudwara Agitation

This agitation which was launched by the Akali Dal in 1924-1925, aimed at wresting control of the Gurudwaras, from the traditional Mahants (priests). These Mahants who held an hereditary position as priests in the Gurudwaras were mostly Sahejdhari Sikhs who had refused to conform to the five outward symbols prescribed by Guru Gobind Singh Ji. The Sahejdhari Mahants some of whom were clean shaven, were all but indistinguishable from the Hindus.

Their natural affinity to Hinduism had led them to introduce elements of Hindu rituals and even image worship in the Gurudwaras and consequently Hindus (Sahejdhari Sikhs in the context of Punjab) and Sikhs (Keshadharis) worshipped together.

The Shiromani Shiromani Gurudwara Prabandhak Committee (SGPC). These Mahants were considered to have uncertain loyalty towards their Sikh faith vis-a-vis Hinduism. And by virtue of the vital position they held as officiating priests at Gurudwaras, they represented a potent force that could merge the Sikhs with Hinduism.

After a protracted struggle the Akali Dal got the British administration to enact a Sikh Gurudwara and Shrines Act. Under this Act the hereditary tenure of the Mahants was abolished and all control Of the Gurudwaras was vested in a Shiromani Gurudwara Prabandhak Committee (SGPC).

Once having ejected the Mahants, the agitationists, threw out the images of Hindu deities, replaced the rituals and ceremonies of the Mahants by those which they considered were in accordance with Sikh scriptures and Maryada. They also appointed priests (Granthis and Jathedars) who were to be the on the payroll of the SGPC. This revivalist movement helped to strengthen the wedge between the Keshadharis and the Sahejdharis whose line of demarcation was blurred due to a common heritage.

The emphasis on Sikhs being a separate community distinct from the Hindus was sought to be expressed in terms of the 5 distinguishing symbols the Keshadhari Sikhs thus implying that the Sahejdhari Sikhs were not true Sikhs and that the religion which bore the name Sikhism was limited to members of the Khalsa Panth.

To a lay observer the insistence of the Keshadhari Sikhs to look upon only those members who observe the 5 visible symbols as Sikhs, and others who give up these symbols as being Patit (heretics) and having lapsed (into Hinduism) would appear gueer when the Muslims or the Christians can retain their identity as members of a religious community as distinct from the Hindus even without any external symbols.

> *Why is it that a Muslim without a beard remains a Muslim while a Keshadharis (Sikh) without one is looked upon as a Hindu?*

The reason perhaps lies in the fact that most of the Muslims and the Christians though like the Keshadharis (Sikhs) being converts from Hinduism, own up traditions that do not originate in Hinduism or for that matter geographically in India itself. They generally look upon the history and traditions of another country as there own while those of their own country, which incidentally are bound up largely with Hinduism are for them either "infidel" or "pagan"!

This is not so among the Keshadharis (Sikhs) whose traditions have been part and parcel with those of the Hindus, in the five centuries of their existence; and for the period beyond that, the history of the Hindus and of India is their history. (The Keshadharis (Sikhs) share with the people of the rest of India, the history of the land of the Seven Rivers-a region where the concept of India first began to take shape Five Thousand years ago, which gave us the four Vedas; which gave birth to vedic seers like Vishwamitra, and Vyasa; Kings like Paurava (Porus), Ambastha (Ombhis), Shakuni, Raja Jai Pal Shahi, and Raja Tirlochan Pal Shahi; Queens like Kaikeyi, Gandhari; Scholars like Kautilya and Pannini; Universities like Takshashila, metropolises like Lav-kush Pur (Lahore), Mulasthana (Multan), Purushapura (Peshwar), Kubha-Kapisa

(Kabul). The list could be endless.) Hence the Keshadharis do not and cannot look to the history or traditions of another country or religion as their own and at the same time they do not want to be identified with the Hindus from whose ranks all of them have emerged at one time or the other, over the last 500 years. To overcome this nagging dilemma the Sikhs (*i.e.* the Keshadharis), place emphasis on the most evident difference between them and the Sahejdharis (commonly termed Punjabis), which is their external symbols. The agitation for a separate Sikh state in the Punjab was in part a desperate attempt to preserve by political means the identity of a community that is precarlously perched on the verge of Hinduism and harbours a horror of going over the brink and disappearing into the quicksands of its mother faith.

Commonality of Sikhs (Keshadharis) with its Mother Faith-The Saffron Colour

This fear on part of the Keshadharis is natural as in the eyes of an average Sikh, the parallels between his faith and that of his Hindu ancestors appear close enough to be confused with each other if sought to be distinguished. The list of parallels could be an endless one. Even a superficial look at Sikhism brings out the common points. A look atop a Gurudwara cannot miss the triangular saffron flag due to which a the place of worship could be considered to be a Hindu temple unless one is aware of the distinguishing architectural features of a Gurudwara.

Sikh spiritual leaders and priests use Saffron cloth for their turbans and dress as they consider the Saffron colour to have a religious significance though in the 1980s it had become a symbol of revivalism and bigotry (for the terrorists).

"Ek Onkar" of the Keshadharis and "Omkar" of the Hindus

The second thing that meets the eye while looking at Gurudwara is the letter "Ek Onkar" which is inscrlbed on most Gurudwaras (it means "One God"). The concept of God as Om is evidently borrowed from the Hindu concept which is also inscribed on many Hindu temples.

"Pheres" as a Wedding Custom among the Keshadharis

In spite of their horror of being called Hindus; till the 1920s, the fire (agni) and the hearth (agnikund) continued to hold a central place in their marriage rituals and a Keshadhari couple was deemed to have been married only after the couple went around the fire four times in the same manner as the Hindus do seven times in a ritual called the Saptapadi (Seven Steps) or Phere. But in the last few decades, the fire has been replaced by the Adi Granth and the rounds have been reduced from seven to four. Although the custom of Pheres has remained. Like the Hindus the Keshadharis cremate their dead. Ritual bathing before performing religious ceremonies in Gurudwaras is still a current practice which is parallel to the Hindu practice of bathing in rivers or tanks considered holy, before entering a temple.

The pond or lotus pond (Pushkara) that is built near many Hindu temples has its parallel to the Amrit-sarovar around the Golden temple at Amritsar. Even the practice of growing a beard and hair and tying it up in a knot atop one's head is not peculiar to the Keshadhairs. Since ancient times those who entered Sanyasa, the last stage of an ideal life for a Hindu, grew beard and hair and tied the hair in a knot atop their heads. The presence of long hair and beard was a sign of a man who had forsaken material pursuits. Those who accepted Sanyasa right since their celibate boyhood (Brahmacharya) had to wear unshorn hair and tie it atop their heads. Such persons were known as Keshin *i.e.* those with hair. All ancient Hindu Rishis (seers) are shown as having unshorn hair. Even today Sadhus and Sanyasis have unshorn hair. A Sikh without a turban appears quite similar to a Hindu Sadhu. It is quite possible that the inspiration for wearing unshorn hair come from the hoary tradition among the Hindus.

The Guru-Shishya Parampara

The Guru-Shishya tradition which is the core of the Keshadharis is a continuation of the same tradition among the Hindus. The Guru in traditional Hindu society is more than a coach or a tutor. He is looked upon as a spiritual guide next only to God. The Guru-Shishya tradition was natured in

Ashramas and Gurukulas where education was imparted since ancient times. Children were sent to Gurukulas at a tender age and for years together they stayed with their Guru who trained them in all arts and sciences. The Guru was normally from the Brahmin caste (at times he could be a Kshatriya) hence in the eyes of his disciples (Shishyas) he could acquire a venerable and semi-divine status.

Even today this tradition of revering Gurus is not absent among Hindus as is evident from the innumerable Swamis, Gurus and Babas who are looked upon as equivalent of Gods and are an object of worship. Buddha and Mahavir (and the other Tirthankaras) also represented the same tradition as did Guru Nanak. Although many tenets of Sikhism are fundamentally different from the (generally recognised) ritualism of the Hindus, the Guru-Shishya tradition around which the Sikh Panth is built evidently betrays its Hindu Origin.

Idol Worship Among the Keshadharis

Though the Sikhs reject idol worship, they look upon the Granth Saheb as their Guru. The Granth Saheb is placed on a throne (takht) where offerings are made to it and as an act of reverence, fans are waved before it so as to keep it comfortable by circulating the wind around in a way similar to that done for Kings in the past. This betrays a kind of respect for the Guru Granth as though it were a living Guru. This personifies the Guru Granth. The Granth being looked upon as an 'object' of reverence rather than only as a text that gives a message of universal brotherhood in itself betrays a trait of object worship which is but one step behind idol worship (moorti puja of the Hindus).

And although the Sikhs worship no idols their reverence for the Granth and the Golden temple betrays a very similar sentiment. One instance is the practice and the structure of the Parikrama that involves going around the Golden Temple in a circle. The concept of Parikrama is an obvious derivation from the Hindu practice of Pradakshna. The suffix Sinqh which is today a common Sikh title has an origin older than may appear.

In ancient times Hindu Kings and princes used to adopt the suffix 'Simha' meaning lion as *e.g.* in Narasimha Deva the ruler of Orissa who resisted the Muslims and built the Konark Temple. In mediaeval ages the Rajputs corrupted the word Simha to Sinh and Singh *e.g.* Gaj Singh, Uday Singh, etc. This title continued to be a trademark of the martial nobility. To inclulcate in the Sikhs, this martial tradition, Guru Gobind Singh Ji made it obligatory for Keshadharis to use this suffix after their first name. Even today the suffix 'Singh' is used by many Hindus of the Rajput and Jat castes and in some cases it has even become a surname.

Despite their insistence on having a cultural identity distinct from the Hindus the Keshadharis continue to celebrate Hindu festivals like Diwali, Holi (Hola Mohalla) and Baisikhi in a popular way. Even other traditional Hindu festivals like Janmastami, Ramnavami, Mahashivratri and Vijaya-Dashmi are observed, though keshadhari participation in these festivals is not as popular) and in recent times it seems to be on the wane.

Concepts of Karma in Sikhism

Though not known and understood popularly, the Sikh concepts about Karma and Salvation are drawn from their counterparts in Hinduism. At this stage one might wonder, why is it that so many vestiges should have survived in Sikhism when the intention of Guru Nanak Dev Ji was not to identify his disciples with any one religions, or even to establish a separate religion but to preach the universal brotherhood of man and the unity of God by whatever name he may be called?

One reason is that despite these aims of the founder, at the practical level Sikhism functioned as a reform movement among the Hindus. Almost all its converts came from the Hindus and so did All the Gurus. Due to historic compulsion like Mughal oppression, Sikhism over a major period of its history remained a spiritual, temporal and political movement of the Hindus, by the Hindus and virtually for the Hindus.

That Keshadhari Sikhism has still not been able to completely circumcise itself of its Hindu heritage is evident from the repeated pronouncements in shrill tones that the Sikhs are not Hindus. This dread of a loss of identity on part of the Sikhs arises from the genetic similarity between-the mother religion and the offspring. The ambivalence of the Sikhs vis-a-vis Hinduism had till recently (in the 1980s) found expression in the form of terrorist violence. And in doing so the terrorists were waging a matricidal war on a people whose religion and religion, history and culture was their own cradle. It is not surprising that several Indians regarded the activities of the terrorists as those of prodigals gone berserk. Though Keshadharis have always tried to ensure their status as an independent religious community, the anti-Hindu slant was of recent origin. Hindus (Sahejadharis in the context of Punjab) and Keshadharis had till recently never looked upon each other as members of different faiths leave alone of rival or enemy faiths.

Common Struggles of the Recent Past

Needless to recall that in defense of their faith and of themselves; they had to throw their lot with each other in the face of a common danger throughout the five hundred years of the history of Sikhism-the last occasion being in 1947.

The anti-Hindu slant of the 1980s among the Keshadharis (or at least among some sections of them) was a recent phenomenon. In its earlier days Sikhism functioned as a reform movement among the Hindus of Punjab from whom came the followers of the Gurus some of whom became Keshadharis.

Although the message of the Gurus was aimed at all humanity, it was given a sympathetic hearing mainly by the Hindus in Punjab. Its converts came almost entirely from Hinduism as did all its Gurus. Though in many respects The principles of Guru Nanak Dev Ji were fundamentally different from the various Hindu sects his message was nevertheless couched in a Hindu terminology and methods of expression. Despite the differences between Hinduism and the views of the Gurus, they could not have openly preached against the tenets of Hinduism before an audience that was made up of Hindus. Also it is doubtful if the Gurus had disowned the caste system completely, as many Sikh converts originally came from the upper castes Jats and Khatris-the **caste** to which Guru Nanak Dev Ji belonged.

The Possible Face of Sikhism without Guru Gobind Singh Ji's Reform

Had the last Guru Gobind Singh not recast Sikhism as the Khalsa Panth, then, it would have today been among the many sects within Hinduism like those of the followers of Sai Baba in Maharashtra, Basaveshwara in Karnataka, or the Brahmo Samaj in Bengal.

The Sahejdhari Sikhs (*i.e.* most Punjabi Hindus) who do not conform to the tenets laid down by Guru Gobind Singh Ji could be considered symptomatic as to how all Sikhs would have been without the tenets of Guru Gobind Singh. Among the Sikhs today there are many sects like the Nirankaris, Namdharis, Nirmalas, Sanyasis, Udasis, Radhasoamis, etc. Many of these sects come quite close to **Hinduism** and for this reason are frowned upon by the Akalis.

The Dharam Yuddh Morcha of the Akalis

The Akalis, who represent the main sect among the Keshadharis had begun the Gurudwara Agitation in 1920s as also the Dharam Yuddh Morcha in the 1980s both of which increasingly acquired an anti-Hindu slant. We all know how the Dharam Yuddh Morcha of Sant Longowal had many just demands like the proclaimation of Chandigarh as a capital of Punjab and not a shared capital with Haryana. This was justified as Chandigarh was made as a capital for East Punjab after independence and partition when Lahore the former capital went to West (Pakistani) Punjab. Other demands like the sharing of river waters were more of administrative issues. The broadcasting of Gurbani on AIR (All India Radio) was an understandable demand in the light of secularism being mis-interpreted in India as religious tolerance. Apart from these issues the demand that the Anandpur Sahib Resolution be accepted so that "Sikhs could enjoy the glow of freedom" was a first step to secessionism and needed to be rejected outright as was done. The colonial administration that could have further divided the country is no more around. (The aim of dividing up any nation further-be it India, Pakistan or any other, is a retrograde one in the 20th century. The objective should be to move towards a single WORLD STATE.)

The Demand for Khalistan

The Akali agitation gradually slipped out of the hands of the Akali leaders and degenerated into the terrorist frenzy of indiscriminate killings of all clean-shaven bus passengers, mowing down of innocent bystanders in market places, targeted assassinations of editors of newspapers (starting with that of Lala Jagat Narain), blowing up of railway tracks and trains all of which was shameful and culminated in an equally shameful slaughter of the the Keshadharis in New Delhi in November 1982 after the assassinations of the then Indian Prime Minister Indira Gandhi.

The politics of the Congress Party of propping up Bhindranwale to embrass the Akali Dal, which at that time was a part of the Janata Party ruling Delhi, was ultimately responsible for the terrorism of the 1980s. The Congress Party exploited the pre-existing feeling among some of the Keshadharis that they are a separate community and ultimately would have to have a separate nation for themselves. This was the ultimate reason for the creation of disturbances in Punjab. The aim of the Congress was to destabilize the then ruling party and ultimately seize power. The politics of the Congress party paid off, but at a tremendous cost to the nation, and to Punjab in particular.

6

BUDDHISM

Buddhism evolved in India. There were periods in India's past when Buddhism was dominant in India. Today less then 1% of India's population is Buddhist. Buddhism has more followers in countries east of India.

Buddhism was established in about 500 BC. Buddhism began with a prince called Siddhartha Gautama. Siddhartha belonged to an aristocratic family. As a prince he had lot of wealth. He never left his palace. At some point Siddharta began to leave his palace and behold for the first time poverty, sickness and misery. After seeing this Siddharta lost interest in his spoiled life and left his palace forever and gave his rich personal belongings to the needy. He joined a group of ascetics who were searching for enlightenment. In those days people searching for enlightenment believed that this could be gained only by people who were capable of resisting their basic needs. These people almost did not eat anything and almost starved themselves to death. Siddharta also adopted this path of searching enlightenment. But at some point he came to a conclusion that this was neither the way towards enlightenment nor the spoiled life he had as a prince was the right path towards enlightenment. According to him the right path was somewhere in the middle and he called it the 'middle path'.

In order to focus on his enlightenment search, Buddha sat under a fig tree and after fighting many temptations he got his enlightenment. In his region 'enlightened' people were called Buddha. And so Siddharta was named Buddha. According to Buddha's theory life is a long suffering. The suffering is caused because of the passions people desire to accomplish. The more one desires and the less he accomplishes the more he suffers. People who do not accomplish their desirable passions in their lives will be born again to this life circle which is full of suffering and so will distant themselves from the world of no suffering-Nirvana.

To get Nirvana, one has to follow the eight-fold path which are to believe right, desire right, think right, live right, do the right efforts, think the right thoughts, behave right and to do the right meditation.

Buddhism emphasis non-violence. Buddha attacked the Brahmanic custom of animal slaughtering during religious ceremonies. Religiously the Buddhists are vegetarians. But a strong narrative in India claims that Buddha, died because he ate a sick animal. Buddhism does not have a God, nor is it atheistic. Many Buddhists keep images of Buddha. Buddha is not seen as the first prophet of the religion, but as the fourth prophet of the religion.

There are two main doctrines in Buddhism, Mahayana and Hinayana. Mahayana Buddhist believe that the right path of a follower will lead to the redemption of all human beings. The Hinayana believe that each person is responsible for his own fate. Along with these doctrines there are other Buddhist beliefs like 'Zen Buddhism' from Japan and the 'Hindu Tantric Buddhism' from Tibet. Zen Buddhism is a mixture of Buddhism as it arrived from India to Japan and original Japanese beliefs. The Hindu Tantric Buddhism is a mixture of Indian Buddhism and original Tibetian beliefs which existed among the Tibetians before the arrival of Buddhism in Tibet, among it magic, ghosts and tantras (meaningless mystical sentences).

Our Message of Peace, Non-violence and Goodwill

The second great religion that originated in India is Buddhism. Ironically though Buddhism flourished overseas; in the land of its birth it was till recently non-existent. It received a lease of life after independence, when Dr. B.R. Ambedkar decided to embrace Buddhism. A significant section of the scheduled **castes** followed Dr. Ambedkar and they today constitute an overwhelming portion of the adherents of Buddhism in India today. But they do not form part of the two traditional sects of Buddhism *viz.*, (Mahanayana and Hinayana) and are generally termed as Neo-Buddhists (Nava-Baudha). The history of Buddhism in India starts with that of its founder Gautama Buddha who lived in the 6th century B.C.E.

Life Story of Buddha

Buddha was born in the Shakya clan that belonged to the warrior (Kshatriya) caste. His father was Shudhodana and his mother Maya. Before Buddha was born his mother had a dream in which a white elephant descended from heaven and entered her womb. Buddha was said to have been born in a grove named Lumbini near the ancient town of Kapilavastu. At birth the name given to him was Gautama, probably after the more ancient Vedic seer to whom some of the hymns in the Rigveda are ascribed. Buddha was also known as Siddhartha which means 'he whose aim is accomplished' The latter name seems to be a title given to him by his disciples} although varying opinions are held on this issue.

The Prophecy of Buddha

At his birth, a sage is said to have told King Shudhodana that Gautama would grow up to be a powerful king. But to become a king he should be kept away from the sorrows of 1ife. And if perchance he happened to see any of the sorrows of life he would become an universal teacher. Keen as King Shudhodhana was to see Gautama to be a successful ruler, he built up special palace for Gautama from where he could set his eyes on none of the world's sufferings. Even when the prince Gautama went out for stroll or ride, all unpleasant objects were removed so as to prevent Gautama's mind from being disturbed.

The Young Gautama is Kept away from Real Life

But the prophesy of Gautama becoming an universal teacher was destined to be fulfilled. One day through some lapse, Gautama managed to slip out unnoticed from the palace. Riding through the streets of the city he saw for the first time in his life, a lame person, a sick person, a dead body and an ascetic. These sights made a deep impact on his tender teenaged mind and he set thinking upon the cause of sufferings and sorrow. Consequently, Gautama began neglecting the affairs of the State which his father had assigned to him. Alarmed at his son's strange behaviour, King Shudhodana, to get his son off this brroding decided to marry him to a princess Yashodhara. Some days after marriage a son was born to them who was named Rahula.

But married life could not distract Gautama from his life's mission for long. When his patience was at the end of its tether, Gautawna decided to forsake family life and one day he slipped out of his palace along with his servant Chandaka. After moving out of the city, Gautema cut off his hair removed his royal ornaments and jewels, his rich garments and sandals and gave them to Chandaka and bid him to return to the palace with the news of his (Gautama's) departure.

Gautama becomes The Buddha—The Enlightened One

Thus Gautama set out on his quest for the cause of sufferings (Klesha). He undertook severe austerities by fasting continuously. In this he was accompanied by five disciples. But his frail and pampered body could not stand up to this self-inflicted punishment and one day he fainted. Realizing that this was not the way to arrive at the truth, he gave up the austerities. Horrified at their Master's apostasy the five disciples left him.

But undaunted, Gautama continued his quest for the cause of sufferings. He seated himself under a fig tree (Mahabodhi tree) and decided not get up unless he found answers to his questions. His enlightenment is said to have come suddenly and was exceedingly simple-*viz.*, that all pain is caused-by desire, and therefore peace comes when one ceases to crave for anything.

This thought was new at that age and it struck him with blinding force, and not only influenced his future life but left a lasting imprint on Buddhist philosophy. Freedom from all desires was said to release a person from the cycle of re-birth and lead to his salvation (Nirvana). After this revelation

Gautama started preaching to people and for this he travelled from place to place. He is said to have delivered his first sermon at a deer park (Isipatana) setting in motion, the wheel of law (Dharma-chakra or Dhammachakra in Pali).

As his teachings impressed people his following grew. Among his early converts were Sariputta, Mogallana and Ananda. He even received the patronage of rich traders like Anathapindika (*i.e.* feeder of poor) and powerful kinqs of the age like Ajatashatru of Magadha. After the revelation (Bodhi), Gautama came to be known as Buddha or Gautama Buddha.

He was also known as Shakyamuni (Sage of the Shakyas). The tree under which he attained enlightenment is known as the Bodhi or Mahabodhi tree But though he received an impressive following Buddha never claimed Divine status. Very few miracles are attributed to him.

"Miracles" by the Buddha

On one occasion a grieving lady carried her dead child to Buddha and asked him to revive it. This was a perfect setting for a miracle to be woven into religious folklore, but Buddhist records state that Buddha calmed the lady and told her that he would require three mustard seeds to revive her child. But the mustard seeds should be from a family where so far no one has ever died.

To fulfill this seemingly simple request the lady went from house to house only to be told that sometime or the other, someone had died in every family. Gradually, the truth dawned upon the grieving lady and going to a cemetery, she laid down her child's body and taking its little hand in hers, she said "Beloved son, I thought that death has overtaken you alone. but no it overtakes all of us". She went back to Buddha and became his disciple.

The Buddhist Sangha and Morality

Buddhism is unique among religions in a fundamental sense. It does not advocate invocation of any God. Salvation can be attained by controlling one's desire; as desire is the cause of suffering. The original Buddhism had neither God nor Devil.

The emphasis was not on prayer but on controlling one's mind. In this sense it was more a worldly philosophy rather than a religion. But with the passage of time it acquired the nature of a religion complete with dogmas and rituals. Buddha's life-story is an eventful one.

The most potent institution that Buddha established during his lifetime was the Sangha (monastic order) into which men were admitted irrsespective of their caste. The members of the Sangha who were known as Bhikkus (beggars)had to lead a rigorous life devoid of all desires. Their daily needs were limited to those necessary for physical survival.

Their only possessions were a begging bowl, yellow coloured loin cloth, a walking stick if necessary and a pair of sandals for the more delicate. They were to sustain themselves by the alms they received but were forbidden from expressly begging for alms. Alms were to be accepted if given willingly and if not the Bhikkus were to move on to the next house. Thus came into being a clergy, but which unlike its Hindu counterpart was not based on caste and which was oriented towards missionary activities rather on the performance and upholding of rituals.

The break of Buddhism from other forms of worship that constituted Hinduism was almost complete in the lifetime of Buddha. This took the form of non-recognition of any personified Gods, spirits or the devil, and the near absence of rituals, repudiation of the caste system and the intense missionary activity of the monks which included rendering social service with the aim of alleviation of human suffering. Another significant aspect was that in the early stages all followers of Buddha were enrolled as members of the Sangha hence it was completely a missionary religion.

The distinction between the Bhikkus and other lay adherents of Buddhism came about later when the following of the religion increased manifold.

From its inception Buddhism received royal patronage. In the lifetime of Buddha Ajatashatru the king of north India's most powerful kingdom Magadha (in present-day Bihar) patronised Buddhism during Buddha's lifetime, and a few years after Buddha attained Nirvana {Salvation), the first religious council of the Buddhists was held at the town Rajagriha, which was the capital of Magadha from where Ajatashatru ruled. Councils such as this one were occasions for formulation and revision of the Buddhist religious code which was supposed to be adhered to by all followers. Thus it kept a check on the emergence of sub-sects-a tendency which is a hallmark o£ Hinduism.

The second such council was held at Vaishali also in Magadha, about a hundred years after the first council *i.e.* in the 5th century B.C.E.

Relations between Buddhism and Hinduism

Buddhism continued to grow steadily in the first few centuries after its birth. The reasons were its universal appeal, humane outlook, emphasis on missionary and social work and finally its peaceable methods that limited confrontation with the established local religions to a philosophical level. Thus even kings who patronised Hinduism did not feel it necessary to make a distinction between Hinduism and Buddhism in policy matters. Buddhism normally returned the sympathy of the ruling power by giving it a moral legitimacy amongst the lay people. And although Brahmin orthodoxy did grudge the inroads made into itself by the new faith there hardly ever was there active confrontation between the two faiths.

On the contrary there was a exchange of beliefs and attitudes between Hinduism and Buddhism. The Hindu insistence of vegetarianism and non-violence (Ahimsa) are borrowed from Buddhism (and Jainism). Hinduism in turn tried to absorb Buddhism within itself by making Buddha one of the incarnations of Vishnu.

Major Royal Patrons-Samrat Ashok Maurya, Kanishka, Harsha Vardhana

The growth of Buddhism received a tremendous boost in the 3rd century B.C.E. when Samrat Ashoka Maurya whose empire covered nearly the whole of India (including present-day Pakistan and Afghanistan) was converted to Buddhism.

Samrat Ashoka elevated Buddhism to the level of a state religion and sent missionaries not only to all parts of India but also to Sri Lanka, West Asia, Central Asia and China. In his days Buddhism is said to have spread in varying degrees up to Egypt and South-western Russia. Since the days of emperor Ashoka, Buddhist missionaries built majestic monasteries known as Viharas, Stupas and Chaityas.

The simple ascetic character of Buddhism had received its first dent under the pampering effect of royal patronage. The religlon continued to grow nevertheless. During the reign of Ashoka the third Religious Council was held at Pataliputra which was the capital of Ashoka's vast empire.

But that Ashoka was not inimical to Hinduism is evident from one of the titles that he took *viz.* Deva-naam-priya (Beloved of the Gods). After the fall of the Maurya empire, Buddhism did not receive official patronage on a comparable scale for a long time. During the period after the Maurya empire, India was beset with invasions from the Indo-Greeks, Kushanas, Parthians, etc. But most of these invaders acculturized themselves in a few years after their coming and many of their kings embraced either Buddhism or Hinduism.

Prominent among them were, Menander (Milinda) who was an Indo-Greek and to whom is ascribed the Buddhist treatise called Milinda-Panho (Questions of Menander) in which thc king, posed certain questions to which answers were given by a Buddhist Sage called Nagasena. The next major royal patron of Buddhism was Kushana who was a Mongol king who ruled north India, Pakistan and Afghanistan in the 1st century B.C.E. In his reign) the fourth religious council was held at Jalandhara (Modern Jullundar in Indian Punjab). Now Buddhism had spread far and wide and had received royal patronage in varying degrees almost continuously from one king or another since Ashoka.

Split into Two Sects — Mahayana (Greater Vehicle) and Hinayana (Lesser Vehicle)

By the time the fourth religious council was held, the religion had vertically split up into two schools. One school had elevated Buddha to the status of a God and introduced worship of the Buddha's image (idol), it also evolved elaborate rituals which were derived largely from Hinduism, and gave up the rigorous ascetic life in monasteries, discarded Pall and accepted Sanskrit as the literary medium. These changes had far-reaching effects in narrowing the breach between Buddhism and Hinduism but at the cost of departing from the essence of the way of life that Buddha established.

This school was called the Mahayana {Greater Vehicle) school or the northern school of Buddhism. On the other hand the Hinayana (Lesser Vehicle) school stuck to the original character of Buddhism with its emphasis on rigorous and simple living although idol worship gradually made its way into Hinayana also. This school is also known as Theravada (from Staieryavada *i.e.* principle of stability) is mainly prevalent in Sri Lanka, Burma and Thailand.

Despite the split, Buddhism continued to grow steadily up to the reign of the Guptas. Since the reign of the Gupta kings (3rd and 4th centuries C.E.) the growth of Buddhism came to a standstill and gradually the decline set in. The reasons for this decline could be many but the principal one was to be the absence of royal patronage since the Gupta period, although there was no persecution either.

The last known royal patron of Buddhism was Harsh Vardhana who ruled over a large part of northern India around the 7th century C.E. Harsha who was an ardent worshipper of the Hindu deity — Shiva, did not embrace Buddhism, but he extended many favours to the religion. During his reign the fifth religious council was held at Prayaga (Allahabad).

No significant event took place thereafter in the history of Buddhism. But it is certain that upto the beginning of the Gupta period the religion was on its ascendance and its following in India was significant. From the Gupta period Hinduism seems to have undergone a revival, partly under the patronage of the Gupta kings. Buddhism then onwards was definitely on the decline. The intellectual onslaught of Brahmanic philosophers like Adi Shankaracharya seems to have had its toll in emasculating what was once a cohesive and vibrant way of life. Whatever the reasons, it is certain that the following of Buddhism declined sharply during and after the Gupta perlod.

It survived nominally as an intellectual tradition kept alive by the select monks who controlled the monastic universities like the one at Nalanda. These universities were highly respected as seats of learning and attracted students from abroad. Fa Hien, Huien Tsiang and I-Tsing who came from China were said to have studied at Nalanda and other centres of Buddhist learning. But from the 5th century Onwards, Buddhism declined as the religion of the masses. Its following seems to have been absorbed into Hinduism, although this could have also been the result not of formal conversion but of a gradual relapse of the Buddhist laity into the parent religion.

The portrayal of Buddha as an incarnation of the Hindu deity Vishnu, and the absorption of many Hindu attitudes by Mahayana Buddhism, along with the absence of royal patronage to Buddhism (and the extension of this patronage to Hinduism during Gupta times) must have contributed to this effect. Whatever Buddhists that remained constituted an elite who inhabited the Monasteries and rarely ventured out of them. Missionary activity was nearly absent.

Muslim Invasions Give the Fatal Blow to Buddhism

The last fatal blow to this once virile religion came from a non-Indian impetus-the Muslim invasion of north India in the 12th century. The defeat of Prithviraj Chauhan and Jaichandra Gahadawal (Rathore) in 1192 and 1194 respectively by the Afghan raider, Mahmud Ghori opened up the Gangetic plains to the ruthless invader where the Buddhist (and Hindu) centres of learning were located. The destruction of monasteries and the slaughter of monks that followed the headlong rush, of the Muslim invaders, down the Ganges stilled the agony of this once glorious order into the silence of death.

Thus passed out of existence in the land of its birth a religion that touched the lives of millions of humans not only in India but in China, Japan, Korea and other countries of Central Asia and South-East Asia. Buddhism in India was to remain a dead religion until the 20th century.

Buddhism Resurrected in India in the 20th Century

In the mid 20th Century, Dr. B.R. Ambedkar, who was one of the architects of India's Constitution, gave Buddhism a fresh lease of life by embracing it a few years after India achieved independence. A significant number of members of those castes who were denied equal rights in the Hindu caste hierarchy also embraced Buddhism. Today an over-whelming proportion of Buddhists in India are these recent converts who term themselves as Nava-Baudha or Neo-Buddhists. A comparatively recent event of significance was the 6th religious council held at Rangoon in 1954 which came 1300 years after the 5th council held at, Prayaga in 643 C.E. in the reign of the last major pan-Indian emperor-Harsha Vardhana. The Rangoon council was also the first one to be held outside India.

Buddhism and Hinduism-Umbilical Marks

In the course of its eventful history Buddhism which began as a departure from the ritualism of the Hindu religion gradually adapted and absorbed many Hindu ideas and practices to the point that at times, the lines of distinction between the two religions (the parent and the offspring) were blurred. The objective of Nirvana towards which every Buddhist is supposed to strive is undoubtedly an adaptation of the Hindu concept of Moksha. The difference is that for the attainment of Moksha righteous behaviour and the conformation of duties as assigned by the caste into which a person has been born is necessary, while for the attainment of Nirvana a person has to be free of all desires. But the essence of both concepts is the release from the cycle of re-birth.

The daily of life of the Buddhist Bhikkus (missionary ascetics) was evidently inspired by the concept and practice of Sanyasa which was the last phase of life a Hindu during which he was supposed to be free of all desires and to roam from place to place in search of spiritual enlightenment while spreading the gospel of rightousness among the people. The yellow coloured robes that the Buddhist Bhikkus donned were borrowed from the Saffron robes of the Hindu ascetic. Although as for the Buddhists the yellow colour was chosen to represent an autumn leaf which was once green but has inevitably turned yellow in conformation with the law that everything born has to decay and pass away.

Among the auxiliary Hindu practices which found their way into Buddhism, idol worship and the use of Sanskrit as the liturgical and scriptural language. The Buddhist conception of Buddha as a God and that in a later period after five thousand years when righteousness suffer an eclipse the Buddha will reappear on the earth. This Buddha who will be known as Maiterya will restore the rule of dhamma (law and religion). This idea implies belief in incarnations and re-incarnations on lines parallel to the Hindu concept of Kalki who, we are told, is to be the future incarnation of Lord Vishnu.

But all said and done though Buddhism precariously came close to Hinduism it maintained its distinct entity unlike the Jaina religion whose proximity to Hinduism nearly made it a part of Hinduism. In its appeal Buddhism was not, like its parent religion Hinduism, restricted to India and Indians but spread far and wide.

Thus in Buddhism, India gave birth to a major international religion, while the Hindus continued their way. Buddhism was the world's first missionary religion and won its triumphs through missionary activity. The ancient Buddhist monks who carried the Master's message of peace, love and universal brotherhood were pioneers in such a mission in Human history. Buddhism is the only trans-national religion which has never preached malice against other faiths, nor have its followers ever indulged in a holy war against those of another faith. Buddhism has won its way by persuasion and never by the sword, nor has it ever used its position or power to compel conformity to its precepts.

> *And whatever its defects, it has unquestionably done much to benefit the human race by introducing and perpetuating a higher standard of conduct in life. One is inclined to bow before the Buddha, not in homage to a deity but in recognition to a superior craftsman in the art of living.*

We now turn to examine Jainism in the next chapter and the influences of Hinduism on Jainism and vice versa.

BUDDHIST PHILOSOPHY

A singing bowl, also known as a Himalayan bowl or cup gong, is a musical instrument used in Buddhist meditation, dating back many centuries. They are traditionally played in Tibet, Nepal, India, China, Japan, and Korea, mostly by Buddhist monks and in monasteries. The instrument is made of metal, often including precious metals such as silver and gold. Many other metals, including copper, tin, zinc, lead, iron, and, nickel also feature in many bowls' metallic makeup. Generally, singing bowls can be made of many different metals. Singing bowls are played by hitting, striking, or slowly rubbing/ stirring a wooden striker/mallet within or on the top outer surface of the bowl. When done correctly, the bowl will produce a continuous harmonic sound, said to be relaxing and good for the chakra.

Some claim that many bowls are "tuned" to a specific chakra. Currently, these bowls are used for meditation, yoga, healing, sound massage, sound therapy, and chakra balancing. Singing bowls can be found in a variety of shapes, sizes, designs, colors, carvings and craftings. They may be found with various religious themes and symbols, like Tibetan mantra chant om mani padme hum, dragon carvings, mandala carvings, *asta mangal* (eight auspicious good luck symbols), Buddhist religious symbols and many more. The making of traditional bowls is now considered a lost art. Most old bowls contain very little, if any, ornamentation.

Most bowls are handmade, apart from some tools used for shining and polishing, and fall into two categories. The first is the hand-hammered (beaten) singing bowl, most of which come from Nepal and India, and are manufactured using traditional processes. Hand-hammered bowls are very much more popular for meditation, healing and sound therapy. The second type is the colored, carved and crafted bowl. These are popular for gifts, decorations and souvenir items, and are mostly from Nepal, the Himalayan Country.

Basic Buddhist Philosophical Doctrines: There are some philosophical doctrines that are so early and so fundamental to Buddhism that denials of them tend to be regarded as profoundly non-Buddhist heterodoxies. All forms of Buddhism endeavor to maintain these principles.

1. *Momentariness:* Nothing exists for any length of time. There is no *substance* or duration to things. Each moment is an entirely new existence, which is succeeded by an entirely new existence. The only connection between one thing and the next is that one causes the next. This doctrine sounds much like the Greek philosopher Heraclitus. The "things" tend to be called the *dharmas* in Buddhist thought.
2. *Relative Existence or No Self Nature:* Nothing has a *essence*, nature, or character by itself. Things in isolation are *shunya*, "empty." The nature of things only exists in relation to everything else that exists. Existence as we know it is thus completely relative and conditioned by everything else. Only *Nirvan.a* would be unconditioned, although we cannot know what it is like. The distinction between the conditioned reality that we know and the unconditioned reality that we do not know is similar to the distinction between *phenomena* and *things-in-themselves* made by the German philosopher Immanuel Kant. The notion that the *dharmas* derive their nature from everything else has led to comparison with the "monads" of another German philosopher, Leibniz. The monads also represent the whole universe. However, since the *dharmas* are momentary, this is actually more like the actual entities postulated by Alfred North Whitehead (1861-1947) in his "Process" philosophy. *Shunyata*, "Emptiness," is easily misunderstood. It is not nothingness. Emptiness is neither existence, nor non-existence, nor both existence and non-existence, nor neither existence nor non-existence. At the very least, this means that we don't know what is left when we take away all conditioned relations. Beyond that, it can mean that we *cannot*

know what that is. No Self Nature means that there are no *essences*, just as Momentariness means that there are no *substances.*

3. *No-Atman:* There is no Self (*atman*) in Buddhism, either as an essence or as a substance. What we call our self is a collection of things, the "aggregates" (*skandhas*): 1) the body, or "form," 2) feelings, 3) ideas, 4) impressions, & 5) momentary consciousness. There is no enduring thing present in the aggregates. This critique of the self as just a collection is very similar to the view of the Scottish philosopher David Hume. An implication of No-Atman is that reincarnation cannot be *transmigration*, since there is nothing to migrate.
4. *No-God:* There is no Brahman or any other such ultimate enduring substance or nature to reality. *Nirvan.a* thus cannot be characterized as realizing either Self, Brahman, or God.
5. *Dependent Origination:* Everything has a cause. A momentary existence occurs as it does because of a previous momentary existence, but the cause itself is also momentary. Dependent Origination combines the doctrines of momentariness and relative existence and is why in the Second Noble Truth desire and ignorance cause each other. That relationship can be expanded:

1. ignorance (*avidya*), causes
2. impressions (*samakaras*), which cause
3. consciousness (*vijnana*), which causes
4. mind-body (*namarupa*), which causes
5. the sense organs (*sadayatana*), which cause
6. contact with objects (*sparsha*), which cause
7. experience (*vedana*), which causes
8. desire, which causes
9. clinging (*upadana*), which causes
10. the will to be born (*bhava*), which causes
11. rebirth (*jati*), which causes

12. suffering (*jaramarana*), which in turn causes
13. ignorance (*avidya*).

Nirvan.a is thus not the removal of an ultimate cause but the simultaneous removal of *all* causes, all of conditioned existence.

6. *Karma:* Because there is no substance or duration in Buddhism, the Buddhist view of karma is different from that in Hinduism or Jainism. Karma is only causation, without the mediation of any substance (*apurva,* causal body, etc.). Reincarnation thus consists in our being *caused* by something in the past, and our karma is simply the effect now of past actions.

In the history of Buddhist philosophy, these doctrines created some difficulties. If there is no self, then what is it that attains enlightenment or Nirvana? It is not me, for I am already gone in an instant; and if it is not me, then why bother? Also, if there is no enduring self, then the rewards and punishments of karma are visited on different beings than those who merited them. Why do I, instead of someone else, deserve the karma of some past existence? The Buddha himself probably would have been irritated with the doctrines that created these difficulties, since he rejected theorizing (it did not "tend to edification"), and he would have expected no less than that such theories would lead to tangled and merely theoretical disputes. The important philosophical lesson of these difficulties, however, is whether the concept of causality can be used as a substitute for the concept of substance.

In all honesty, no. Something rather like the Buddhist position, however, can be formulated by Kant, for whom the concept of substance applies to phenomena but has only uncertain meaning when applied to things-in-themselves. Phenomena are only "provisional existence" to Buddhism, and the Buddhist doctrine of no enduring Self could easily be adapted to the Kantian transcendent.

Stages in the History of Buddhism: The history of Buddhism in India, which lasted about 1500 years, can be divided into 500 year periods, during which distinctive forms of Buddhism emerged. This is an idealized and schematic picture, but it is convenient, and it can be matched up with where Buddhism spread during these periods and what forms of Buddhism became dominant there.

Buddhist doctrine and practice in the earliest period were agreed upon in a series of Councils, sometimes reckoned to be three, or four.

1. The First Council was held shortly after the Buddha's death, at Rajagriha. Issues about the conduct of the Sangha, the monastic community, in the absence of the Buddha appear to have been settled.
2. The Second Council was held about a century after the Buddha's death, at Vaisali. Sometimes this is considered the First Council, or is confused with the previous one. It began to agree on the content of the Buddhist Canon and on the monastic discipline, the vinaya.
3. The Third Council was called by the Emperor Ashoka and held at Pataliputra. The content of the Pali Tripitaka, "Three Baskets," is supposed to have been settled at this Council, or there abouts in this period, consisting of the Sutra-pit.aka [Sutta in Pali], the sermons of the Buddha, the Vinaya-pitaka, the monastic discipline, and the Abhidharma-pitaka [dharma is dhamma in Pali], the philosophical development of Buddhist doctrine. Buddhism was introduced into Sri Lanka (Ceylon) as the result of Ashoka's own efforts, and the Canon in Pali was preserved there.
4. The Fourth Council was called under the Emperor Kanishka I and held at Jalandhara. This is not attested in Pali sources, and so one often hears that there were only three Councils. The Council is supposed to have supervised the translation of the Tripit.aka into Sanskrit. The Canon apparently had not only existed in Pali, but in other Prakrits, which were all consulted for a standard Sanskrit version. It appears to be the Sanskrit texts that were subsequently spread to China. The sutras of the Mahayana may have existed only in Sanskrit from the beginning.

Theravada (Teaching of the Elders) Buddhism (called "Hinayana," the "Lesser Vehicle," by the Mahayana): In India, 5th century BC to 1st century AD.

1. Distinctive doctrines:
2. The Buddha (Siddhartha Gautama, Shakyamuni) is gone, and individual practitioners must work out their salvation on their own.
3. The Buddha was unique, and individual practitioners cannot become Buddhas, only *arhats* (saints). There will be a future Buddha, Maitreya, but not for thousands of years.
4. *Nirvana* (liberation) and *samsara* (the place of death and rebirth) are definitely different. *Samsara* is a place of suffering to be left behind. *Nirvana* is a liberation that is free of death and rebirth but is beyond description and rational understanding.

Mahayana (Great Vehicle) Buddhism: In India, 1st century AD to 6th century. is not gone, and individual practitioners are not on their own. Instead, the Buddha taught the dharma out of compassion, and his compassion would prevent him from being unavailable to practitioners now. Indeed, to emulate the compassion of the Buddha, practitioners become bodhisattvas, who vow to carry all beings with them into salvation. Bodhisattvas are also available, like the Buddhas, to help people work out their salvation. Maitreya is presently a bodhisattva, but the most important bodhisattva is probably Avalokiteshvara, who became identified with the Chinese goddess of Mercy, Guanyin (Kwan-in in Wade-Giles, Kannon in Japan).

The Buddha was not unique, and individual practitioners who have become bodhisattvas can become Buddhas. There are already multiple Buddhas besides Shakyamuni. Most important are Mahavairocana and Amitabha. Amitabha is famous for his Western Paradise, or Pure Land, where he has Vowed to cause anyone who calls on him for help to be born, so they will be free of the world of suffering to work out their ultimate liberation. In Japan Amitabha is known as Amida and Mahavairocana as

Dainichi. Most of the famous Buddha statues in Japan are not Shakyamuni: the great outdoor bronze Buddha at Kamakura is Amida, and the Buddha enshrined in the Todaiji ("Great Eastern") Temple in Nara (the largest wooden building in the world), is another Buddha named Locana.

Nirvana and samsara are no longer definitely different. The "Fourfold Negation" is applied to the relationship between the two. Samsara and nirvan.a are thus neither the same, nor different, nor both the same and different, nor neither the same nor different.

This allows some room for maneuver, which may have made Buddhism more palatable in China, where Confucianism never did approve either of the world-denying metaphysics or the monasticism of Buddhism. Distinctively Chinese schools of Buddhism developed, like T'ien-t'ai (Tendai in Japan) and Ch'an (Seon [Son] in Korea, Thien in Vietnam, Zen in Japan), for whom samsara and nirvan.a were virtually identical, so that enlightenment and nirvan.a transformed the world rather than eliminated it. The paradoxical metaphysics of Buddhism could be assimilated to the similar paradoxical doctrines of the native Chinese philosophical school of Taoism.

- *Places where Mahayana spread:* Mahayana Buddhism is presently practiced in China, Korea, Vietnam, and Japan. Buddhism was propagated in China by missionaries from India, like Kumarajiva (344-413), who arrived in China in 401, and Buddhabhadra (359-429), who arrived in 408, and by Chinese pilgrims who traveled to India, like Fa-Hsien (Fa^{3}xian^3), who travelled to India between 399 and 414, and Hsüan-tsang (Xuánzang^3, 600-664), who went to India between 629 and 645. These were difficult journeys, either by sea around Malaya, where many ships were attacked by pirates or sunk by storms, or by land through Central Asia, on the "Silk Road" caravan route, through deserts and over some of the highest mountains in the world. The highest peaks of the Pamirs and related mountain chains, called Bam-e Donya in Persian, "the Roof of the World," are all over

24,000 feet [note]. One story of a Buddhist missionary crossing the Pamirs, Kumarayana, father of Kumarajiva, is that he carried a Buddha image during the day—and the Buddha image carried him during the night! Kumarajiva, Fa-Hsien, and Hsüan-tsang all brought Buddhist texts from India to China and translated them.

The Buddhist canon as it arrived in China was in Sanskrit, and it included many special Mahayana Sutras that are not in the Pali Canon (though many are now suspected of being Chinese forgeries). The stories of Fa-Hsien and Hsüan-tsang's travels are important parts of Chinese literature, and Fa-Hsien's account of India during the reign of Chandra Gupta II (375-415) is an important document for the history of India.

Vajrayana ("Thunderbolt Vehicle") Buddhism: In India, 6th to 11th Century

- *Distinctive doctrines:* Vajrayana Buddhism is Tantric Buddhism, often called "esoteric" Buddhism. Although it is sometimes also translated as "diamond" (*i.e.* "hard"), the vajra (kongo in Japanese) was originally the thunderbolt of Indra; and in Vajrayana it symbolizes the magical power of Tantrism. Tantric magic could be worked through man.d.alas, sacred diagrams, mantras, sacred formulas for recitation (the most famous one being, " Om, mane padme hum" — "The jewel is in the lotus") and mudras, sacred gestures. This Tantric magic could be merely thaumaturgical ("wonder working") or could be regarded as means of achieving liberation in addition to or apart from meditative or meritorious practices. Just as Hindu Tantrism expresses its magical power through goddesses like Kali, Vajrayana emphasizes female figures. Vajrayana comes to balance male Bodhisattvas with female Bodhisattvas as attendants of the various Buddhas. And while Buddhas tend to be regarded as male in all branches of Buddhism, Tibetan Buddhism supplies female figures corresponding to each Buddha, like the "savioresses" Green Tara, White Tara, and Mamaki, who actually vow to always be reborn as women in the process of leading all beings to salvation. Vajrayana symbolism always balances male and female: the Vajra Man.d.ala (or the "jewel" above) corresponds to the Womb (or Matrix) Mandala (the lotus). The extent to which Vajrayana practiced real sexual union, been the physical male "vajra" and the physical female womb, as part of its Tantrism is unclear and disputed. Often "right-handed"

Tantrism is distinguished from "left-handed" Tantrism, in which the former practiced the union of male and female, in symbolic, iconographic form, while the latter practiced it literally.

While the "right-handed" forms are mainly what remain in Tibet and in Japanese Shingon today, there is little doubt that real "left-handed" practices existed in the past and survive to an extent in the present, and Tibetan art sometimes still portrays the more violent and disturbing aspects of Tantric practice — rape, bestiality, etc.

- *Places where Vajrayana spread:* Vajrayana Buddhism most importantly spread to Tibet and then Mongolia. In Tibet it assumed distinctive forms that are usually called Lamaism, since the monks are called Lamas. The present Dalai Lama, who was the priestly ruler of Tibet until he fled the Communist Chinese in 1959, is from a line that is reputed to be successive incarnations of the Bodhisattva Avalokiteshvara.

Vajrayana Buddhism also entered China, Japan, etc. as special "esoteric" schools, like the Japanese Shingon school. The great temple at Borobudur, outside Jakarta on the island of Java, dates from this period (c. 800) and embodies Vajrayana man.d.ala forms; but in Indonesia Buddhism soon thereafter gave way to Islam.

The End of Buddhism in India: Buddhism may have died out in India in the 11th century because:

1. It had become almost indistinguishable from the Tantric forms of Hinduism. Sophisticated Buddhist doctrine did not appeal to most people, and the actual practices and

iconography of Vajrayana could easily be assimilated into Hinduism. And,

2. Islam arrived in earnest in India with the Afghan prince Mah.mud of Ghazna, who defeated a coalition of Hindu princes in 1008 and soon annexed the Punjab. As Buddhism was persecuted, conversions to Islam increased, and Buddhism declined. By the time the British arrived, about 25% of India was Moslem. That ultimately led to the partition of the country into India and Pakistan. The Gautama Buddha himself has ended up being regarded as the 9th Incarnation (Avatar) of the great Hindu God Visnu, although the unflattering take on it is that he deliberately taught a false doctrine (*i.e.* Buddhism) in order to deceive and destroy demons.

The Final Dharma Age: Another way of dividing the history of Buddhism emerged in the Buddhist tradition as a way of dealing with the prediction of the Buddha himself that the Dharma would only last 500 years. This became a matter of concern in China, where Buddhism did not even become established until nearly 1000 years after the time of the Buddha. Indeed, there was uncertainty about when the time of the Buddha had been, but soon enough it was obvious that far more than 500 years had passed. The doctrine that was formulated in response to this we find in K'uei-chi (Tz'u-en, 632-682), founder of the Fa-hsian school early in the T'ang Dynasty, in his I-lin-chang, "The Grove of Meanings." There we find a division into three periods based on the existence of Buddhist teaching, Buddhist practice and Buddhist "proof," *i.e.* results—supernatural powers and Nirvana:

- The Age of the True Dharma (Sanskrit Saddharma, Japanese shobo). In the first 500 years of Buddhism (sometimes put at 1000 years, however), the teaching, the practice, and the proof of Buddhism are all evident and effective. This becomes the Buddhist equivalent of the "age of the Apostles" in Christianity or of the "companions of the Prophet" in Islam — when the best exemplars of the religion lived, people whose achievements are now largely beyond the reach of believers (as most Protestants do not believe that any modern Christians can perform miracles on the scale of the Apostles). It becomes, naturally, particularly associated with Buddhism in India, the first step in the Sangoku, or "three nations," ideology that later developed in Japan.

- The Age of the Counterfeit Dharma (Sanskrit Saddharma-pratirupaka, Japanese zoho). In the 1000 years following the True Dharma, the teaching and the practice of Buddhism are evident but the proof fails. While uncertainty about the length of the True Dharma Age could postpone a reckoning, Buddhism in China — which now becomes particularly associated with the second Age — eventually had to face the fact that the full force of the Dharma, as defined by the Buddha himself, was spent. This would seem to remove the point of Buddhist belief and practice altogether, but it was also something whose full implications most Buddhists were unwilling to accept. One result was the popularity of devotionalistic forms of Buddhism, which substitute intermediate goals before final Nirvan.a. In Pure Land practice, the Vow of the Buddha Amitabha enables devotees to be reborn in a Pure Land, where they will be free of suffering, let alone the Hells, and can work out their salvation without distractions (like hunger or sex). Pure Land Buddhism, indeed, became the most popular form of Buddhism in China and Japan. Another approach, which we see in the T'ien-tai (Japanese Tendai) and Ch'an (Zen) Schools, was to redefine the "proof," so that avoiding rebirth was no longer the goal of Buddhist practice. Instead, life in the world of samsara can become the equivalent of Nirvan.a. This gives to Buddhism itself a very different character, unlike the world-denying tendencies of India and more conformable to the sensibilities of both Confucianism and Taoism. This goes along with discussions about whether it was really necessary to keep Buddhist Precepts. Nevertheless, we do have a continuation of traditional monasticism, and of course not everyone agrees with the new tendencies in thinking.

- The Age of the Final Dharma (Sanskrit Saddharma-vipralopa, Japanese mappo). If the Counterfeit Dharma posed a disturbing challenge for Buddhism, the Final Dharma was even worse. At that point the real practice and proof of Buddhism are both supposed to no longer be possible. Only the teaching remains. While K'uei-chi didn't yet quite have to worry about that, by the time we get to the Kamakura Period (1186-1336) in Japanese history, it becomes widely accepted that the Final Dharma, Mappo, is upon them. This is expected to last no less than 10,000 years. After that, Buddhism will simply be forgotten, and ages will pass, perhaps a million years, before the arrival of the Future Buddha, Maitreya. By this time, of course, Buddhism was already vanishing in India itself. Some Japanese expected this, or were aware of it, others didn't believe it. But it was the kind of thing to reinforce the sense of the fading of the Dharma.

The response was a period of religious creativity, in which a number of Chinese schools were adopted and reworked (Tendai, Zen, Jodo), and some original Japanese schools (Jodo Shin, Nichiren) emerged. Japanese monks ceased taking full monastic vows, clerical marriage became tolerated, sometimes sanctioned (in Jodo Shin), later even expected, and Japanese monks could easily gain reputations as formidable drinkers, despite the Precept against intoxicants. To Buddhists elsewhere, this kind of thing often makes it seem that Japanese monks are no longer proper Buddhists.

In the Japanese tradition, however, this is all of a piece with Mappo, and the development of Japanese Buddhism was seen as actually making it the living center of the Buddhist world. Thus, in the Sangoku ideology, Japan itself becomes the exemplar of the third Age. This would have some unfortunate implications, when Imperial Japan saw itself as exporting its superiority to the rest of Asia. Japanese Buddhist "missions" in Korea helped discredit Buddhism to many, resulting in large numbers of Koreans converting to Christianity. Nevertheless, Japanese religious creativity remains impressive, as groups of

"New Religions" continue to draw on Buddhist and various eclectic sources, and some schools, like Nichiren, have managed to establish themselves among non-Japanese around the world.

While many Buddhists now no longer worry about the problem of the fading Dharma, there is no denying the statement of the Buddha, or the role that dealing with this has played in the history of Buddhism.

Culmen Mundi, the Roof of the World: Most people think of the Himalayas, on the border between Tibet and India and Nepal, as the "Roof of the World" (which would be Culmen Mundi in Latin), since Mt. Everest, at 29,035 ft., is the highest mountain in the world. There was no easy route across the

Himalayas, however, so the term actually originates in Persian (Bam-e Donya) to refer to those ranges that were more familiar to travellers. The Pamirs are very nearly the center from which the other ranges radiate, and thus the focus of overland travel to and from India:

- The highest peak in the Pamirs, now in Tajikistan is Imeni Ismail Sumani Peak, formerly Communism Peak, formerly Stalin Peak (1933-1962), originally Garmo Peak, 24,590 ft. This was the highest point in the old Soviet Union.
- The highest peak in the Karakorum Range, on the border between Pakistani Kashmir and China, is K2 (Mount Godwin Austen), 28,250 ft. (second highest mountain in the world).
- The highest peak in the Hindu Kush, in Pakistan, is Tirich Mir, 25,230 ft.
- The highest peak in the Kunlun Range, in China, is Ulugh Muztagh (Mu-tzu-t'a-Ko), 25,340 ft.
- The highest peak in the Tien Shan (Tian Shan in Pinyin), on the border between China and Kyrgyzstan, is Pobedy Peak (Jengish Chokusu), 24,406 ft.

The Silk Road route from the Middle East to China mainly went through the Tarim Basin, either on the north side, below the Tian Shan, or the south side, above the Kunlun. The center of the Basin, the Taklimakan Desert, is waterless, uninhabited, and, really, uninhabitable. There was also a route north of the Tian Shan. That was a bit further, but the Dzungaria Basin, which I've heard described as a " sage brush and jack rabbit desert," is not as lifeless as the Taklimakan. Today, the through rail line and the larger cities (like Ürümqi) are on the north side on the Tian Shan.

All this is now in the Chinese territory of Sinkiang [Xinjiang]. The passes trough the Pamirs are so high, that familiar pack animals like horses and mules simply die. Only yaks are adapted to the altitude. But then yaks can't live at lower altitudes. Every caravan (from Perisan karvan), consequently, must begin down below with one kind of animal and then change over to yaks, and then back again once over the mountains. Perhaps the most famous Silk Road site, the caves full of Buddhist art and manuscripts at Dunhuang, is just north of the Nanshan ranges, still in the Chinese province of Kansu [Gansu].

Following Central Asia, the Andes have the highest peaks, culminating in Aconcagua at 22,834 ft. North America comes next, with Mt. McKinley at 20,320 ft. Then Africa, with Mt. Kilimanjaro at 19,340 ft. The Culmen Europae, the highest range in Europe, are the Caucasus mountains, whose highest peak is Mt. Elbrus (18,510 ft.). This is far from the population, historical, and cultural center of Europe. The Culmen Franciae is in the Alps, whose highest peak is Mt. Blanc at 15,771 ft. This lay in the historic Kingdom of Burgundy but is now on the border between France and Italy.

Just to round things off, the highest peak in Antarctica is the Vinson Massif, at 16,864 ft. The highest peak in the remaining continent, Australia, is Mt. Kosciusko at only 7,310 ft. This is beat on two nearby islands, Mt. Jaya on New Guinea, at 16,500 ft., and Mt. Cook in New Zealand, at 12,349 ft. However, the highest peak in Polynesia is Mauna Kea on the Island of Hawai'i, at 13,796 ft. Measured from base to summit, Mauna Kea is itself actually the tallest mountain in the world. Mt. Everest is at the edge of the 10,000 foot Tibetan Plateau, meaning that it only rises about 19,000 feet. Mauna Kea, however, rises directly from the sea floor, which is at least 15,000 feet (three miles) down. Base to summit, Mauna Kea is at least 5.6 miles, or 29,568 ft. high (or perhaps as much as 33,000 feet, depending on the reference depth—sea level certainly makes this kind of thing easier).

Philosophy of History

Buddhist philosophy is the branch of Eastern philosophy based on the teachings of Gautama Buddha, a.k.a. Siddhartha Gautama (c. 563 BCE-c. 483 BCE). Buddhist philosophy deals extensively with problems in metaphysics, phenomenology, ethics, and epistemology. From its inception, Buddhism has had a strong philosophical component. Buddhism is founded on the rejection of certain orthodox philosophical concepts, in which the Buddha had been instructed by various teachers. Buddhism rejects atheism, theism, monism, and dualism alike. The Buddha criticized all concepts of metaphysical being and non-being, and this critique is inextricable from the founding of Buddhism.

Particular points of Buddhist philosophizing have often been the subject of disputes between different schools of Buddhism. Metaphysical questions such as "Is there a god?" and "Does the soul (Atman) really exist?" have divided the Buddha's followers even during his own lifetime, and epistemological debates over the proper modes of evidence have always been lively in Buddhism.

Readers should note that theory for its own sake is not valued in Buddhism, but theory pursued in the interest of enlightenment for oneself or others is fully consistent with Buddhist values and ethics.

Buddhism as Philosophy

Some have asserted that Buddhism as a whole is a philosophy rather than a religion. Proponents of such a view may argue that (a) Buddhism is non-theistic (*i.e.*, it has no special use for the existence or nonexistence of a god or gods) or atheistic and (b) religions necessarily involve some form of theism. Others might contest either part of such an argument. Other arguments for Buddhism "as" philosophy may claim that

Buddhism does not have doctrines in the same sense as other religions; the Buddha himself taught that a person should accept a teaching only if one's own experience verifies it and it is praised by the wise.

Arguments against Buddhism as a philosophy might call attention to the way Buddhism's pervasive inclusion of supernatural entities (not "gods" in the sense of Western monotheism, of course), to what most scholars identify as worship practices (ceremonial reverence of saints, etc.), to Buddhism's thoroughly developed hierarchies of clergy (not usually characteristic of a "philosophy"), and its overall religious organization. A third perspective might take the position that Buddhism can be practiced either as a religion or as a philosophy. A similar distinction is often made with reference to Taoism.

Lama Anagorika Govinda expressed it as follows in the book 'A Living Buddhism for the West':

> *"Thus we could say that the Buddha's Dharma is, as experience and as a way to practical realisation, a religion; as the intellectual formulation of this experience, a philosophy; and as a result of self-observation and analysis, a psychology. Whoever treads this path acquires a norm of behaviour that is not dictated from without, but is the result of an inner process of maturation and that we-regarding it from without-can call morality."*

It should also be noted that in the South and East Asian cultures in which Buddhism achieved most of its development, the distinction between philosophy and religion is somewhat unclear and possibly quite spurious, so this may be a semantic problem arising in the West alone.

Epistemology: Decisive in distinguishing Buddhism from what is commonly called Hinduism is the issue of epistemological justification. The schools of Indian logic recognize a certain set of valid justifications for knowledge, while Buddhism recognizes a smaller set.

Both accept perception and inference, for example, but for the orthodox schools (of Hinduism), the received textual tradition (*e.g.*, the Vedas) is in itself an epistemological category equal to perception and inference (although this is not necessarily true for some of the non-orthodox schools, like Vedanta). Thus, in the orthodox schools, if a claim was made that could not be substantiated by appeal to the textual canon, it would be viewed as ridiculous as a claim that the sky was green. Buddhism, on the other hand, rejected an inflexible reverence of accepted doctrine. As the Buddha said:

> *Do not accept anything by mere tradition... Do not accept anything just because it accords with your scriptures... Do not accept anything merely because it agrees with your pre-conceived notions... But when you know for yourselves — these things are moral, these things are blameless, these things are praised by the wise, these things, when performed and undertaken, conduce to well-being and happiness — then do you live acting accordingly.*

Metaphysics and Phenomenology: In earliest Buddhism and today still in Theravda and the Madhyamaka, any metaphysical essence or being underlying the play of phenomenal experience is rejected. No "soul" or permanent self was recognized, and the perception of a continuous identity was held to be an illusion.

Any feeling whatsoever, any perception whatsoever, any mental processes whatsoever, any consciousness whatsoever—past, future, or present; internal or external; blatant or subtle, common or sublime, far or near; every consciousness—is to be seen as it actually is with right discernment as "This is not mine. This is not my self. This is not what I am."

From within the context of the Madhyamaka, we find Candrakirti:

> *"Self is an essence of things that does not depend on others; it is an intrinsic nature. The non-existence of that is selflessness".*

This anti-essentialist teaching, known as anatta, brought up many questions. If there is no atman or Brahman underlying the objects and events of the universe, how could they be explained? What gave them their existence? And if there was no "self", who makes the decisions we think we make, and what gets reincarnated? Early Buddhist philosophers and exegetes created a pluralist metaphysical and phenomenological system in which all experiences of people, things, and events, can be broken down into smaller and smaller perceptual or perceptual-ontological units called dharmas.

These dharmas (roughly synonymous with "phenomena") were interpreted differently by different schools: some held they were real, some held only some were real, some held all were illusory, some held they were empty, some held they were intrinsically associated with suffering, etc.

Other debates in metaphysics and phenomenology include the issue of the Pudgala, or "person", which was inserted by the Pudgalavada school to replace the atman as that which transmigrates and that which carries the burden of karma from one life to another.

Other schools made unsurprising objection to this. There were further sub-debates regarding whether the pudgala was real or illusory or something in between. The Yogacara school, somewhat later, would later elevate the mind to act as a substitute for Brahman, much as the Pudgala replaces the atman.

In many or all of these debates, some would point out the irony of pursuing questions which the Buddha was often prone to refuse to answer, on the grounds that they were non-conducive to enlightenment. For more detailed information, see Schools of Buddhism and the individual schools themselves.

Dependent Origination: The original positive Buddhist contribution to the field of metaphysics is prat+tyasamutpda, which arises from the Buddhist critique of Indian theories of causality. It states that events are not predetermined, nor are they random, and it rejects notions of direct causation owing to the need for such theories in the Indian context to be undergirded by a substantialist metaphysics. Instead, it posits the arising of events under certain conditions which are inextricable, such that the units in question at no time have independent existence.

This being, that becomes.

From the arising of this, that arises.

This not being, that does not become.

From the ceasing of this, that ceases. — Samyutta Nikaya

Pratitya-samutpada goes on to posit that certain specific events, concepts, or realities are always dependent on other specific things. Craving, for example, is always dependent on, and caused by, emotion. Emotion is always dependent on contact with our surroundings. This chain of causation purports to show that the cessation of decay, death, and sorrow is indirectly dependent on the cessation of craving, and ultimately dependent on an all-encompassing stillness.

Ngrjuna, one of the most influential Buddhist philosophers, asserted a direct connection between, even identity of, dependent origination, anatta, and [knyat.

He pointed out that implicit in the early Buddhist concept of dependent origination is the lack of any substantial being (anatta) underlying the participants in origination, so that they have no independent existence, a state identified as emptiness ([knyat), or emptiness of a nature or essence (sva-bhva). This element of Ngrjuna's thought is relatively uncontroversial, but it opens the way for his identification of samsara and nirvana, which was revolutionary.

Interpenetration: This doctrine comes from the Avatamsaka Sutra and its associated schools. It holds that all phenomena are intimately connected. Two images are used to convey this idea. The first is known as Indra's net. The net is set with jewels which have the extraordinary property that they reflect all of the other jewels. The second image is that of the world text. This image portrays the world as consisting of an enormous text which is as large as the universe itself. The 'words' of the text are composed of the phenomena that make up the world. However, every atom of the world contains the whole text within it. It is the work of a Buddha to let out the text so that beings can be liberated from suffering.

This idea was enormously influential on the Japanese monk kkkai in founding the Shingon school of Buddhism.

Ethics

Although there are many ethical tenets in Buddhism that differ depending on whether one is a monk or a layman, and depending on individual schools, the Buddhist system of ethics can always be summed up in the Eightfold Path.

And this, monks, is the noble truth of the way of practice leading to the cessation of suffering — precisely this Noble Eightfold Path — right view, right resolve, right speech, right action, right livelihood, right effort, right mindfulness, right concentration.

The purpose of living an ethical life is to escape the suffering inherent in (unenlightened) worldly life. Although early Buddhism (Hinayana) is contrasted with later Buddhism (Mahayana) in that the latter emphasizes striving for the enlightenment of all (apparent) beings rather than simply oneself, in neither case can the motivation for ethical living be called 'selfish', because Buddhist doctrine holds the notion of a 'self' to be illusory.

Buddhist teachings claim that there is no real difference between ourselves and others; therefore one should attempt to increase the happiness of all living things as eagerly as one's own. This is why many Buddhists choose to be vegetarians.

Early Development

The philosophical outlook of Earliest Buddhism was primarily negative, in the sense that it focused on what doctrines to reject more than on what doctrines to accept. This dimension has been preserved by the Madhyamaka school. It includes critical rejections of all views, which is a form of philosophy, but it is reluctant to posit its own. Only knowledge that is useful in achieving enlightenment is valued. The cycle of philosophical upheavals that in part drove the diversification of Buddhism into its many schools and sects only began once Buddhists began attempting to make explicit the implicit philosophy of the Buddha and the early Suttas. After the death of the Buddha, attempts were made to gather his teachings and transmit them in a commonly agreed form, first orally, then also in writing (The Tripitaka). In addition to collecting the

Buddha's speeches and rules for monastic life (Vinaya), monks soon undertook to condense what they considered the essential elements of Buddhist doctrine into lists of categories, provided with extensive commentary. This process took shape from about the 2nd century BCE to probably the 2nd century CE.

Early Buddhism: Before the royal sponsorship of Ashoka the Great in the 3rd century BCE, Buddhism seems to have remained a relatively minor phenomenon, and the historicity of its formative events is poorly established. Two formative councils are supposed to have taken place, although our knowledge of them is based on much later accounts. The councils tend to explain the formalization of the Buddhist doctrine, and the various subsequent schisms inside the Buddhist movement.

Buddhist Council: The first Buddhist council was held soon after the death of the Buddha under the patronage of king Ajatasatru of the Magadha empire, and presided by a monk named Mahakasyapa, at Rajagriha (today's Rajgir). The objective of the council was to record the Buddha's sayings (sutra) and codify monastic rules (vinaya): Ananda, one of the Buddha's main disciples and his cousin, was called upon to recite the discourses of the Buddha, and Upali, another disciple, recited the rules of the vinaya. These became the basis of the Pali Canon, which has been the orthodox text of reference throughout the history of Buddhism.

The second Buddhist council was convened by King Kalasoka and held at Vaisali, following conflicts between the traditional schools of Buddhism and a more liberal interpretational movement called the Mahasanghikas. The traditional schools considered the Buddha as a human being who reached enlightenment, which could be most easily attained by monks following the monastic rules and practicing the teaching for the sake of overcoming suffering and attaining Arahantship.

The secessionist Mahasangikas, however, tended to consider this approach too individualistic and selfish. They considered the objective of becoming an arhat insufficient, and instead proposed that the only true goal was to reach full buddhahood, in a sense opening the way to future Mahyna thought. They became proponents of more relaxed monastic rules, which could appeal to a large majority of monastic and lay people (hence their name the "great" or "majority" assembly).

The council ended with the rejection of the Mahasanghikas. They left the council and maintained themselves for several centuries in northwestern India and Central Asia according to Kharoshti inscriptions found near the Oxus and dated c. 1st century CE.

Ashokan Proselytism

Fragment of the 6th Pillar Edict of Ashoka (238 BCE), in Brahmi, sandstone. British Museum. The Mauryan emperor Ashoka the Great (273–232 BCE) converted to Buddhism after his bloody conquest of the territory of Kalinga (today's Orissa) in eastern India. Regretful of the horrors brought by the conflict, the king decided to renounce violence, and propagate the faith by building stupas and pillars urging for the respect of all animal life, and enjoining people to follow the Dharma. He also built roads, hospitals, resthouses, universities and irrigation systems around the country. He treated his subjects as equals regardless of their religion, politics or caste.

This period marks the first spread of Buddhism beyond India. According to the plates and pillars left by king Ashoka (the Edicts of Ashoka), emissaries were sent to various countries in order to spread Buddhism, as far as the Greek kingdoms in the West, in particular the neighboring Greco-Bactrian Kingdom, and possibly even farther to the Mediterranean according to the stone inscriptions left by Ashoka.

King Ashoka convened the third Buddhist council around 250 BCE at Pataliputra (today's Patna). It was held by the monk Moggaliputta. The objective of the council was to reconcile the different schools of Buddhism, to purify the Buddhist movement, particularly from opportunistic factions which had been attracted by the royal patronage, and to organize the dispatch of Buddhist missionaries throughout the known world.

The Pali canon (Tipitaka, or Tripitaka in Sanskrit, literally the "Three Baskets"), which comprises the texts of reference of traditional Buddhism and is considered to be directly transmitted from the Buddha, was formalized at that time. It consists of the doctrine (the Sutra Pitaka), the monastic discipline (Vinaya Pitaka) and an additional new body of subtle philosophy (the Abhidharma Pitaka).

The efforts of Ashoka to purify the Buddhist faith also had the effect of segregating against other emerging movements. In particular, after 250 BCE, the Sarvastivadin (who had been rejected by the 3rd council, according to the Theravada tradition) and the Dharmaguptaka schools became quite influential in northwestern India and Central Asia, up to the time of the Kushan Empire in the first centuries of the common era. The Dharmaguptakas were characterized by a belief that Buddha was separate, and above, the rest of the Buddhist community. The Sarvastivadin believed that past, present, and future are all simultaneous.

Hellenistic World: Some of the Edicts of Ashoka inscriptions describe the efforts made by Ashoka to propagate the Buddhist faith throughout the Hellenistic world, which at that time formed an uninterrupted continuum from the borders of India to Greece. The Edicts indicate a clear understanding of the political organization in Hellenistic territories: the names and location of the main Greek monarchs of the time are identified, and they are claimed as recipients of Buddhist proselytism: Antiochus II Theos of the Seleucid Kingdom (261–246 BCE), Ptolemy II Philadelphos of Egypt (285–247 BCE), Antigonus Gonatas of Macedonia (276–239 BCE), Magas of Cyrene (288–258 BCE), and Alexander II of Epirus (272–255 BCE).

Buddhist Proselytism at the Time of King Ashoka

"The conquest by Dharma has been won here, on the borders, and even six hundred yojanas (5,400-9,600 km) away, where the Greek king Antiochos rules, beyond there where the four kings named Ptolemy, Antigonos, Magas and Alexander rule, likewise in the south among the Cholas, the Pandyas, and as far as Tamraparni (Sri Lanka)." (Edicts of Ashoka, 13th Rock Edict, S. Dhammika). Furthermore, according to Pali sources, some of Ashoka's emissaries were Greek Buddhist monks, indicating close religious exchanges between the two cultures:

"When the thera (elder) Moggaliputta, the illuminator of the religion of the Conqueror (Ashoka), had brought the (third) council to an end (...) he sent forth theras, one here and one there: (...) and to Aparantaka (the "Western countries" corresponding to Gujarat and Sindh) he sent the Greek (Yona) named Dhammarakkhita". (Mahavamsa XII).

Bilingual inscription (Greek and Aramaic) by king Ashoka, from Kandahar. Kabul Museum.

It is not clear how much these interactions may have been influential, but some authors have commented that some level of syncretism between Hellenist thought and Buddhism may have started in Hellenic lands at that time. They have pointed to the presence of Buddhist communities in the Hellenistic world around that period, in particular in Alexandria (mentioned by Clement of Alexandria), and to the pre-Christian monastic order of the Therapeutae (possibly a deformation of the Pali word "Theravada"), who may have "almost entirely drawn (its) inspiration from the teaching and practices of Buddhist asceticism" (Robert Lissen).

Buddhist gravestones from the Ptolemaic period have also been found in Alexandria, decorated with depictions of the Dharma wheel (Tarn, "The Greeks in Bactria and India"). Commenting on the presence of Buddhists in Alexandria, some scholars have even pointed out that "It was later in this very place that some of the most active centers of Christianity were established" (Robert Linssen "Zen living").

In the 2nd century CE, the Christian dogmatist Clement of Alexandria recognized Bactrian Buddhists (Sramanas) and Indian Gymnosophists for their influence on Greek thought:

> *"Thus philosophy, a thing of the highest utility, flourished in antiquity among the barbarians, shedding its light over the nations. And afterwards it came to Greece. First in its ranks were the prophets of the Egyptians; and the Chaldeans among the Assyrians; and the Druids among the Gauls; and the Sramanas*

among the Bactrians; and the philosophers of the Celts; and the Magi of the Persians, who foretold the Saviour's birth, and came into the land of Judaea guided by a star. The Indian gymnosophists are also in the number, and the other barbarian philosophers. And of these there are two classes, some of them called Sramanas and others Brahmins." Clement of Alexandria "The Stromata, or Miscellanies".

Asian Expansion

In the areas east of the Indian subcontinent (today's Burma), Indian culture strongly influenced the Mons. The Mons are said to have been converted to Buddhism around 200 BCE under the proselytizing of the Indian king Ashoka, before the fission between Mahayana and Hinayana Buddhism. Early Mon Buddhist temples, such as Peikthano in central Burma, have been dated between the 1st and the 5th century CE.

Mons Wheel of the Law (Dharmacakra), art of Dvaravati, c.8th century.

The Buddhist art of the Mons was especially influenced by the Indian art of the Gupta and post-Gupta periods, and their mannerist style spread widely in South-East Asia following the expansion of the Mon kingdom between the 5th and 8th centuries. The Theravada faith expanded in the northern parts of Southeast Asia under Mon influence, until it was progressively displaced by Mahayana Buddhism from around the 6th century CE.

Sri Lanka was allegedly proselytized by Ashoka's son Mahinda and six companions during the 2nd century BCE. They converted the king Devanampiya Tissa and many of the nobility. This is when the Mahavihara monastery, a center of Sinhalese orthodoxy, was built. The Pali Canon was put in writing in Sri Lanka during the reign of king Vittagamani (r. 29–17 BCE), and the Theravada tradition flourished there, harbouring some great commentators such as Buddhaghosa (4th–5th century). Although Mahayana Buddhism gained some influence at that time, Theravada ultimately prevailed, and Sri Lanka turned out to be the last stronghold of Theravada

Buddhism, from where it would expand again to South-East Asia from the 11th century. There is also a legend, not directly validated by the edicts, that Ashoka sent a missionary to the north, through the Himalayas, to Khotan in the Tarim Basin, then the land of the Tocharians, speakers of an Indo-European language.

MENTAL DEVELOPMENT (SAMADHI)

The "mental development" subdivision of the Noble Eightfold Path is constituted by those elements that deal with how a Buddhist practitioner can best go about shaping his or her outlook towards the world.

Right Effort: Right effort can also be translated as "right endeavor", and involves the Buddhist practitioner's continuous effort to, essentially, keep his or her mind free of thoughts that might impair his or her ability to realize or put into practice the other elements of the Noble Eightfold Path; for example, wishing ill towards another living being would contradict the injunction—contained in the "Right thought" element—to have good will towards others, and the "Right effort" element refers to the process of attempting to root out such an ill wish and replace it with a good wish. The Buddhist monk Ajahn Chah, of the Thai forest tradition of Theravada Buddhism, described right effort as follows:

> *Proper effort is not the effort to make something particular happen. It is the effort to be aware and awake in each moment, the effort to overcome laziness and defilement, the effort to make each activity of our day meditation.*

By making right effort, a Buddhist practitioner is considered to be engaging in an effort that is wholesome in terms of karma; that is, in terms of that effort's ultimate consequences to the practitioner.

Right Mindfulness: Right mindfulness also translated as "right memory", together with right concentration, is concerned broadly with the practice of Buddhist meditation. Roughly speaking, "mindfulness" refers to the practice of keeping the mind alert to phenomena as they are affecting the body and mind. In the Magga-vibhanga Sutta, this aspect of the Noble Eightfold Path is explained as follows:

And what, monks, is right mindfulness?

(i) There is the case where a monk remains focused on (his/her) body in and of itself... ardent, aware, and mindful... having already put aside worldly desire and aversion.

(ii) (He/she) remains focused on feelings in and of themselves... ardent, aware, and mindful... having already put aside worldly desire and aversion.

(iii) (He/she) remains focused on the mind in and of itself... ardent, aware, and mindful... having already put aside worldly desire and aversion.

(iv) (He/she) remains focused on mental qualities in and of themselves... ardent, aware, and mindful... having already put aside worldly desire and aversion.

This, monks, is called right mindfulness.

Bhikkhu Bodhi, a monk of the Theravadin tradition, further glosses the concept of mindfulness as follows:

The mind is deliberately kept at the level of bare attention, a detached observation of what is happening within us and around us in the present moment. In the practice of right mindfulness the mind is trained to remain in the present, open, quiet, and alert, contemplating the present event. All judgments and interpretations have to be suspended, or if they occur, just registered and dropped.

Right Concentration: Right concentration together with right mindfulness, is concerned broadly with the practice of Buddhist meditation.

And what, monks, is right concentration?

(i) Quite withdrawn from sensuality, withdrawn from unwholesome states, a monk enters in the first jhna: rapture and pleasure born from detachment, accompanied by movement of the mind onto the object and retention of the mind on the object.

(ii) With the stilling of directed thought and evaluation, he enters and remains in the second jhna: rapture and pleasure born of concentration; fixed single-pointed awareness free from movement of the mind onto the object and retention of the mind on the object; assurance.

(iii) With the fading of rapture, he remains in equanimity, mindful and fully aware, and physically sensitive of pleasure. He enters and remains in the third jhna which the Noble Ones declare to be "Equanimous and mindful, (he/she) has a pleasurable abiding."

(iv) With the abandoning of pleasure and pain...as with the earlier disappearance of elation and distress...he enters and remains in the fourth jhna: purity of equanimity and mindfulness, neither in pleasure nor in pain.

This, monks, is called right concentration.

The Ninth and Tenth Elements: In the Great Forty Sutra (Mahcattr+saka Sutta), which appears in the Pli Canon, the Buddha explains that cultivation of the Eightfold Path leads to the development of two further stages once enlightenment has been reached. These also fall under the category of pann and are Right Knowledge (sammnGa) and Right Liberation (or Right Release; sammvimutti). Some consider Right Association as an implicit ninth aspect of the Path.

The Noble Eightfold Path and Cognitive Psychology: From the standpoint of modern cognitive psychology, the Noble Eightfold Path can be seen as rooted in what is called cognitive dissonance, which is the perception of incompatibility between two cognitions. In the essay " Buddhism Meets Western Science", Gay Watson explains this dissonance as it relates to Buddhist teaching:

Buddhism has always been concerned with feelings, emotions, sensations, and cognition. The Buddha points both to cognitive and emotional causes of suffering. The emotional cause is desire and its negative opposite, aversion. The cognitive cause is ignorance of the way things truly occur, or of three marks of existence: that all things are unsatisfactory, impermanent, and without essential self. The Noble Eightfold Path is, from this psychological viewpoint, an attempt to resolve this dissonance by changing patterns of thought and behavior. It is for this reason that the first element of the path is right understanding (samm-dimmhi), which is how one's mind views the world. Under the wisdom (pann) subdivision of the Noble Eightfold Path, this worldview is intimately connected with the second element, right thought (samm-saEkappa), which concerns the patterns of thought and intention that controls one's actions. These elements can be seen at work, for example, in the opening verses of the Dhammapada:

Preceded by perception are mental states,
For them is perception supreme,
From perception have they sprung.
If, with perception polluted, one speaks or acts,
Thence suffering follows
As a wheel the draught ox's foot.
Preceded by perception are mental states,
For them is perception supreme,
From perception have they sprung.
If, with tranquil perception, one speaks or acts,
Thence ease follows
As a shadow that never departs.

Thus, by willfully altering one's distorted worldview as well as the behaviors stemming from that worldview and bringing out "tranquil perception" in the place of "perception polluted", one is enabled to potentially escape from suffering and develop one's mind. Watson points this out from a psychological standpoint:

Research has shown that repeated action, learning, and memory can actually change the nervous system physically, altering both synaptic strength and connections. Such changes may be brought about by cultivated change in emotion and action; they will, in turn, change subsequent experience.

As such, Buddhism can essentially be seen as mind cultivation and rehabilitation.

Panchasila

Pancha or Pancas+la (Pli) means the five precepts, which are the fundamental code of ethics, undertaken by lay followers of the Buddha Gautama.

The laity undertake to follow these training rules at the same time as they become Buddhists, taking refuge in the Triple Gem: In the Buddha (teacher), in the Dharma (teaching) and thirdly in the Sangha (community of monks and nuns).

The Buddha taught the five precepts out of compassion, not out of any desire to control his followers, and so they are to be undertaken voluntarily rather than as "commandments" from a god. The following are rendered in English and then Pali.

1. I undertake the precept to refrain from destroying living beings. Pntipt veramani sikkhpadam samdiymi
2. I undertake the precept to refrain from stealing. Adinndn veramani sikkhpadam samdiymi
3. I undertake the precept to refrain from sexual misconduct (adultery, rape, etc). Kmesu micchcra veramani sikkhpadam samdiymi
4. I undertake the precept to refrain from false speech (lying). Musvda veramani sikkhpadam samdiymi
5 I undertake the precept to refrain from intoxicants which lead to heedlessness. Sur meraya majja pamdatthn veramani sikkhpadam samdiymi

Nirvana

Nirvana is, further, the abiding of a fully enlightened being (see terms Arhat and Buddha) in pure unobstructed awareness of reality as-it-is. It is accompanied by and synonymous with a state of spiritual awakening (Enlightenment). The Buddha describes the abiding in nirvana as a state of 'deathlessness' (Pali: amata or amaravati) and the "unconditioned" and as the highest spiritual attainment, the natural result that accrues to one who lives a life of virtuous conduct in accordance with Dharma.

There are many synonyms for Nirvana, as shown by the following passage:

> *World Honored One, the ground of fruition is bodhi, nirvana, true suchness, the Buddha-nature, the amala-consciousness, the empty treasury of the Thus Come One, the great, perfect mirror-wisdom. But although it is called by these seven names, it is pure and perfect, its substance is durable, like royal vajra, everlasting and indestructible. (Surangama Sutra IV 207)*

Nirgna (Pali nibbna) in sutra is "bhavanirodha nibbnam" (The cessation of becoming means Nirvna). Nirvna in sktra is never conceived of as a place, but the antinomy of samsra (see below) which itself is synonymous with ignorance (avidy, Pli avijj). "This said:

> *'the liberated mind/will (citta) which does not cling' means Nibbna" (Majjhima Nikaya 2-Att. 4.68).*

Nibbna is meant specifically as pertains gnosis that which ends the identity of the mind (citta) with empirical phenomena. Doctrinally Nibbna is said of the mind which no "longer is coming (bhava) and going (vibhava)", but which has attained a status in perpetuity, whereby "liberation (vimutta) can be said".

It carries further connotations of stilling, cooling, and peace; the realizing of nirvana is compared to the ending of avidy (ignorance) which perpetuates the will (citta/mind) from passing through samsra life after life, which causes (and is caused by) among other things craving, consciousness, birth, death, greed, hate, delusion, ignorance. Nirgna, then, is not a place nor a state, it is an absolute truth to be realized, and a person can do so without dying.

When a person who has realized nirvna dies, his death is referred as his parinirvna, his fully passing away, as his life was his last link to the cycle of death and rebirth (samsara), and he will not be reborn again. Buddhism holds that the ultimate goal and end of samsaric existence (of ever "becoming" and "dying" and never truly being) is realization of nirvna; what happens to a person after his parinirvna cannot be explained, as it is outside of all conceivable experience.

Undefinable Nature: Ergo the freed mind is equal to Nibbana in Buddhist doctrine. Elsewhere the Buddha calls nirvna 'the unconditioned element' (*i.e.*, that which is not subject to causation). Nirvna in doctrinal citation the "subjugation of becoming" (bhavanirodha nibbanam) and is relavent to Ignorance (avijja) only, such that Samsara is the will/mind (citta) in ignorance, and Nirvana/Nibbana the will/mind devoid of said ignorance; it can only be experienced in dirrect Subjective gnosis. While some of the associated effects of nirvna can be identified, a definition of nirvna can only be approximated by what it is not.

It is not the clinging existence with which man is understood to be afflicted. It is not any sort of becoming. It has no origin or end. It is not made or fabricated. It has no dualities, so that it cannot be described in words. It has no parts that may be distinguished one from another. It is not a subjective state of consciousness. It is not conditioned on or by anything else.

It should also be noted that the Buddha discouraged certain lines of speculation, including speculation into the state of an enlightened being after death, on the grounds that these were not useful for pursuing enlightenment; thus definitions of nirvna might be said to be doctrinally unimportant.

In the Samyutta Nikaya, the Buddha describes Nibbna as:

> *"the far shore, the subtle, the very difficult to see, the unaging, the stable, the undisintegrating, the unmanifest, the unproliferated, the peaceful, the deathless, the sublime, the auspicious, the secure, the destruction of craving, the wonderful, the amazing, the unailing, the unailing state, the unafflicted, dispassion, purity, freedom, the unadhesive, the island, the shelter, the asylum, the refuge..."*

At the end of the Mahsatipammhna Sutta in D+gha Nikya, the Buddha describes Success of Four Pammhna Meditations as: "One who is honest to himself and practice this four

Pammhna Meditations without a delay, he should be willing to achieve Arahat or Angami level, in seven days to seven years in time which would ultimately direct to Nirgna."

What Nirvana is Not?

Nirvana is the complete realization of the middle way (majjhena dha"mma"m deseti) and is neither the extremist views of nihilism (Pali: Ucchedavaada) nor eternalism (Pali: Sassatavaada) nor the monism of "oneness with brahman".

In the Saamannaphala Sutta of the Digha Nikaya, Buddha clearly outlines the differences between his teachings and these schools which are considered pasanda or schools which lead to wrong views. Nirvana is not eternalism as Buddhism posits Anatta (not-self), so there is no personal immortality of a self.

Nirvana is not Nihilism: Which identifies the psycho-physical person (naama-ruupa) with the body (ruupa), rejecting human effort and the world hereafter (para loka). When the body is dead, it entails the total annihilation of the psycho-physical person, without the continuity of the consciousness for bearing moral retribution of his deeds done;

Similarly, Nirvana is not equivalent to the Vedic concept of Brahman, nor is the same as Heaven in many other religions:

> *The Buddha emphasized that the atman is like a mountain stream, which flows fast and is forever changing. There is no being (sat), there is only becoming (bhava) in it. The arising (uppaada), disappearance (vyaya) and changing of what exists (a~n~natatha) are the three signs of compounded things. The belief in a permanent self (atman) not only negates the activities of moral life but also falls in a form of grasping, a hindrance to spiritual liberation.*

In more precise terms, it is the non-Self (*i.e.*, the mundane body and unawakened mind, not the "Self") which is, according to the pronouncements of the Buddha in the Nikayas, linked to impermanence and change. Clutching onto this non-Self and the latter's suffering-generating mutations is what deprives sentient beings of the attainment of Nirvana.

Nirvna and Samsra: In Mahyna Buddhism, calling nirvna the "opposite" of samsra or implying that it is apart from samsra is doctrinally problematic. According to early Mahyna Buddhism, they can be considered to be two aspects of the same perceived reality. By the time of Ngrjuna, there are teachings of the identity of nirvna and samsara. However, even here it is assumed that the natural man suffers from at the very least a confusion regarding the nature of samsra.

The Theravda school makes the antithesis of samsara and Nibbna the starting point of the entire quest for deliverance. Even more, it treats this antithesis as determinative of the final goal, which is precisely the transcendence of samsara and the attainment of liberation in Nibbna. Where Theravada differs significantly from the Mahyna schools, which also start with the duality of samsara and Nirgna, is in not regarding this polarity as a mere preparatory lesson tailored for those with blunt faculties, to be eventually superseded by some higher realization of non-duality. From the standpoint of the Pli Suttas, even for the Buddha and the Arahants suffering and its cessation, samsra and Nibbna, remain distinct.

In the experience of some, Nirvna is a state which all six bases (Eye, Ear, Nose, Tongue, Body and Mind) cannot feel.

It is probably best to understand the relationship between Nirvana and samsara in terms of the Buddha while on earth. Buddha was both in Samsara while having attained to Nirvana so that he was seen by all, and simultaneously free from samsara.

Nirvana in Buddhist Commentaries: Sarvastivàdin commentary, Abhidharma-mahavibhàsa-sàstra, gives the complete context of the possible meanings from it's sanskrit roots:

- Vàna, implying the path of rebirth, + nir, meaning leaving off' or 'being away from the path of rebirth.'
- Vàna, meaning 'stench', + nir, meaning 'freedom': ' freedom from the stench of distressing kamma.'
- Vàna, meaning 'dense forests', + nir, meaning 'to get rid of' = 'to be permanently rid of the dense forest of the

five aggregates (panca skandha), or the 'three roots of greed, hate and delusion (lobha, dosa, moha)' or 'three characteristics of existence (impermanence, anitya; unsatisfactoriness, dukkha, soullessness, anàtma).

- Vàna, meaning 'weaving', + nir, meaning 'knot' = ' freedom from the knot of the distressful thread of kamma.'

Nirvna in the Mahparinirvna Sktra: The nature of Nirvana assumes a differently aspected Mahayana focus in what alleges to be the final of all Mahayana sutras, allegedly delivered by the Buddha on his last day of life on earth-the Mahaparinirvana Sutra or Nirvana Sutra. Here, as well as in a number of linked "tathagatagarbha" sutras, in which the Tathagatagarbha is equated with the Buddha's eternal Self or eternal nature, Nirvana is spoken of by the Mahayana Buddha in very "cataphatic", positive terms. Nirvana, or "Great Nirvna", is indicated to be the sphere or domain (vishaya) of the True Self. It is seen as the state which constitutes the attainment of what is "Eternal, the Self, Bliss, and the Pure". Mah-nirvna ("Great Nirvana") thus becomes equivalent to the ineffable, unshakeable, blissful, all-pervading and deathless Selfhood of the Buddha himself-a mystery which no words can adequately reach and which, according to the Nirvana Sutra, can only be fully known by an Awakened Being-a perfect Buddha-directly.

Strikingly, the Buddha of the Mahaparinirvana Sutra gives the following definition of the attributes of Nirvana, which includes the ultimate reality of the Self (not to be confused with the "worldly ego" of the 5 skandhas):

> *"The attributes of Nirvana are eightfold. What are these eight? Cessation [nirodha], loveliness/ wholesomeness [subha], Truth [satya], Reality [tattva], eternity [nitya], bliss [sukha], the Self [atman], and complete purity [parisuddhi]: that is Nirvana."*

He further states: "Non-Self is Samsara [the cycle of rebirth]; the Self (atman) is Great Nirvana."

An important facet of Nirvna in general is that it is not something that comes about from a concatenation of causes, that springs into existence as a result of an act of creation or an agglomeration of causative factors: it was never created; it always was, is and will be. But due to the moral and mental darkness of ordinary, samsarically benighted sentient beings, it remains hidden from unawakened perception. The Buddha of the MahpariNirgnasktra insists on its eternal nature and affirms its identity with the enduring, blissful Self, saying:

> *"It is not the case that the inherent nature of Nirvna did not primordially exist but now exists. If the inherent nature of Nirgna did not primordially exist but does now exist, then it would not be free from taints (sravas) nor would it be eternally (nitya) present in nature. Regardless of whether there are Buddhas or not, its intrinsic nature and attributes are eternally present... Because of the obscuring darkness of the mental afflictions (kle[as), beings do not see it. The Tathgata, endowed with omniscient awareness (sarvajn-jnna), lights the lamp of insight with his skill-in-means (upya-kau[alya) and causes Bodhisattvas to perceive the Eternal, Bliss, the Self, and the Pure of Nirvna."*

Vitally, according to these Mahyna teachings, any being who has reached Nirvana is not blotted out or extinguished: there is the extinction of the impermanent and suffering-prone "worldly self" or ego (comprised of the five changeful skandhas), but not of the immortal "supramundane" Self of the indwelling Buddha Principle [Buddha-dhatu]. Spiritual death for such a Nirvana-ed being becomes an utter impossibility. The Buddha states in the "Mahyna Mahparinirvna Sutra" (Tibetan version): "Nirvna is deathless... Those who have passed into Nirvna are deathless. I say that anybody who is endowed with careful assiduity is not compounded and, even though they involve themselves in compounded things, they do not age, they do not die, they do not perish."

Quotations

- Gautama Buddha:
- " Nirvana is the highest happiness."

- "Where there is nothing; where naught is grasped, there is the Isle of No-Beyond. Nirgna do I call it — the utter extinction of aging and dying."
- "There is, monks, an unborn — unbecome — unmade— unfabricated. If there were not that unborn— unbecome— unmade — unfabricated, there would not be the case that emancipation from the born — become— made — fabricated would be discerned. But precisely because there is an unborn — unbecome — unmade — unfabricated, emancipation from the born — become— made — fabricated is discerned."
- This said: 'the liberated mind/will (citta) which does not cling' means Nibbna"
- "The subjugation of becoming means Nirvana'; this means the subjugation of the five aggregates means Nirvana."
- "Parinibbuto thitatto"-"Parinirvana is to be fixed in the Soul"
- Said immediately after the physical death of Gotama Buddha wherein his mind (citta) is= parinirvana=the essence of liberation:
- "No longer with (subsists by) in-breath nor out-breath, so is him (Gotama) who is steadfast in mind (citta), inherently quelled from all desires the mighty sage has passed beyond. With mind (citta) limitless (Brahman) he no longer bears sensations; illumined and unbound (nibbana), his mind (citta) is definitely (ahu) liberated."
- "The mind (citta) being so liberated and arisen from defilements, one is fixed in the Soul as liberation, one is quelled in fixation upon the Soul. Quelled in the Soul one is unshakable. So being unshakable, the very Soul is thoroughly unbound (parinirvana)."
- Sutta Nipta, tr. Rune Johansson:
- Like a flame that has been blown out by a strong wind goes to rest and cannot be defined, just so the sage who is freed from name and body goes to rest and cannot be defined.

For him who has gone to rest there is no measure by means of which one could describe him; that is not for him. When all (dharmas) have gone, all signs of recognition have also gone.

- Venerable Sariputta:
- The destruction of greed, hatred and delusion is Nirvana.

Three Jewels

The Three Jewels, also rendered as Three Treasures, Three Refuges or Triple Gem (Sanskrit: Triratna, also Ratna-traya, Pali: Tiratana, Tisarana are the three things that Buddhists give themselves to, and in return look toward for guidance, in the process known as taking refuge.

Taking the the Triple Gem is generally considered makes one officially a Buddhist. Thus, in many Buddhist communities, the following Pali chant, the Vandana Ti-sarana is often recited by both monks and lay people:

- Buddham Sharanam Gacchami I go for refuge in the Buddha.
- Dhammam Sharanam Gacchami I go for refuge in the Dharma
- Sangham Sharanam Gacchami I go for refuge in the Sangha

Taking refuge in the Three Jewels is central to Buddhist lay and monastic ordination ceremonies, as originated by Gautama Buddha.

These three types of persons are found in the world: One with a mind like an open sore; one with a mind like a flash of lightning; one with a mind like a diamond.

- One who is irascible and very irritable, displaying anger, hatred and sulkiness; such a one is said to be a person with a mind like an open sore.
- One who understands the Four Noble Truths correctly is said to have a mind like a flash of lightning.
- One who has destroyed the mind-intoxicating defilements and realized the liberation of mind and the

liberation by knowledge is said to have a mind like a diamond

With this we understand that to take refuge in the Buddha is to take refuge in the mind like a diamond, the hardest natural substance that can cut through all delusion. The Three Gems when used in the process of taking refuge, become the Three Refuges.

The expression Three Gems are found in the earliest Buddhist literature of the Pali Canon, besides other works there is one sutta in the Sutta-nipata, called the Ratana-sutta which contains a series of verses on the Jewels in the Buddha, Dharma, and Sangha. In the Ratana-sutta, all the qualities of the Sangha mentioned are attributes of the Buddha's enlightened disciples. The Three Refuges occur very frequently in the ancient Buddhist Texts, and here the Sangha is used more broadly to refer to either the Sangha of Bhikkhus, or the Sangha of Bhikkhunis.

"I go to Master Gotama for refuge and to the Dhamma, and to the Sangha of Bhikkhus."

Triratna Symbol: The compound Buddhist symbols: Shrivatsa within a triratana, over a Dharmacakra wheel, on the Tonana gate at Sanchi. 1st century BCE.

The Three Jewels are also symbolized by the triratna, composed of (from bottom to top):

- A lotus flower within a circle.
- A diamond rod, or vajra.
- A trident, or trisula, with three branches, representing the threefold jewels of Buddhism: Buddha, the Dharma and the Sangha.

On representations of the footprint of the Buddha, the Triratna is usually also surmounted by the Dharma wheel. The Triratna can be found on frieze sculptures at Sanchi as the symbol crowning a flag standard (2nd century BCE), as a symbol of the Buddha installed on the Buddha's throne (2nd century BCE), as the crowning decorative symbol on the later gates at the stupa in Sanchi (2nd century CE), or, very often on the Buddha footprint (starting from the 1st century CE). 2nd century BCE coin of the Kunindas, incorporating on the reverse the Buddhist triratna symbol on top of a stupa.

The Triratna is also on the 1st century BCE coins of the Kingdom of Kuninda in northern Punjab, surmounting depictions of stupas, on some the coins of the Indo-Parthian king Gondophares, or the coins of some of the Kushan kings such as Vima Kadphises. The triratna can be further reinforced by being surmounted with three dharma wheels (one for each of the three jewels of Buddhism: the Buddha, the Dharma and the Sangha).

The triratna symbol is also called nandipada, or "bull's hoof", by Hindus.

Qualities of the Buddha, Dharma, and Sangha: The Triratna or "Three Jewels" symbol, on a Buddha footprint. 1st century CE, Gandhara.

The qualities of the Buddha, Dharma, and Sangha are frequently repeated in the ancient texts. It is a Buddhist practise to reflect upon them.

- *The Buddha:* "The Blessed One is an Arahant, perfectly enlightened, accomplished in true knowledge and conduct, fortunate, knower of the world, unsurpassed leader of persons to be tamed, teacher of devas and humans, the Enlightened One, the Blessed One."
- *The Dharma:* "The Dhamma is well expounded by the Blessed One, directly visible, immidiate, inviting one to come and see, applicable, to be personally experienced by the wise."
- *The Sangha:* "The Sangha of the Blessed One's disciples is practising the good way, practising the straight way, practising the true way, practising the proper way; that is, the four pairs of persons, the eight types of individuals-This Sangha of the Blessed One's disciples is worthy of gifts, worthy of hospitality, worthy of offerings, worthy of reverential salutation, the unsurpassed field of merit for the world."

Three marks of existence:

After much meditation, the Buddha concluded that everything in the physical world (plus everything in the phenomenology of psychology) is marked by three characteristics, known as the three characteristics of existence, three signs of being or Dharma Seals. Together the three characteristics of existence are called ti-lakkhana, in Pali; or tri-laksana, in Sanskrit.

- Dukkha or unsatisfactoriness. Nothing found in the physical world or the psychological realm can bring lasting deep satisfaction.
- Anicca or impermanence. This refers not only to the fact that all conditioned things eventually cease to exist, but also that all conditioned things are in a constant state of flux. (A convenient way to visualize this would be to recall that the atoms constituting your body are constantly being replaced.)
- Anatta, impersonality, or non-Self. The human personality, "soul", or Self, is a conventional appellation applied to the assembly of physical and psychological components, each individually subject to constant flux; there is no central core (or essence); this is somewhat similar to a bundle theory of mind or soul.

There is often a fourth Dharma Seal mentioned:

- Nirvana is peace. Nirvana is the 'other shore' from Samsara.

By bringing the three (or four) seals into moment-to-moment experience through concentrated awareness, we are said to achieve Wisdom-the third of the three higher trainings-the way out of Samsara.

In this way we can identify that, according to Sutra, the recipe (or formula) for leaving Samsara is achieved by a deep-rooted change to our Weltanschauung. According to the Buddhist tradition, all phenomena (dharmas) are marked by three characteristics, sometimes referred to as the Dharma seals, that is dukkha (suffering), anicca (impermanence), and anatta (non-Self).

Dukkha

Whatever is impermanent is subject to change. Whatever is subject to change is subject to suffering. — The Buddha

Striving for what we desire, we may experience stress and suffering—dukkha. Getting what we desired, we may find delight and happiness. Soon after, the novelty may wear out and we may get bored with it. Boredom is a form of dissatisfaction (or suffering) and to escape from it, we divert ourselves from such boredom by indulging in a pursuit of new forms of pleasure. Sometimes not willing to relinquish objects that we are already disinterested in, we start to collect and amass possessions instead of sharing with others who may have better use in it than we do. Boredom is a result of change. Change of our interest in that object of desire that so captivated us in the first place.

If we do not get bored already, then change may instead occur in the object of desire. Silverware may becom tarnished, a new dress worn thin or a gadget gone obsolete. Or it may become broken, causing us to grieve. In some cases it may get lost or stolen. In some cases, we may worry about such losses even before they happen. Husbands and wives worry about losing their spouses even though their partners are faithful. Unfortunately, sometimes our very worry and fear drives us to act irrationally, resulting in distrust and breaking up of the very relationship that we cherished so much.

While we like changes such as becoming an adult when we are in our teens, we dislike the change called aging. While we strive for change to become rich, we fear the change of retrenchment. We are selective in our attitude towards the transient nature of our very existence. Unfortunately, this transient nature is unselective. We can try to fight it, just as many have tried since beginningless time, only to have our efforts washed away through the passages of time. As a result, we continually experience dissatisfaction or suffering due to the very impermanence of compounded phenomena.

Only in the realm of Nirvana — so Mahayana Buddhism insists — can true and lasting happiness be found. Nirvana is the opposite of the conditional, the transitory and the painful (dukkha), so it does not result in disappointment or deterioration of the state of bliss. Nirvana is the refuge from the otherwise universal tyranny of change and suffering. In other schools of Buddhism, nirvana is not viewed as the goal, but merely as a projection from the state of samsara. According to these schools samsara (confusion) and nirvana (perfection) are two sides of the same coin that must be transcended through diligent practice of meditation.

Anicca

All compounded phenomena (things and experiences) are inconstant, unsteady, and impermanent. (Practically) everything is made up of parts, and is dependent on the right conditions for its existence. Everything is in constant flux, and so conditions and the thing itself is constantly changing. Things are constantly coming into being, and ceasing to be. Nothing lasts. The important point here is that phenomena arise and cease according to (complex) conditions and not according to our whims and fancy. While we have limited ability to effect change to our possessions and surroundings, experience tells us that our feeble attempts are no guarantee that the results of our efforts will be to our likings. More often than not, the results fall short of our expectations.

In Mahayana Buddhism, a caveat is added: one should indeed always meditate on the impermanence and changefulness of compounded structures and phenomena, but one must guard against extending this to the realm of Nirvana, where impermanence holds no sway and eternity alone obtains. To see Nirvana or the Buddha (in his ultimate Dharmakaya nature) as impermanent would be to indulge in "perverted Dharma" and would be seriously to go astray, according to the Buddha's final Mahayana doctrines. Other schools of Buddhism, however, feel uneasy with such a teaching.

Anatta

In Indian philosophy, the concept of a Self is called atman (that is, "soul" or metaphysical Self), which refers to an unchanging, permanent essence conceived by virtue of existence.

This concept and the related concept of Brahman, the Vedantic monistic ideal, which was regarded as an ultimate atman for all beings, were indispensable for mainstream Indian metaphysics, logic, and science; for all apparent things there had to be an underlying and persistent reality, akin to a Platonic form.

The Buddha rejected all concepts of atman, emphasizing not permanence, but changeability. He taught that all concepts of a substantial personal Self were incorrect, and formed in the realm of ignorance. However, in a number of major Mahayana sutras (*e.g.* the Mahaparinirvana Sutra, the Tathagatagarbha Sutra, the Srimala Sutra, among others), the Buddha is presented as clarifying this teaching by saying that, while the skandhas (constituents of the ordinary body and mind) are not the Self, there does truly exist an eternal, unchanging, blissful Buddha-essence in all sentient beings, which is the uncreated and deathless Buddha-nature (" Buddha-dhatu") or "True Self" of the Buddha himself.

This immaculate Buddhic Self (atman) is in no way to be construed as a mundane, impermanent, suffering "ego", of which it is the diametrical opposite. On the other hand, this Buddha-essence or Buddha-nature is also often explained as the potential for achieving Buddhahood, rather than an existing phenomenon one can grasp onto as being me or Self. It is the opposite of a personalised, samsaric "I" or "mine". The paradox is that as soon as the Buddhist practitioner tries to grasp at this inner Buddha potency and cling to it as though it were his or her ego writ large, it proves elusive.

It does not "exist" in the time-space conditioned and finite mode in which mundane things are bodied forth. It is presented by the Buddha in the relevant sutras as ultimately inexplicable, primordially present Reality itself-the living potency for Buddhahood inside all beings.

It is finally revealed (in the last of the Buddha's Mahayana sutras, the Nirvana Sutra) not as the circumscribed "non-Self", the clinging ego (which is indeed anatta/anatman), but as the ever-enduring, egoless Great Self or Dharmakaya of the Buddha.

The scriptural evidence of the Nikyas and gamas is ambivalent with regard to the Buddha's reported views on the existence or otherwise of a permanent Self (atman/atta). Though he is clearly reported to have criticized many of the heterodox concepts concerning an eternal personal Self and to have denied the existence of an eternal Self with regards to any of the constituent elements (skandha) of a being, he is nevertheless not reported to have explicitly denied the existence of a non-personal, permanent Self, contrary to the popular, orthodox view of the Buddha's teachings.

Moreover, when the Buddha predicates "antman" (anatta) with regards to the constituents of a being, there is a grammatical ambivalence in the use of the term. The most natural interpretation is that he is simply stating that "the constituents are not the Self" rather than "the constituents are devoid of Self". This ambivalence was to prove troublesome to Buddhists after the Buddha's passing. Some of the major schools of Buddhism that developed subsequently maintained the former interpretation, but other influential schools adopted the latter interpretation and took measures to establish their view as the orthodox Buddhist position.

One such proponent of this hard-line "non-Self" position was the monk Nagasena, who appears in the Questions of King Milinda, composed during the period of the Hellenistic Indo-Greek kingdom of the 2nd and 1st centuries BCE. In this text, Nagasena demonstrates the concept of absolute 'non-Self' by likening human beings to a chariot and challenges the Greek king "Milinda" (Menander) to find the essence of the chariot. Nagasena states that just as a chariot is made up of a number of things, none of which are the essence of the chariot in isolation, without the other pieces, similarly no one part of a person is a permanent entity; we can be broken up into five constituents — body, sensations, ideation, mental formations and consciousness— the consciousness being closest to the permanent idea of 'Self', but is ever-changing with each new thought according to this view point.

According to some thinkers both in the East and the West, the doctrine of "non-Self", may imply that Buddhism is a form of nihilism or something similar. However, as thinkers like Nagarjuna have clearly pointed out, Buddhism is not simply a rejection of the concept of existence (or of meaning, etc.) but of the hard and fast distinction between existence and non-existence, or rather between being and nothingness. Phenomena are not independent from causes and conditions, and do not exist as isolated thing as we perceive them to be. Philosophers such as N stress that the lack of a permanent, unchanging, substantial Self in beings and things does not mean that they do not experience growth and decay on the relative level.

But on the ultimate level of analysis, one cannot distinguish an object from its causes and conditions, or even object and subject. (This is an idea appearing relatively recently in Western science.) Buddhism thus has much more in common with Western empiricism, pragmatism, anti-foundationalism, and even poststructuralism than with nihilism.

In the Nikyas, the Buddha and his disciples are commonly found to ask in question or declare "Is that which is impermanent, subject to change, subject to suffering fit to be considered thus: 'This I am, this is mine, this is my self'?" The question which the Buddha posts to his audience is whether compounded phenomena is fit to be cosidered as self, in which the audience agrees that it is unworthy to be considered so. And in relinquishing such an attachment to compounded phenomena, such a person gives up delight, desire and craving for compounded phenomena and is unbounded by its change. When completely free from attachments, craving or desire to the five aggregates, such a person experiences then transcends the very causes of suffering.

In this way, the insight wisdom or prajn of non-Self gives rise to cessation of suffering, and not an intellectual debate over whether a self exists or not.

It is by realizing (not merely understanding intellectually, but making real in one's experience) the three marks of conditioned existence that one develops prajn, which is the antidote to the ignorance that lies at the root of all suffering. From the "tathagatagarbha-Mahayana" perspective (which diverges from the Theravadin understanding of Buddhism), however, a further step is required if full Buddhahood is to be attained: not only seeing what is impermanent, suffering and non-Self in the samsaric sphere, but equally recognising that which is truly Eternal, Blissful, Self, and Pure in the transcendental realm — the realm of Mahaparinirvana.

Interpretations of the Three Marks by Various Schools

Some Buddhist traditions assert that Anatta pervades everything, and is not limited to personality, or soul. These traditions assert that Nirvana also has the quality of Anatta, but that Nirvana (by definition) is the cessation of Dukkha and Anicca.

In Nagarjuna's says:

There is not the slightest difference.

Between Samsara and Nirvana: This verse points us to an interesting stress between dukkha and nirvana, through an argument based in anatta. This specific stress can be seen to be the key to (and possibly source for the development of) the deity yogas of vajrayana.

The sutra path enjoins us to identify the entire world (internally and externally) as samsara — a continual churning of suffering that nobody wants to be part of. Our practice is that of leaving the shores of samsara.

On the other hand, we are told that unconditioned, enlightened activity is not actually different from samsara.

Whereas the deity yoga of vajrayana enjoins us to identify the entire world as nirvana — a continual play of enlightening activity that everyone wishes to be a part of. Our practice here is that of arriving at the shores of nirvana.

At this level, the distinction between Sutra and Vajrayana remain that of view (departing vs. arriving), but basically the practitioner remains involved in undergoing a transformative development to his or her Weltanschauung, and in this context, these practices remain rooted in psychological change, grounded in the development of Samatha, or training in concentration.

However, there are certain practices in Tantra which are not solely concerned with psychological change; these revolve around the basic idea that it is possible to induce deep levels of concentration through psycho-physical methods as a result of special exercises. The purpose remains the same (to achieve liberating view), but the method involves a 'short cut' for the training in Samatha.

Skandha

The five skandhas (Sanskrit) or five khandhas (Pli) are the five "aggregates" which constitute individual experience according to Buddhist phenomenology. Moreover, in Buddhism, a "person" is made up of the five skandhas, beyond which there is no "self."

In the Theravada tradition, suffering arises when one identifies with or otherwise clings to an aggregate; hence, suffering is extinguished by relinquishing attachment to aggregates. The Mahayana tradition further puts forth that ultimate freedom is realized by deeply penetrating the instrinsically empty nature of all aggregates.

Outside of Buddhist contexts, "skandha" can mean heap, bundle or tree trunk.

Definition: Buddhist doctrine describes one physical and four mental skandhas, which conveys the relative experience of the world by an individual. The five skandhas are:

1. "form" or "matter" (sa., pi. rkpa):includes both external and internal matter. Externally, rupa is the physical world. Internally, rupa includes the material body and the physical sense organs.
2. "sensation" or "feeling" (sa., pi. vedan):sensing pleasant, unpleasant or neutral (neither-pleasant-nor-unpleasant). Generally considered not to include "emotions."
3. "perception" or "cognition" (sa. samjn, pi. sann):registers whether sense data is recognized or not (for instance, the sound of a bell or the shape of a tree). From samyutta-nana, conditioned knowledge. It is ordinarily conditioned by ones past sankhara, and therefore conveys a coloured image of reality.

4. "mental formations" or "volition" (sa. samskra, pi. sankhra) :all types of mental habits, thoughts, ideas, opinions, compulsions, and decisions. Sankhra arise from contact with form or from other mental factors. Sankhra are the source of karma.
5. "consciousness" (sa. vijnna, pi. vinnGa):conscious base that support all experience. Alternately, the Abhidhamma envisions consciousness as series of rapidly changing interconnected discrete acts of cognizance.

See examples of definitional references to the aggregates in Buddhist primary sources.

The aggregates are causally related as follows:

- The four "Great Elements" (mahbhkta: earth, wind, fire and water) give rise to form (rkpa).
- Through the contact (phassa) of an external object, a sense organ and consciousness (vinnGa), form (rkpa) gives rise to the three "name" (nma) aggregates of feeling, perception and mental formation. (The nma aggregates are caused by either contact with an object or the arising of concomitant mental factors.)

Bhikkhu Bodhi (2000b, p. 840) states that an examination of the aggregates has a "critical role" in the Buddha's teaching for multiple reasons, including:

1. *Understanding the Four Noble Truths:* The five aggregates are the "ultimate referent" in the Buddha's elaboration on suffering (dukkha) in his First Noble Truth (see excerpted quote below) and "since all four truths revolve around suffering, understanding the aggregates is essential for understanding the Four Noble Truths as a whole."
2. *Future Suffering's Cause:* The five aggregates are the substrata for clinging and thus "contribute to the causal origination of future suffering."
3. *Release:* Clinging must be removed from the five aggregates in order to achieve release.

Below, excerpts from the Pli literature will bear out Bhikkhu Bodhi's assessment.

Suffering's Ultimate Referent: In the Buddha's first discourse, the "Dhammacakkappavattana Sutta" ("The Setting in Motion the Wheel of Truth Discourse," SN 56:11), he provides a classic elaboration on the first of his Four Noble Truths, "The Truth of Suffering" (Dukkhasacca):

> *"The Noble Truth of Suffering (dukkha), monks, is this: Birth is suffering, aging is suffering, sickness is suffering, death is suffering, association with the unpleasant is suffering, dissociation from the pleasant is suffering, not to receive what one desires is suffering—in brief the five aggregates subject to grasping are suffering." [Boldface added.] (Trans. from the Pali by Piyadassi Thera, 1999.)*

According to Thanissaro (2002)

> *"Prior to the Buddha, the Pali word khandha had very ordinary meanings: A khandha could be a pile, a bundle, a heap, a mass. It could also be the trunk of a tree. In his first sermon, though, the Buddha gave it a new, psychological meaning, introducing the term 'clinging-khandhas' to summarize his analysis of the truth of stress and suffering. Throughout the remainder of his teaching career, he referred to these psychological khandhas time and again."*

In what way are the aggregates suffering? For this we can turn to Khandhavagga suttas.

Future Suffering's Cause: The Samyutta Nikaya contains a book entitled the "Khandhavagga" ("The Book of Aggregates") compiling over a hundred suttas related to the five aggregates. Typical of these suttas is the "Upadaparitassana Sutta" ("Agitation through Clinging Discourse," SN 22:7), which states in part:

> *The instructed noble disciple... does not regard form [or other aggregates] as self, or self as possessing form, or form as in self, or self as in form. That form of his changes and alters. Despite the change and alteration of form, his consciousness does not become preoccupied with the change of form.... [T]hrough non-clinging he*

does not become agitated." (Trans. by Bodhi, 2000b, pp. 865-866.)

Put another way, if we were to self-identify with an aggregate then we would cling (upadana) to such; and, given that all aggregates are impermanent (anicca), it would then be likely that at some level we would experience agitation (paritassati) or loss or grief or stress or suffering (see dukkha). Therefore, if we want to be free of suffering, it is wise to experience the aggregates clearly, without clinging or craving (tanha), as apart from any notion of self (anatta). Many of the suttas in the Khandhavagga express the aggregates in the context of the following sequence:

I. An uninstructed worldling (assutav puthujjana)

1. regards: form as self; self as possessing form; form as in self; self as in form.
2. lives obsessed by the notions: I am form; and/or, form is mine
3. this form changes
4. with the changes of form, there arises dukkha

II. An instructed noble disciple (sutav ariyasvaka) does not regard form as self, etc., and thus, when form changes, dukkha does not arise. (Note that, in each of the suttas where the above forumla is used, subsequent verses replace "form" with each of the other aggregates: sensation, perception, volition and consciousness.)

Example of Aggregate-Clinging to give a simplistic example, if one believes "this body is mine" or "I exist within this body," then as their body ages, becomes ill and approaches death, such a person will likely experience longing for youth or health or eternal life, will likely dread aging and sickness and death, and will likely spend much time and energy lost in fears and fantasies.In the Nikayas, such is likened to shooting oneself with a second arrow, where the first arrow is a physical phenomenon (such as, in this case, a bodily manifestation associated with aging or illness or dying) and the second is the mental anguish of the undisciplined mind associated with the physical phenomenon (see the Sallatha Sutta).On the other hand, one with a disciplined mind who is able to see this body as a set of aggregates will be free of such fear, frustration and time-consuming escapism.

But how does one become aware of and then let go of ones own identification with or clinging to the aggregates? Below is an excerpt from the classic Satipatthana Sutta that shows how traditional mindfulness practices can awaken understanding, release and wisdom.

Release through Aggregate-contemplation: In the classic Theravada meditation reference, the "Satipammhna Sutta" ("The Foundations of Mindfulness Discourse," MN 10), the Buddha provides four bases for establishing mindfulness: body (kaya), sensations (vedana), mind (citta) and mental objects (dhamma). When discussing mental objects as a basis for meditation, the Buddha identifies five objects, including the aggregates. Regarding meditation on the aggregates, the Buddha states:

> *"How, monks, does a monk live contemplating mental objects in the mental objects of the five aggregates of clinging?*
>
> *"Herein, monks, a monk thinks, 'Thus is material form; thus is the arising of material form; and thus is the disappearance of material form. Thus is feeling; thus is the arising of feeling; and thus is the disappearance of feeling. Thus is perception; thus is the arising of perception; and thus is the disappearance of perception. Thus are formations; thus is the arising of formations; and thus is the disappearance of formations. Thus is consciousness; thus is the arising of consciousness; and thus is the disappearance of consciousness.'*
>
> *"Or his mindfulness is established with the thought, 'Mental objects exist,' to the extent necessary just for knowledge and mindfulness, and he lives detached, and clings to nothing in the world. Thus also, monks, a monk lives contemplating mental objects in the mental objects of the five aggregates of clinging." (Nyanasatta, trans., 1994.)*

Thus, through mindfulness contemplation, one sees an "aggregate as an aggregate" — sees it arising and dissipating. Such clear seeing creates a space between the aggregate and clinging, a space that will prevent or enervate the arising and propagation of clinging, thereby diminishing future suffering. As clinging disappears, so too empty notions of self. In the Mahasunnata Sutta ("The Greater Discourse on Emptiness," MN 122), after reiterating the aforementioned aggregate-contemplation instructions (for instance, "Thus is form; thus is the arising of form; and, thus is the disappearance of form"), the Buddha states:

> *"When he [a monk] abides contemplating rise and fall in these five aggregates affected by clinging, the conceit 'I am' based on these five aggregates affected by clinging is abandoned in him...." (Nanamoli & Bodhi, 2001, p. 975.)*

In a complementary fashion, in the Buddha's second discourse, the Anattalakkhana Sutta ("The Characteristic of Nonself," SN 22:59), the Buddha instructs:

> *"Monks, form is nonself. For if, monks, form were self, this form would not lead to affliction, and it would be possible to [manipulate] form [in the following manner]: 'Let my form be thus; let my form not be thus....' [Identical statements are made regarding feeling, perception, volitional formations and consciousness.]*
>
> *"Seeing thus [for instance, through contemplation], monks, the instructed noble disciple becomes disenchanted with form [and the other aggregates].... Being disenchanted, he becomes dispassionate. Through dispassion [his mind] is liberated." (Bodhi, 2005, pp. 341-2.)*

As seen below, the Mahayana tradition continues this use of the aggregates to achieve self-liberation.

Mahayana Perspectives: In one of Mahayana Buddhism's most famous declarations, the aggregates are referenced:

"Form is emptiness, emptiness is form."

What does this mean? To what degree is it a departure from the aforementioned Theravada perspective? Moreover, more generally, how are the aggregates used in the Mahayana literature? These questions are addressed below.

The intrinsic emptiness of all things

The classic "Prajnaparamita Hridaya Sutra" ("Heart Sutra") begins:

The Bodhisattva Avalokita,

while moving in the deep course of Perfect Understanding,

shed light on the five skandhas

and found them equally empty [of self].

After this penetration, he overcame all pain.

From its very first verse, the Heart Sutra introduces an alternative practice and worldview to the Theravada perspective of the aggregates:

- *Prajnaparamita:* Whereas Theravada meditation practices with the aggregates generally use change-penetrating vipassana meditation, here the non-dualistic prajnaparamita practice is invoked.
- *Svabhava:* In Theravada texts, when "emptiness of self" is mentioned, the English word "self" is a translation of the Pali word "atta" (Sanskrit, "atman"); in the Heart Sutra, the English word "self" is a translation of the Sanskrit word "sva-bhava". According to Red Pine, "The 'self' (sva)... was more generalized in its application than 'ego' (atman) and referred not only to beings but to any inherent substance that could be identified as existing in time or space as a permanent or independent entity." (Italics added.)

In other words, whereas the Sutta Pitaka typically instructs one to apprehend the aggregates without clinging or self-identification, Prajnaparamita leads one to apprehend the aggregates as having no intrinsic reality. In the Heart Sutra's second verse, after rising from his aggregate meditation, Avalokiteshvara declares:

"Form is emptiness, emptiness is form, form does not differ from emptiness, emptiness does not differ from form.

The same is true with feelings, perceptions, mental formations and consciousness."

Red Pine Comments:

"That form is empty was one of the Buddha's earliest and most frequent pronouncements. But in the light of Prajnaparamita, form is not simply empty, it is so completely empty, it is emptiness itself, which turns out to be the same as form itself.... All separations are delusions. But if each of the skandhas is one with emptiness, and emptiness is one with each of the skandhas, then everything occupies the same indivisible space, which is emptiness.... Everything is empty, and empty is everything.

D.T. Suzuki further states:

"When the sutra says that the five Skandhas have the character of emptiness..., the sense is: no limiting qualities are to be attributed to the Absolute; while it is immanent in all concrete and particular objects, it is not in itself definable."

We can see in sutra form, an expounding of the Buddha's doctrine of Anatman (No-self, No-I).

Here the doctrine of the Five Skandha supports the concept of Anatman.

For if there is "No-self", "No-I", then what experiences? The answer lies in the five skandha.

The Truth of Our Insubstantiality: According to Chogyam Trungpa (1976, pp. 20-22), the five skandhas are "a set of Buddhist concepts which describe experience as a five-step process" and that "the whole development of the five skandhas...is an attempt on our part to shield ourselves from the truth of our insubstantiality," while "the practice of meditation is to see the transparency of this shield." (ibid, p.23)

Relation to Other Buddhist Concepts

Other fundamental Buddhist concepts associated with the five skandhas include:

- *Samsara:*It is through the five skandhas that the world (samsara) is experienced, and nothing is experienced apart from the five skandhas.
- *Three Characteristics:* It is through the five skandhas that impermanence (anicca) is experienced, that suffering (duhkha) arises, and that "non-self" (anatta or anatman) can be realized.
- *Four Paramatthas:*The Abhidhamma and post-canonical Pali texts create a meta-scheme for the Sutta Pitaka's conceptions of aggregates, sense bases and elements. This meta-scheme is known as the four paramatthas or four ultimate realities:
- consciousness
- mental factors
- material phenomena
- Nibbna The mapping between the ultimate realities and the aggregates is represented in the chart to the right.
- Twelve Nidanas/Dependent Origination:

It is through the five skandhas that clinging (upadana) occurs, a pivotal link in the endless chain of suffering.

- *Eighteen Dhatus :*The eighteen dhatus function through the five aggregates. The eighteen dhatus can be arranged into six triads, where each triad is composed of a sense organ, a sense object and sense consciousness. In regards to the aggregates:
- The first five sense organs (eye, ear, nose, tongue, body) are derivates of form. The sixth sense organ (mind) is part of consciousness.
- The first five sense objects (visible forms, sound, smell, taste, touch) are also derivatives of form. The sixth sense object (mental object) includes form, sensation, perception and mental formations.
- The six sense consciousness are the basis for consciousness.

References in Buddhist Literature

The table below briefly cites Buddhist primary sources that characterize different aspects of the aggregates. This table is by no means exhaustive.

Buddhist Cosmology the Canonical Buddhist Scriptures and Commentaries

The self-consistent Buddhist cosmology which is presented in commentaries and works of Abhidharma in both Theravda and Mahyna traditions, is the end-product of an analysis and reconciliation of cosmological comments found in the Buddhist sktra and vinaya traditions. No single sktra sets out the entire structure of the universe. However, in several sktras the Buddha describes other worlds and states of being, and other sktras describe the origin and destruction of the universe. The synthesis of these data into a single comprehensive system must have taken place early in the history of Buddhism, as the system described in the Pli Vibhajyavda tradition (represented by today's Theravdins) agrees, despite some trivial inconsistencies of nomenclature, with the Sarvstivda tradition which is preserved by Mahyna Buddhists.

The picture of the world presented in Buddhist cosmological descriptions cannot be taken as a literal description of the shape of the universe. It is inconsistent, and cannot be made consistent, with astronomical data that were already known in ancient India. However, it is not intended to be a description of how humans perceive their world; rather, it is the universe as seen through the divyacakcus (Pli: dibbacakkhu), the "divine eye" by which a Buddha or an arhat who has cultivated this faculty can perceive all of the other worlds and the beings arising (being born) and passing away (dying) within them, and can tell from what state they have been reborn and into what state they will be reborn.

Buddhist cosmology can accordingly be divided into two related kinds: spatial cosmology, which describes the arrangement of the various worlds within the universe, and temporal cosmology, which describes how those worlds come into existence, and how they pass away.

Spatial Cosmology

Spatial cosmology can also be divided into two branches. The vertical cosmology describes the arrangement of worlds in a vertical pattern, some being higher and some lower. The sahasra cosmology describes the grouping of these vertical worlds into sets of thousands, millions or billions.

Vertical Cosmology

In the vertical cosmology, the universe exists of many worlds (lok) – one might say "planes" – stacked one upon the next in layers. Each world corresponds to a mental state or a state of being. A world is not, however, a location so much as it is the beings which compose it; it is sustained by their karma and if the beings in a world all die or disappear, the world disappears too. Likewise, a world comes into existence when the first being is born into it.

The physical separation is not so important as the difference in mental state; humans and animals, though they partially share the same physical environments, still belong to different worlds because their minds perceive and react to those environments differently.

The vertical cosmology is divided into three realms, or dhtus, each corresponding to a different type of mentality. These three (Tridhtu) are the rkpyadhtu, the Rkpadhtu, and the Kmadhtu. This technical division does not correspond to the more informal categorization of the "six realms". In the latter scheme, all of the beings born in the rkpyadhtu and the Rkpadhtu may be classified as "gods" or "deities" (dev), as can a considerable fraction of the beings born in the Kmadhtu, even though the deities of the Kmadhtu differ more from those of the rkpyadhtu than they do from humans.

It is to be understood that deva is an imprecise term referring to any being living in a longer-lived and generally more blissful state than humans. Most of them are not "gods" in the common sense of the term, having little or no concern with the human world and rarely if ever interacting with it; only the lowest deities of the Kmadhtu correspond to the gods described in many polytheistic religions.

The term "brahm" is used both as a name and as a generic term for one of the higher devas. In its broadest sense, it can refer to any of the inhabitants of the rkpyadhtu and the Rkpadhtu. In more restricted senses, it can refer to an inhabitant of one of the nine lower worlds of the Rkpadhtu, or in its narrowest sense, to the three lowest worlds of the Rkpadhtu. A large number of devas use the name "Brahm", *e.g.* Brahm Sahampati, Brahm Sanatkumra, Baka Brahm, etc. It is not always clear which world they belong to, although it must always be one of the worlds of the Rkpadhtu below the Zuddhvsa worlds. There are four types of rkpyadhtu devas, corresponding to the four types of arkpadhynas:

- *Nevasannnsannyatana:* "Sphere of neither perception nor non-perception". In this sphere the formless beings have gone beyond a mere negation of perception and have attained a liminal state where they do not engage in "perception" (saCjn, recognition of particulars by their marks) but are not wholly unconscious. This was the sphere reached by Udraka Rmaputra (Pli: Uddaka Rmaputta), the second of the Buddha's two teachers, who considered it equivalent to enlightenment.
- *Kincannyatana:* "Sphere of Nothingness" (literally "lacking anything"). In this sphere formless beings dwell contemplating upon the thought that "there is no thing". This is considered a form of perception, though a very subtle one. This was the sphere reached by r.
- A Klma the first of the Buddha's two teachers; he considered it to be equivalent to enlightenment.
- *Vinnmnancyatana:* "Sphere of Infinite Consciousness". In this sphere formless beings dwell meditating on their consciousness (vijnna) as infinitely pervasive.
- *Ksnancyatana:* "Sphere of Infinite Space". In this sphere formless beings dwell meditating upon space or extension as infinitely pervasive.

Rkpadhtu

The Rkpadhtu or "Form realm" is, as the name implies, the first of the physical realms; its inhabitants all have a location and bodies of a sort, though those bodies are composed of a subtle substance which is of itself invisible to the inhabitants of the Kmadhtu. According to the Janavasabha Sutta, when a brahma (a being from the Brahma-world of the Rkpadhtu) wishes to visit a deva of the TryastriC[a heaven (in the Kmadhtu), he has to assume a "grosser form" in order to be visible to them.

The beings of the Form realm are not subject to the extremes of pleasure and pain, or governed by desires for things pleasing to the senses, as the beings of the Kmadhtu are. The bodies of Form realm beings do not have sexual distinctions.

Like the beings of the rkpyadhtu, the dwellers in the Rkpadhtu have minds corresponding to the dhynas (Pli: jhnas). In their case it is the four lower dhynas or rkpadhynas. However, although the beings of the Rkpadhtu can be divided into four broad grades corresponding to these four dhynas, each of them is subdivided into further grades, three for each of the four dhynas and five for the Zuddhvsa devas, for a total of seventeen grades (the Theravda tradition counts one less grade in the highest dhyna for a total of sixteen).

Physically, the Rkpadhtu consists of a series of planes stacked on top of each other, each one in a series of steps half the size of the previous one as one descends. In part, this reflects the fact that the devas are also thought of as physically larger on the higher planes. The highest planes are also broader in extent than the ones lower down, as discussed in the section on Sahasra cosmology. The height of these planes is expressed in yojanas, a measurement of very uncertain length, but sometimes taken to be about 4,000 times the height of a man, and so approximately 4.54 miles or 7.32 kilometers.

Zuddhvsa Worlds

The Zuddhvsa (Pli: Suddhvsa; Tib: gnas gtsang.ma) worlds, or "Pure Abodes", are distinct from the other worlds of the Rkpadhtu in that they do not house beings who have been born there through ordinary merit or meditative attainments, but only those Angmins ("Non-returners") who are already on the path to Arhat-hood and who will attain enlightenment directly from the Zuddhvsa worlds without being reborn in a lower plane (Angmins can also be born on lower planes). Every Zuddhvsa deva is therefore a protector of Buddhism. Because a Zuddhvsa deva will never be reborn outside the Zuddhvsa worlds, no Bodhisattva is ever born in these worlds, as a Bodhisattva must ultimately be reborn as a human being.

Since these devas rise from lower planes only due to the teaching of a Buddha, they can remain empty for very long periods if no Buddha arises.

However, unlike the lower worlds, the Zuddhvsa worlds are never destroyed by natural catastrophe. The Zuddhvsa devas predict the coming of a Buddha and, taking the guise of brahmins, reveal to human beings the signs by which a Buddha can be recognized.

They also ensure that a Bodhisattva in his last life will see the four signs that will lead to his renunciation.

The five Zuddhvsa worlds are:

- *Akanicmha or Akanimmha:* World of devas "equal in rank" (literally: having no one as the youngest). The highest of all the Rkpadhtu words, it is often used to refer to the highest extreme of the universe. The current Zakra will eventually be born there. The duration of life in Akanicmha is 16,000 kalpas (Vibhajyavda tradition). The height of this world is 167,772,160 yojanas above the Earth.
- *Sudarana or Sudass:* The "clear-seeing" devas live in a world similar to and friendly with the Akanicmha world. The height of this world is 83,886,080 yojanas above the Earth.
- *Suda or Sudassa:* The world of the "beautiful" devas are said to be the place of rebirth for five kinds of angmins. The height of this world is 41,943,040 yojanas above the Earth.
- *Atapa or Atappa:* The world of the "untroubled" devas, whose company those of lower realms wish for. The height of this world is 20,971,520 yojanas above the Earth.

- *Avaha or Aviha:* The world of the "not falling" devas, perhaps the most common destination for reborn Angmins. Many achieve arhatship directly in this world, but some pass away and are reborn in sequentially higher worlds of the Pure Abodes until they are at last reborn in the Akanicmha world. These are called in Pli uddhaCsotas, "those whose stream goes upward". The duration of life in Av[ha is 1,000 kalpas (Vibhajyavda tradition). The height of this world is 10,485,760 yojanas above the Earth.

Bhatphala Worlds

The mental state of the devas of the B[hatphala worlds corresponds to the fourth dhyna, and is characterized by equanimity (upekc). The B[hatphala worlds form the upper limit to the destruction of the universe by wind at the end of a mahkalpa (see Temporal cosmology below), that is, they are spared such destruction.

- *Asannasatta:* "Unconscious beings", devas who have attained a high dhyna (similar to that of the Formless Realm), and, wishing to avoid the perils of perception, have achieved a state of non-perception in which they endure for a time. After a while, however, perception arises again and they fall into a lower state.
- *Behatphala:* Devas "having great fruit". Their lifespan is 500 mahkalpas. (Vibhajyavda tradition). Some Angmins are reborn here. The height of this world is 5,242,880 yojanas above the Earth.
- *Punyaprasava:* The world of the devas who are the "offspring of merit". The height of this world is 2,621,440 yojanas above the Earth.
- *Anabhraka:* The world of the "cloudless" devas. The height of this world is 1,310,720 yojanas above the Earth.

Zubhaktsna Worlds

The mental state of the devas of the Zubhaketsna worlds corresponds to the third dhyna, and is characterized by a quiet joy (sukha). These devas have bodies that radiate a steady light. The Zubhaketsna worlds form the upper limit to the destruction of the universe by water at the end of a mahkalpa (see Temporal cosmology below), that is, the flood of water does not rise high enough to reach them.

- *Zubhaktsna:* The world of devas of "total beauty". Their lifespan is 64 mahkalpas (some sources: 4 mahkalpas) according to the Vibhajyavda tradition. 64 mahkalpas is the interval between destructions of the universe by wind, including the Zubhaketsna worlds. The height of this world is 655,360 yojanas above the Earth.
- *Apramnaeubha:* The world of devas of "limitless beauty". Their lifespan is 32 mahkalpas (Vibhajyavda tradition). They possess "faith, virtue, learning, munificence and wisdom". The height of this world is 327,680 yojanas above the Earth.
- *Parittaeubha:* The world of devas of "limited beauty". Their lifespan is 16 mahkalpas. The height of this world is 163,840 yojanas above the Earth.

Bhasvara Worlds

The mental state of the devas of the bhsvara worlds corresponds to the second dhyna, and is characterized by delight (priti) as well as joy (sukha); the bhsvara devas are said to shout aloud in their joy, crying aho sukham! ("Oh joy!"). These devas have bodies that emit flashing rays of light like lightning. They are said to have similar bodies (to each other) but diverse perceptions.

The bhsvara worlds form the upper limit to the destruction of the universe by fire at the end of a mahkalpa (see Temporal cosmology below), that is, the column of fire does not rise high enough to reach them. After the destruction of the world, at the beginning of the vivartakalpa, the worlds are first populated by beings reborn from the bhsvara worlds.

- *Bhsvara or Bhassara:* The world of devas "possessing splendor". The lifespan of the bhsvara devas is 8 mahkalpas (others: 2 mahkalpas). Eight mahkalpas is the interval between destructions of the universal by water, which includes the bhsvara worlds. The height of this world is 81,920 yojanas above the Earth.

- *Apramnbha or Appamnbha:* The world of devas of "limitless light", a concept on which they meditate. Their lifespan is 4 mahkalpas. The height of this world is 40,960 yojanas above the Earth.
- *Parittbha or Parittbha:* The world of devas of "limited light". Their lifespan is 2 mahkalpas. The height of this world is 20,480 yojanas above the Earth.

Brahm Worlds

The mental state of the devas of the Brahm worlds corresponds to the first dhyna, and is characterized by observation (vitarka) and reflection (vicra) as well as delight (priti) and joy (sukha). The Brahm worlds, together with the other lower worlds of the universe, are destroyed by fire at the end of a mahkalpa (see Temporal cosmology below).

- *Mahbrahm:* The world of "Great Brahm", believed by many to be the creator of the world, and having as his titles "Brahm, Great Brahm, the Conqueror, the Unconquered, the All-Seeing, All-Powerful, the Lord, the Maker and Creator, the Ruler, Appointer and Orderer, Father of All That Have Been and Shall Be." According to the Brahmajla Sutta (DN.1), a Mahbrahm is a being from the bhsvara worlds who falls into a lower world through exhaustion of his merits and is reborn alone in the Brahma-world; forgetting his former existence, he imagines himself to have come into existence without cause. Note that even such a high-ranking deity has no intrinsic knowledge of the worlds above his own. Mahbrahm is $1^{1}D_{2}$ yojanas tall. His lifespan variously said to be 1 kalpa (Vibhajyavda tradition) or $1^{1}D_{2}$ kalpas long (Sarvstivda tradition), although it would seem that it could be no longer than $^{3}D_{4}$ of a mahkalpa, *i.e.*, all of the mahkalpa except for the Samvartasthyikalpa, because that is the total length of time between the rebuilding of the lower world and its destruction. It is unclear what period of time "kalpa" refers to in this case. The height of this world is 10,240 yojanas above the Earth.

- *Brahmapurohita:* The "Ministers of Brahm" are beings, also originally from the bhsvara worlds, that are born as companions to Mahbrahm after he has spent some time alone. Since they arise subsequent to his thought of a desire for companions, he believes himself to be their creator, and they likewise believe him to be their creator and lord. They are 1 yojana in height and their lifespan is variously said to be $^{1}D_{2}$ of a kalpa (Vibhajyavda tradition) or a whole kalpa (Sarvstivda tradition). If they are later reborn in a lower world, and come to recall some part of their last existence, they teach the doctrine of Brahm as creator as a revealed truth. The height of this world is 5,120 yojanas above the Earth.
- *Brahmapricadya or Brahmaprisajja:* The "Councilors of Brahm" or the devas "belonging to the assembly of Brahm". They are also called Brahmakyika, but this name can be used for any of the inhabitants of the Brahma-worlds. They are half a yojana in height and their lifespan is variously said to be $^{1}D_{3}$ of a kalpa (Vibhajyavda tradition) or $^{1}D_{2}$ of a kalpa (Sarvstivda tradition). The height of this world is 2,560 yojanas above the Earth.

Kamadhtu

The beings born in the Kmadhtu (Pli: Kmaloka; Tib: 'dod.pa'i khams) differ in degree of happiness, but they are all, other than arhats and Buddhas, under the domination of Mra and are bound by desire, which causes them suffering.

Heavens

The following four worlds are bounded planes. each 80,000 yojanas square, which float in the air above the top of Mount Sumeru. Although all of the worlds inhabited by devas (that is, all the worlds down to the Cturmahrjikakyika world and sometimes including the Asuras) are sometimes called "heavens", in the western sense of the word the term best applies to the four worlds listed below:

- *Parinirmita-vasavartin or Paranimmita-vasavatti:* The heaven of devas "with power over (others') creations". These devas do not create pleasing forms that they desire for themselves, but their desires are fulfilled by the acts of other devas who wish for their favor. The ruler of this world is called Va[avartin (Pli: Vasavatti), who has longer life, greater beauty, more power and happiness and more delightful sense-objects than the other devas of his world. This world is also the home of the devaputra (being of divine race) called Mra, who endeavors to keep all beings of the Kmadhtu in the grip of sensual pleasures. Mra is also sometimes called Va[avartin, but in general these two dwellers in this world are kept distinct. The beings of this world are 4,500 feet tall and live for 9,216,000,000 years (Sarvstivda tradition). The height of this world is 1,280 yojanas above the Earth.
- *Nirmnarati or Nimmnarati:* The world of devas "delighting in their creations". The devas of this world are capable of making any appearance to please themselves. The lord of this world is called Sunirmita (Pli Sunimmita); his wife is the rebirth of Viskh, formerly the chief of the upsiks (female lay devotees) of the Buddha. The beings of this world are 3,750 feet tall and live for 2,304,000,000 years (Sarvstivda tradition). The height of this world is 640 yojanas above the Earth.
- *Tucita or Tusita:* The world of the "joyful" devas. This world is best known for being the world in which a Bodhisattva lives before being reborn in the world of humans. Until a few thousand years ago, the Bodhisattva of this world was Zvetaketu (Pli: Setaketu), who was reborn as Siddhrtha, who would become the Buddha Zkyamuni; since then the Bodhisattva has been Ntha (or Nthadeva) who will be reborn as Ajita and will become the Buddha Maitreya (Pli Metteyya). While this Bodhisattva is the foremost of the dwellers in Tucita,

the ruler of this world is another deva called Santucita (Pli: Santusita). The beings of this world are 3,000 feet tall and live for 576,000,000 years (Sarvstivda tradition). The height of this world is 320 yojanas above the Earth.

- *Yma:* Sometimes called the "heaven without fighting", because it is the lowest of the heavens to be physically separated from the tumults of the earthly world. Its ruler is the deva Suyma; according to some, his wife is the rebirth of Sirim, a courtesan of Rjag[ha in the Buddha's time who was generous to the monks. The beings of this world are 2,250 feet tall and live for 144,000,000 years (Sarvstivda tradition). The height of this world is 160 yojanas above the Earth.

Worlds of Sumeru

The world-mountain of Sumeru is an immense, strangely shaped peak which arises in the center of the world, and around which the Sun and Moon revolve. Its base rests in a vast ocean, and it is surrounded by several rings of lesser mountain ranges and oceans.

The three worlds listed below are all located on or around Sumeru: the TryastriC[a devas live on its peak, the Cturmahrjikakyika devas live on its slopes, and the Asuras live in the ocean at its base. Sumeru and its surrounding oceans and mountains are the home not just of these deities, but also vast assemblies of fantastic fairy-tale creatures who only rarely intrude on the human world.

Earthly Realms

- *Manucyaloka:* This is the world of humans and human-like beings who live on the surface of the earth. The mountain-rings that engird Sumeru are surrounded by a vast ocean, which fills most of the world. The ocean is in turn surrounded by a circular mountain wall called Cakrav.
- A which marks the horizontal limit of the world. In this ocean there are four continents which are, relatively speaking, small islands in it. Because of the immenseness of the ocean, they cannot be reached from each other

by ordinary sailing vessels, although in the past, when the cakravartin kings ruled, communication between the continents was possible by means of the treasure called the cakraratna (Pli cakkaratana), which a cakravartin and his retinue could use to fly through the air between the continents.

- Jambudvipa or Jambudipa is located in the south and is the dwelling of ordinary human beings. It is said to be shaped "like a cart", or rather a blunt-nosed triangle with the point facing south. (This description probably echoes the shape of the coastline of southern India.) It is 10,000 yojanas in extent (Vibhajyavda tradition) or has a perimeter of 6,000 yojanas (Sarvstivda tradition) to which can be added the southern coast of only 3 $^{1}D_{2}$ yojanas' length. The continent takes its name from a giant Jambu tree (Syzygium cumini), 100 yojanas tall, which grows in the middle of the continent. Every continent has one of these giant trees. All Buddhas appear in Jambudv+pa. The people here are five to six feet tall and their length of life varies between 80,000 and 10 years.
- Pkrvavideha or Pubbavideha is located in the east, and is shaped like a semicircle with the flat side pointing westward (*i.e.*, towards Sumeru). It is 7,000 yojanas in extent (Vibhajyavda tradition) or has a perimeter of 6,350 yojanas of which the flat side is 2,000 yojanas long (Sarvstivda tradition). Its tree is the acacia. The people here are about 12 feet tall and they live for 250 years.
- Aparagodniya or Aparagoyna is located in the west, and is shaped like a circle with a circumference of about 7,500 yojanas (Sarvstivda tradition). The tree of this continent is a giant Kadambu tree. The human inhabitants of this continent do not live in houses but sleep on the ground. They are about 24 feet tall and they live for 500 years.
- Uttarakuru is located in the north, and is shaped like a square. It has a perimter of 8,000 yojanas, being 2,000

yojanas on each side. This continent's tree is called a kalpavskca or kalpa-tree, because it lasts for the entire kalpa. The inhabitants of Uttarakuru are said to be extraordinarily wealthy. They do not need to labor for a living, as their food grows by itself, and they have no private property. They have cities built in the air. They are about 48 feet tall and live for 1,000 years, and they are under the protection of Vaisravaga.

- *Tiryagyoniloka or Tiracchnayoni :* This world comprises all members of the animal kingdom that are capable of feeling suffering, from the smallest insect to the elephant.
- *Pretaloka or Petaloka:* The pretas, or "hungry ghosts", are mostly dwellers on earth, though due to their mental state they perceive it very differently from humans. They live for the most part in desert and waste places.

Narakas

Naraka or Niraya is the name given to one of the worlds of greatest suffering, usually translated into English as "hell" or "purgatory". As with the other realms, a being is born into one of these worlds as a result of his karma, and resides there for a finite length of time until his karma has achieved its full result, after which he will be reborn in one of the higher worlds as the result of an earlier karma that had not yet ripened. The mentality of a being in the hells corresponds to states of extreme fear and helpless anguish in humans.

Physically, Naraka is thought of as a series of layers extending below Jambudv+pa into the earth. There are several schemes for counting these Narakas and enumerating their torments. One of the more common is that of the Eight Cold Narakas and Eight Hot Narakas.

Cold Narakas

- Arbuda – the "blister" Naraka
- Nirarbuda – the "burst blister" Naraka
- Amama – the Naraka of shivering
- Hahava – the Naraka of lamentation

- Huhuva – the Naraka of chattering teeth
- Utpala – the "blue lotus" Naraka
- Padma – the "lotus" Naraka
- Mahpadma – the "great lotus" Naraka

The Foundations of the Earth: All of the structures of the earth, Sumeru and the rest, extend downward to a depth of 80,000 yojanas below sea level – the same as the height of Sumeru above sea level. Below this is a layer of "golden earth", a substance compact and firm enough to support the weight of Sumeru. It is 320,000 yojanas in depth and so extends to 400,000 yojanas below sea level. The layer of golden earth in turn rests upon a layer of water, which is 8,000,000 yojanas in depth, going down to 8,400,000 yojanas below sea level. Below the layer of water is a "circle of wind", which is 16,000,000 yojanas in depth and also much broader in extent, supporting 1,000 different worlds upon it.

Sahasra Cosmology

While the vertical cosmology describes the arrangement of the worlds vertically, the sahasra (Sanskrit: "thousand") cosmology describes how they are grouped horizontally. The four heavens of the Kmadhtu, as mentioned, occupy a limited space no bigger than the top of Mount Sumeru. The three Brahm-worlds, however, stretch out as far as the mountain-wall of Cakrav-a, filling the entire sky. This whole group of worlds, from Mahbrahm down to the foundations of water, constitutes a single world-system. It corresponds to the extent of the universe that is destroyed by fire at the end of one mahkalpa.

Above Mahbrahm are the bhsvara worlds. These are not only higher but also wider in extent; they cover 1,000 separate world-systems, each with its own Sumeru, Cakrav a, Sun, Moon, and four continents. This system of 1,000 worlds is called a shasra-ck-ika-lokadhtu, or "small chiliocosm". It corresponds to the extent of the universe that is destroyed by water at the end of 8 mahkalpas.

Above the bhsvara worlds are the Zubhaketsna worlds, which cover 1,000 chiliocosms, or 1,000,000 world-systems. This larger system is called a dvishasra-madhyama-lokadhtu, or "medium dichiliocosm". It corresponds to the extent of the universe that is destroyed by wind at the end of 64 mahkalpas.

Likewise, above the Zubhaketsna worlds, the Zuddhvsa and Behatphala worlds cover 1,000 dichiliocosms, or 1,000,000,000 world-systems. This largest grouping is called a trishasra-mahshasra-lokadhtu or "great trichiliocosm".

Temporal Cosmology

Buddhist temporal cosmology describes how the universe comes into being and is dissolved. Like other Indian cosmologies, it assumes an infinite span of time and is cyclical. This does not mean that the same events occur in identical form with each cycle, but merely that, as with the cycles of day and night or summer and winter, certain natural events occur over and over to give some structure to time.

The basic unit of time measurement is the mahkalpa or "Great Eon". The exact length of this time in human years is never defined exactly, but it is meant to be very long, to be measured in billions of years if not longer. A mahkalpa is divided into four kalpas or "eons", each distinguished from the others by the stage of evolution of the universe during that kalpa. The four kalpas are:

- Vivartakalpa "Eon of evolution" – during this kalpa the universe comes into existence.
- Vivartasthyikalpa "Eon of evolution-duration" – during this kalpa the universe remains in existence in a steady state.
- Samvartakalpa "Eon of dissolution" – during this kalpa the universe dissolves.
- Samvartasthyikalpa "Eon of dissolution-duration" – during this kalpa the universe remains in a state of emptiness.

Each one of these kalpas is divided into twenty antarakalpas (Pli antarakappa, "inside eons") each of about the same length. For the Samvartasthyikalpa this division is merely nominal, as nothing changes from one antarakalpa to the next; but for the other three kalpas it marks an interior cycle within the kalpa.

Vivartakalpa

The Vivartakalpa begins with the arising of the primordial wind, which begins the process of building up the structures of the universe that had been destroyed at the end of the last mahkalpa. As the extent of the destruction can vary, the nature of this evolution can vary as well, but it always takes the form of beings from a higher world being born into a lower world.

The example of a Mahbrahm being the rebirth of a deceased bhsvara deva is just one instance of this, which continues throughout the Vivartakalpa until all the worlds are filled from the Brahmaloka down to Naraka. During the Vivartakalpa the first humans appear; they are not like present-day humans, but are beings shining in their own light, capable of moving through the air without mechanical aid, living for a very long time, and not requiring sustenance; they are more like a type of lower deity than present-day humans are.

Over time, they acquire a taste for physical nutriment, and as they consume it, their bodies become heavier and more like human bodies; they lose their ability to shine, and begin to acquire differences in their appearance, and their length of life decreases. They differentiate into two sexes and begin to become sexually active. Then greed, theft and violence arise among them, and they establish social distinctions and government and elect a king to rule them, called Mahsammata, "the great appointed one". Some of them begin to hunt and eat the flesh of animals, which have by now come into existence. These developments are described in the Agganna Sutta (DN.27).

Vivartasthyikalpa

The Vivartasthyikalpa begins when the first being is born into Naraka, thus filling the entire universe with beings. During the first antarakalpa of this eon, human lives are declining from a vast but unspecified number of years (but at least several tens of thousands of years) toward the modern lifespan of less than 100 years. At the beginning of the antarakalpa, people are still generally happy. They live under the rule of a universal monarch or "wheel-turning king" (cakravartin), who conquer. The Mahsudassana-sutta (DN.17) tells of the life of a cakravartin king, Mahsudassana (Sanskrit: Mahsudar[ana) who lived for 336,000 years.

The Cakkavatti-s+handa-sutta (DN.26) tells of a later dynasty of cakravartins, Da7hanemi (Sanskrit: Dhanemi) and five of his descendants, who had a lifespan of over 80,000 years. The seventh of this line of cakravartins broke with the traditions of his forefathers, refusing to abdicate his position at a certain age, pass the throne on to his son, and enter the life of a [ramaGa. As a result of his subsequent misrule, poverty increased; as a result of poverty, theft began; as a result of theft, capital punishment was instituted; and as a result of this contempt for life, murders and other crimes became rampant.

The human lifespan now quickly decreased from 80,000 to 100 years, apparently decreasing by about half with each generation (this is perhaps not to be taken literally), while with each generation other crimes and evils increased: lying, adultery, evil speech, greed and hatred, wrong views, incest and other sorts of sexual abnormalities, disrespect for parents and elders. During this period, according to the Mahpadna-sutta (DN.14) three of the four Buddhas of this antarakalpa lived: Krakucchanda Buddha (Pli: Kakusandha), at the time when the lifespan was 40,000 years; Kanakamuni Buddha (Pli: Kongamana) when the lifespan was 30,000 years; and K[yapa Buddha (Pli: Kassapa) when the lifespan was 20,000 years.

Our present time is taken to be toward the end of the first antarakalpa of this Vivartasthyikalpa, when the lifespan is less than 100 years, after the life of Zkyamuni Buddha (Pli: Sakyamuni), who lived to the age of 80.

The remainder of the antarakalpa is prophesied to be miserable: lifespans will continue to decrease, and all the evil tendencies of the past will reach their ultimate in destructiveness. People will live no longer than ten years, and will marry at five; foods will be poor and tasteless; no form of morality will be acknowledged. The most contemptuous and hateful people will become the rulers. Incest will be rampant. Hatred between people, even members of the same family, will grow until people think of each other as hunters do of their prey.

Eventually a great war will ensue, in which the most hostile and aggressive will arm themselves and go out to kill each other. The less aggressive will hide in forests and other secret places while the war rages. This war marks the end of the first antarakalpa.

Second Antarakalpa

At the end of the war, the survivors will emerge from their hiding places and repent their evil habits. As they begin to do good, their lifespan increases, and the health and welfare of the human race will also increase with it. After a long time, the descendants of those with a 10-year lifespan will live for 80,000 years, and at that time there will be a cakravartin king named SaEkha. During his reign, the current bodhisattva in the Tucita heaven will descend and be reborn under the name of Ajita. He will then be known by the name of Maitreya (Pli: Metteyya).

After Maitreya's time, the world will again worsen, and the lifespan will gradually decrease from 80,000 years to 10 years again, each antarakalpa being separated from the next by devastating war, with peaks of high civilization and morality in the middle. After the 19th antarakalpa, the lifespan will increase to 80,000 and then not decrease, because the Vivartasthyikalpa will have come to an end.

Samvartakalpa

The Samvartakalpa begins when beings cease to be born in Naraka. This cessation of birth then proceeds in reverse order up the vertical cosmology, *i.e.* pretas then cease to be born, then animals, then humans, and so on up to the realms of the deities.

When these worlds as far as the Brahmaloka are devoid of inhabitants, a great fire consumes the entire physical structure of the world. It burns all the worlds below the bhsvara worlds. When they are destroyed, the Samvartasthyikalpa begins.

Sachvartasthyikalpa

There is nothing to say about the Samvartasthyikalpa, since nothing happens in it below the bhsvara worlds. It ends when the primordial wind begins to blow and build the structure of the worlds up again.

Other Destructions: The destruction by fire is the normal type of destruction that occurs at the end of the Samvartakalpa. But every eighth mahkalpa, after seven destructions by fire, there is a destruction by water. This is more devastating, as it eliminates not just the Brahma worlds but also the bhsvara worlds. Every sixty-fourth mahkalpa, after 56 destructions by fire and 7 destructions by water, there is a destruction by wind. This is the most devastating of all, as it also destroys the Zubhaketsna worlds. The higher worlds are never destroyed.

Buddhism Dharma: Dharma (Sanskrit) or Dhamma (Pli) in Buddhism has two primary meanings: the teachings of the Buddha which lead to enlightenment, and the constituent factors of the experienced world. In East Asia, the character for Dharma is Ol, pronounced fI in Mandarin and hM in Japanese. The Tibetan translation of this term is chos (chö).

Buddha's Teachings: For practicing Buddhists, references to " dharma" (in English often "the" Dharma) primarily mean the teachings of the Buddha – sometimes called Buddhadharma by other schools of thought. Some Buddhists object to this type of terminology on the grounds that the Dharma is the universal and singular law of nature and to call it Buddhadharma misleadingly suggests that other kinds of Dharma may exist. Buddha Dharma itself, however, means "Path of Awakening" and so is a universal understanding of Dharma.

The status of the Dharma is regarded variably by different traditions. Some regard it as an ultimate and transcendent truth which is utterly beyond worldly things, somewhat like the Christian logos. Others, who regard the Buddha as simply an enlightened human being, see the Dharma as the 84,000 different teachings (the Kangyur/bka.'gyur) that the Buddha gave to various types of people based on their needs. The teachings are expedient means of raising doubt in the hearer's own cherished beliefs and view of life; when doubt has opened the door to the Truth, the teaching can be put aside.

" Dharma" usually refers inclusively not just to the sayings of the Buddha but to the later traditions of interpretation and addition that the various schools of Buddhism have developed to help explain and expand upon the Buddha's teachings. For others still, they see the dharma as referring to the "truth" or ultimate reality or "the way things are".

The Dharma is one of the Three Jewels of Buddhism of which practitioners of Buddhism seek refuge in (what one relies on for his/her lasting happiness). The three jewels of Buddhism are the Buddha (mind's perfection of enlightenment), the Dharma (teachings and methods), and the Sangha (awakened beings who provide guidance and support).

Buddha's Dharma Body: The qualities of the Dharma (Law, truth) is the same as the qualities of the Buddha and forms his "truth body" or "Dhamma Kaya": In the Samyutta Nikaya, Vakkali Sutta, Buddha said to his disciple Vakkali that:

"Yo kho Vakkali dhammam passati so mam passati"

Vakkali, whoever sees Dhamma, sees me [the Buddha]

Another reference from the Agganna Sutta of the Digha Nikaya, says to his disciple Vasettha:

"Tathagatassa h'etam Vasettha adivacanam Dhamma-kayo iti pi...":

O Vasettha! The Word of Dhammakaya is indeed the name of the Tathagata

Knowing these attributes, Buddhists believe that they will attain the greatest peace and happiness through the practice of the Dhamma. Each person is therefore fully responsible for himself to put it in the real practice.

Here the Buddha is compared to an experienced and skilful doctor, and the Dhamma to proper medicine. However efficient the doctor or wonderful the medicine may be, the patients cannot be cured unless they take the medicine properly. So the practice of the Dhamma is the only way to attain the final deliverance of Nibbna. These teachings ranged from understanding karma (Pli: kamma) (cause and effect) and developing good impressions in one's mind, to how to reach full enlightenment by recognizing the nature of mind.

Dharmas in Buddhist Phenomenology: Other uses include dharma, normally spelled with a small "d" (to differentiate), which refers to a phenomenon or constituent factor of human experience. This was gradually expanded into a classification of constituents of the entire material and mental world. Rejecting the substantial existence of permanent entities which are qualified by possibly changing qualities, Buddhist Abhidharma philosophy, which enumerated seventy-five dharmas, came to propound that these "constituent factors" are the only type of entity that truly exists.

This notion is of particular importance for the analysis of human experience: Rather than assuming that mental states inhere in a cognizing subject, or a soul-substance, Buddhist philosophers largely propose that mental states alone exist as "momentary elements of consciousness", and that a subjective perceiver is assumed.

One of the central tenets of Buddhism, is the denial of a separate permanent "I", and is outlined in the three marks of *e*. The three signs: 1. Du%kha (Pali: Dukkha)-Suffering, 2. Anitya (Pali: Anicca)-Change/Impermanence, 3. Antman (Pali: Anatta)-Non-self. At the heart of Buddhism, is the denial of a "self" or "I" (and hence the delusion) as a separate self-existing entity.

Later, Buddhist philosophers like Ngrjuna would question whether the dharmas (momentary elements of consciousness) truly have a separate existence of their own. (*i.e.* Do they exist apart from anything else?) Rejecting any inherent reality to the dharmas, he asked (rhetorically):

What is impermanent and permanent? What is neither?

Auspicious is the pacification of phenomenal metastasis,
the pacification of all apprehending;

There is no dharma whatsoever taught by the Buddha to whomever, whenever, wherever. Dharma as Righteousness.

According to S.N. Goenka, teacher of Vipassana Meditation, the original meaning of dhamma is "dhareti ti dhamma', or "that which is contained". Dharma in the Buddhist scriptures has a variety of meanings, including "phenomenon", and " nature" or "characteristic". Dharma also means 'mental contents', and is paired with citta, which means heart/mind. The pairing is paralleled with the pairing of kaya (body) and vedana (feelings or sensations, that which arise within the body but experienced through the mind), in major sutras such as the Mahasatipatthana sutra. Dharma is also used to refer to the teachings of the Buddha, not in the context of the words of one man, even an enlightened man, but as a reflection of natural law which was re-discovered by this man and shared with the world. A person who lives their life with an understanding of this natural law, is a "dhammic" person, which is often translated as "righteous".

Dharma (Sanskrit) or Dhamma (Pli) in Buddhism has two primary meanings: the teachings of the Buddha which lead to enlightenment, and the constituent factors of the experienced world. In East Asia, the character for Dharma is Ol, pronounced fI in Mandarin and hM in Japanese. The Tibetan translation of this term is chos (cho).

Samsara (Buddhism): Samsara, the Sanskrit and Pli term for "continous movement" or "continuous flowing" refers in Buddhism to the concept of a cycle of birth (jti) and consequent decay and death (jarmarana), in which all beings in the universe participate and which can only be escaped through enlightenment. It is generally opposed to Nirgna or nibbna.

Samsara in Nikya Buddhism: Whereas in Hinduism some being (atman, jiva, etc.) is regarded as being subject to Samsara, Buddhism was founded on a rejection of such metaphysical substances, and originally accounts for the process of rebirth/reincarnation by appeal to phenomenological or psychological constituents. Later schools of Buddhism such as the Pudgalavda, however, re-introduce the concept of a "person" which transmigrates. The basic idea that there is a cycle of birth and rebirth is, however, not questioned in early Buddhism and its successors, and neither is, generally, the concept that samsara is a negative condition to be abated through religious practice concluding in the achievement of final Nirgna.

Samsara in Mahyna Buddhism: According to several strands of the Mahyna Buddhist tradition, the division of samsara and Nirgna is attacked using an argument that extends some of the basic premises of antman and of Buddha's attack on orthodox accounts of existence. This is found poetically in the "Perfection of Wisdom" literature and more analytically in the philosophy of Ngrjuna and later writers. It is not entirely clear which aspects of this theoretical move were developed first in the sutras and which in the philosophical tradition.

Samsara in Tibetan Buddhism: Samsara is uncontrollably recurring rebirth, filled with suffering and problems (according to Klacakra tantra as explained by Dr. A. Berzin).

Rebirth (Buddhism): Rebirth in Buddhism is the doctrine that streams of consciousness composed of aggregates called skandha causes a new form to emerge and would continue as long as those aggregates abide in ignorance or avidya (Buddhism), which is the root cause of existence in Buddhism.

Although the cessation of a life is not in itself a sufficient condition for the inception of a new life (since arhats, pratyekabuddhas and buddhas pass away without rebirth), the supporting conditions for a new birth are almost always present. From an external perspective, each life appears as a link in a beginningless sequence of lives, varying in length and in quality.

In traditional Buddhist cosmology, these lives can be in any of a large number of states of being, including those of humans, any kind of animal, and several types of supernatural being (see Six realms). The type of rebirth that arises at the end of one life is conditioned by the karmas (actions of body, speech and mind) of the previous life; good karmas will yield a happier rebirth, bad karmas will produce one which is more unhappy. In the traditional Buddhist languages of Sanskrit and Pli, there is no word corresponding exactly to the English

" rebirth". A rebirth, that is, the state one is born into, is referred to as jti, *i.e.* simply " birth", also referring to the process of being born or coming into the world in any way. The entire process of change from one life to the next is called punarbhava (Sanskrit) or punabbhava (Pli), literally "becoming again"; it is also known simply as bhava, *i.e.* "becoming". The process seen from a universal perspective, encompassing all living beings, is called samsara.

From an interior perspective, a person who remembers or imagines a past life is likely to think of it as representing a continuity of existence between lifespans, *i.e.*, that the same person (however defined) was formerly one person (with a certain name and body) and is now a different person (with another name and body).

This perspective is objectionable from the point of view of Buddhist philosophy on two counts. First, because it seems to postulate an enduring, self-existing entity that exists separate from the elements of mind and body, contrary to the Buddhist philosophical position of antman. Second, because it overlooks the characterization of this process as one of constant change, both within and between lives, in which the newly-arising life is conditioned by but in no respect identical to the predecedent life. Nonetheless, the Buddha is represented using language reflecting the interior perspective in stories about his past lives in both jtakas and sktras. For instance, "At that time I was the Brahmin, the Great Steward..." (Mahgovinda-sutta, DN.19) or "Six times, nanda, I recall discarding the body in this place, and at the seventh time I discarded it as a wheel-turning monarch..." (Mahsudassana-sutta, DN.17). This can be regarded as a concession to the needs of conventional speech.

Rebirth as Cycle of Consciousness: Another view of rebirth describes the cycle of death and rebirth in the context of consciousness rather than the birth and death of the body. In this view, remaining impure aggregates, skandhas, reform consciousness into a new form.

Buddhist meditation teachers suggest that through careful observation of the mind, it is possible to see consciousness as being a sequence of conscious moments rather a continuum of awareness. Each moment is an experience of an individual mind-state: a thought, a memory, a feeling, a perception. A mind-state arises, exists and, being impermanent, ceases following which the next mind-state arises. Thus the consciousness of a sentient being can be seen as a continuous series of birth and death of these mind-states. In this context rebirth is simply the persistence of this process. Clearly this explanation of rebirth is wholly divorced from rebirth which may follow bodily death and it is possible for a Buddhist to believe in either, both or neither definition.

The explanation of rebirth as a cycle of consciousness is consistent with other core Buddhist beliefs, such as anicca (impermanence), dukkha (unsatisfactoriness) and anatta (non-self). Furthermore it is possible to observe a karmic link between these mind-states.

In the practice of Vipassana meditation, the meditator uses "bare attention" to observe the endless round of mind-states. This observation derives insight and understanding from seeing this cycle of birth, death and rebirth without interfering, owning or judging the individual states of mind that arise and pass away. This understanding enables them to limit the power of desire, which according to the second noble truth of Buddhism is the cause of Dukkha (suffering, unsatisfactoriness) thus making possible the realisation of Nibbana. So it can be concluded that the understanding of rebirth in the context of the cycle of consciousness is an invaluable and practical component of the fundamental aim of Buddhism.

Rebirth as Buddhist Reincarnation: Within Buddhism, the term rebirth or re-becoming (Sanskrit: punarbhava) is preferred to "reincarnation", as the latter is taken to imply there is a fixed entity that is reborn. However, this still leaves the question as to what exactly the process of rebirth entails. The lack of a fixed self does not mean lack of continuity. One of the metaphors used to illustrate this is that of fire. For example, a flame is transferred from one candle to another, or a fire spreads from one field to another. In the same way that it depends on the original fire, there is a conditioned relationship between one life and the next; they are not identical but neither are they completely distinct. The early Buddhist texts make it clear that there is no permanent consciousness that moves from life to life.

Early Buddhists had to deal with the problems of establishing the nature of the causal link between two lives, especially the crucial one of how one being could receive the fruits of the actions of a previous being, now dead, and how saCskras, or volitional tendencies to act and think in particular ways can be transferred from one being to another.

The Puggalavda school (now extinct) believed in a personal entity (puggala) separate from the five skandhas that provided a link of personal continuity that allows for karma to act on an individual over time. The medieval Pali scholar Buddhaghosa posited a ' rebirth-linking consciousness' (patisandhi), which connected the arising of a new life with the moment of death, but how one life came to be associated with another was still not made clear. Some schools were led to the conclusion that karma continued to exist in some sense and adhere to a particular person until it had worked out its consequences. Another school, the Sautrantika, made use of a more poetic model to account for the process of karmic continuity. For them, each act 'perfumed' the individual and led to the planting of a 'seed' that would later germinate as a good or bad karmic result.

While all Buddhist traditions seem to accept some notion of rebirth, there is no unified view about precisely how events unfold after the moment of death. Theravada Buddhism generally asserts that rebirth is immediate. The Tibetan schools, on the other hand, hold to the notion of a bardo (intermediate state) which can last up to forty-nine days, and this has led to the development of a unique 'science' of death and rebirth, a good deal of which is set down in what is popularly known as The Tibetan Book of the Dead. Also, Rick Strassman's book "The Spirit Molecule" touches on the association between the intermediate state and a possible scientific explanation. While Theravada Buddhism generally denies there is an intermediate state, some early Buddhist texts seem to support it. One school that adopted this view was the Sarvstivda, who believed that between death and rebirth there is a sort of limbo in which beings do not yet reap the consequences of their previous actions but in which they may still influence their rebirth. The death process and this intermediate state were believed to offer a uniquely favourable opportunity for spiritual awakening.

There are many references to rebirth in the early Buddhist scriptures. These are some of the more important: Mahakammavibhanga Sutta (Majjhima Nikaya 136); Upali Sutta (Majjhima Nikaya 56); Kukkuravatika Sutta (Majjhima Nikaya 57); Moliyasivaka Sutta (Samyutta Nikaya 36.21); Sankha Sutta.

Rebirth in the Context of Other Religions and Other Buddhist Beliefs: In the religions of Middle Eastern origin, Judaism, Christianity and Islam, life and death are believed to be linear: a being is born (usually understood as a new creation), lives, and then dies, at which point their soul or other part that survives death, passes to a domain that is inaccessible to living beings and remains there indefinitely, or until the end of the world. (Note that reincarnation, in the limited form of gilgul neshamot plays a role in some forms of Judaism. An even more restricted belief in reincarnation (tanasukh) is found in the Druze religion which is derived from Islam.)

The Buddha lived at a time of great philosophical creativity in India, and many different concepts of the nature of life and death that were proposed at that time. Some thinkers were materialists, believing that there was no existent consequent upon the end of a life, and that there was an atman (self) which was annihilated upon death. Others believed in a form of cyclic existence, where a being is born, lives, dies and then is re-born, but in the context of a type of determinism or fatalism, in which karma played no role. Others were "eternalists", postulating an eternally existent atman, comparable to the Western concept of the soul: when a being (or his body) dies, the atman survives death and is re-embodied (reincarnates) as another living being, based on its karmic inheritance. This last belief is the one that has come to be dominant (with certain modifications) in modern Hinduism.

The Buddha taught a concept of rebirth that was distinct from that of any Indian teacher contemporary with him. This concept was consistent with the common notion of a sequence of related lives stretching over a very long time, but was constrained by two core Buddhist concepts: anatt, that there is no irreducible atman or "self" tying these lives together; and anicca, that all compounded things are subject to dissolution, including all the components of the human person and personality. The Buddha's detailed conception of the connections between action (karma), rebirth, and their ultimate causes is set out in the twelve links of dependent origination.

Shunyata

Zknyat, (Sanskrit) or Sunnat (Pli) is a term, translated as "Emptiness" or "Voidness", which constitutes an aspect of the Buddhist metaphysical critique as well as Buddhist epistemology and phenomenology. Zknyat signifies that everything one encounters in life is empty of soul, permanence, and self-nature. Everything is inter-related, never self-sufficient or independent; nothing has independent reality. Yet [knyat never connotes nihilism, which Buddhist doctrine considers to be a delusion, just as it considers materialism to be a delusion.

In the Mahayana Tathagatagarbha sutras, in contrast, only impermanent, changeful things and states (the realm of samsara) are said to be empty in a negative sense-but not the Buddha or Nirvana, which are stated to be Real, eternal and filled with inconceivable, enduring virtues.

Origin and Development of Zknyat: The theme of Sknyat emerged from the Buddhist doctrines of Anatta (Pali, Sanskrit:Antman—the nonexistence of the self, or atman) and Paticcasamuppada (Pali, Sanskrit: prat+tyasamktpda, Interdependent Arising). The Sunna Sutta, part of the Pali Canon, relates that the monk Ananda, the attendant to Gautama Buddha asked, "It is said that the world is empty, the world is empty, lord. In what respect is it said that the world is empty?" The Buddha replied, "Insofar as it is empty of a self or of anything pertaining to a self: Thus it is said, Ananda, that the world is empty."

Zknyat is a key theme of the Heart Sutra, which is commonly chanted by Mahayana Buddhists worldwide. Zknyat was further developed by Ngrjuna and the Madhyamaka school, which is usually counted as an early Mahayana school. Zknyat ("positively" interpreted-see Tathagatagarbha section below) is also an important element of the Tathagatagarbha literature, which played a formative role in the evolution of subsequent Mahayana doctrine and practice. It should be noted that the exact definition and extent of shunyata varies within the different Buddhist schools of philosophy. In the Tibetan Buddhist tradition, detailed dialogs between the perspectives of the various schools are preserved in order to train students.

Zknyat in Presecular Buddhism, in the Nikayas: Sunnata "Emptiness" (sunnata) in Pali contexts is not the metaphysical Zero (Nonbeing as the principle of Being, Infinite Possibility as distinguished from Indefinite Actuality), but a characteristic of this world, where it has been explained that when the Almsman returns from a deathlike Contemplation in which consciousness and feeling have been arrested, "three touches touch him," "emptiness (sunnato)," "formlessness (animito)" and "making no plans (appanihito phasso)," and he discriminates (viveka) accordingly; and the meaning of "emptiness" 'is explained at M 1.29, "emancipation of the mind by Emptiness (sunnata ceto vimutti) being consequent upon the realization that this world is empty of spirit or anything spiritual'; sunnata is synonymous with anatta; of which it really only paraphrases and isolates the privative AN.

It is no doubt in the same sense that in A 1.72, "the texts are coupled with `emptiness' (suttanta... sunnata patisannuta)"; there is, in fact, nothing more characteristic of Buddhist teaching than its constant resort to negatives (above all in the sense of the word anatta), which even some contemporary hearers found perplexing.

The denial of spirituality to contingent things in particular is a denial of any real essence to these things in themselves, and thus forms the basis of the more sweeping sunyavada doctrine which in the Mahayana denies not any "value" but any essence to even the Buddha's appearance and to the promulgation of the Dhamma itself.

If such a doctrine disturbs us, it may be found more palatably expressed in the Vajracchedika Sutra thus, "Those who see me in the body (rupena) and think of me in sounds (ghosaih), their way of thinking is false, they do not see me at all.... The Buddha cannot be rightly understood (rjuboddhum) by any means (upayena). Not that "means" are not dispositive to a right understanding, but that if regarded as ends, even the most adequate means are a hindrance. In such a radical iconoclasm as this all traditional teachings are finally agreed. What is true of ethics is also true of the supports of contemplation: as in the well known Parable of the Raft, the means are of no more use when the goal has been reached.

"What is non-emptiness' monks? It is the Soul (attano), Self-Nature (sabhava) is non-emptiness, is the refuge to be sought". What friend is emancipation of the mind by means of devoidness (sunnata)? Herein a follower has gone to a clearing in the forest and the root of a tree and investigates thusly: 'This is devoid (sunnamidam) of the Soul and what the Soul subsists upon." This is called emancipation of the mind by means of devoidness (sunnata cetovimmuti).

The fixed unshakable emancipation of the mind is devoid of lusts, devoid of hate, and devoid of delusions. "What is shunyata liberation? He considers: 'this is void of the Soul and what belongs to the Soul'.

Zunyata in the Heart Sutra: The Heart Sutra (one of the Mahayana Perfection of Wisdom Sutras) declares that the skandhas, which constitute our mental and physical existence, are empty in their nature or essence, *i.e.*, empty of any such nature or essence. But it also declares that this emptiness is the same as form (which connotes fullness)—*i.e.*, that this is an emptiness which is at the same time not different from the kind of reality which we normally subscribe to events; it is not a nihilistic emptiness that undermines our world, but a "positive" emptiness which defines it.

- "The noble bodhisattva, Avalokitesvara, engaged in the depths of the practice of the perfection of wisdom, looked down from above upon the five skandhas (aggregates), and saw that they were empty in their essential nature."
- "Here, O Sariputra, emptiness is form; form is just emptiness. Apart from form, emptiness is not; emptiness, form is not. Emptiness is that which is form, form is that which is emptiness. Just thus are perception, cognition, mental construction, and consciousness."
- "Here, O Sariputra, all phenomena of existence are marked by emptiness: not arisen, not destroyed, not unclean, not clean not deficient nor fulfilled."

Zknyat in Nagrjuna: For Nagrjuna, who provided the most important philosophical formulation of [knyat, emptiness as the mark of all phenomena means is a natural consequence of dependent origination; indeed, he identifies the two. In his analysis, any enduring essential nature (*i.e.*, fullness) would prevent the process of dependent origination, would prevent any kind of origination at all, for things would simply always have been and always continue to be. That things happen is proof that things lack the kind of nature attributed to them in mainstream Indian metaphysics.

An interesting consequence of this is that this enables Ngrjuna to put forth a bold argument regarding the relation of nirvna and saAsra. If all phenomenal events (*i.e.*, the events that constitute saAsra) are empty, then they are empty of any compelling ability to cause suffering. For Ngrjuna, Nirgna is neither something added to saAsra nor any process of taking away from it (*i.e.*, removing the enlightened being from it). In other words, Nirgna is simply saAsra rightly experienced in light of a proper understanding of the emptiness of all things.

Sunyata in the Tathagatagarbha Sutras: The class of Buddhist scriptures known as the Tathagatagarbha sutras presents a seemingly variant understanding of Emptiness, according to which the Buddha and Nirvana, unlike compounded, conditioned phenomena, are not empty of intrinsic existence, but merely empty of the impermanent, the painful and the Self-less.

In the "Srimala Sutra" the Buddha is seen as empty of all defilement and ignorance, not of intrinsic Reality. The "Mahayana Mahaparinirvana Sutra" supports such a vision and views Ultimate Emptiness as the Buddhic cognition ("jnana") which perceives both Emptiness and non-Emptiness, wherein "the Empty is the totality of Samsara and the non-Empty is Great Nirvana".

The Buddha in the Mahayana Mahaparinirvana Sutra further indicates that to view absolutely everything as empty is an unbalanced approach and constitutes a deviation from the middle path of Buddhism: "The wise perceive Emptiness and non-Emptiness, the Eternal and the Impermanent, Suffering and Bliss, the Self and the non-Self.... To perceive the Emptiness of everything and not to perceive non-Emptiness is not termed the Middle Way; to perceive the non-Self of everything and not to perceive the Self is not termed the Middle Way."

Moreover, this particular sutra contains a passage in which the Buddha castigates those who view the Tathagatagarbha (which is the indwelling, immortal Buddha-element) in each being as empty, declaring of them that they are effectively committing a form of painful spiritual suicide through their wrongheaded stance: "By having cultivated non-Self in connection with the Tathagatagarbha and having continually cultivated Emptiness, suffering will not be eradicated but one will become like a moth in the flame of a lamp." (Tibetan version of the Mahayana Mahaparinirvana Sutra).

The attainment of nirvanic Liberation ("moksha"), by contrast, is said to open up a realm of "utter bliss, joy, permanence, stability, [and] eternity" (ibid), in which the Buddha is "fully peaceful" (Dharmakshema "Southern" version). Perhaps the clearest statement of Tathagatagarbha Buddhism's understanding of Emptiness is found in the Angulimaliya Sutra, where we read the following clarifying explanation:

> *"... by cultivating extreme emptiness and continually considering things to be empty, one will behold the utter destruction of all phenomena. Though Liberation is not empty, one will see and think it to be empty. Thus, for*

example, having thought hail-stones to be jewels, one comes to think that real gems are empty [[knya]. Likewise, you too think of phenomena which are not empty [a[knya] to be empty [[knya], for viewing phenomena as empty, you dissolve into emptiness ([knya) even those phenomena which are not empty.

Some phenomena are empty [of existence] and some phenomena are not empty [of existence]. Just like the hail-stones, the billions of kleshas [mental and moral afflictions] are empty [of existence], like the hail-stones, those phenomena appertaining to ignorance are empty [of existence] and swiftly fade away. Like the real beryl gems, the Buddha is eternal. Liberation is like the real beryl gems."

Thus in the distinctive Tathagatagarbha sutras a balance is drawn between the empty, impermanent and coreless realm of samsara and the lasting, liberating Reality of the Buddha and Nirvana.

Pratitya-samutpada: Dependant Arising is an important part of Buddhist metaphysics. Common to all Schools of Buddhism, it states that phenomena arise together in a mutually interdependent web of cause and effect. It is variously rendered into English as "dependent origination," "conditioned genesis," "dependent co-arising," "interdependent arising," etc.

Dependent Origination

The enlightenment (Bodhi) of the Buddha Gautama was simultaneously his liberation from suffering and his insight into the nature of the universe – particularly the nature of the lives of 'sentient beings' (principally humans and animals). What the Buddha awakened to (Bodhi means 'to awaken') was the truth of dependent origination. This is the understanding that any phenomenon 'exists' only because of the 'existence' of other phenomena in an incredibly complex web of cause and effect covering time past, time present and time future. Because all things are thus conditioned and transient (anicca), they have no real independent identity (anatta) so do not truly 'exist', though to ordinary deluded minds this appears to be the case. All phenomena are thus fundamentally insubstantial and 'empty' (sunya). Wise human beings, who 'see things as they are' (yatha-bhuta-nana-dassana), renounce attachment and clinging, transform the energy of desire into awareness and understanding, and eventually transcend the conditioned realm of form becoming Buddhas or Arahants.

General Formulation

A general formulation of this concept goes:

With this as condition,

That arises.

With this NOT as condition,

That does NOT arise.

An example to illustrate:

You go on summer holiday to a hot climate, such as Arizona, Spain or Australia. It's a hot clear day and you're sunbathing by the hotel pool with the sun beating down on you. You will begin to feel hot, sweaty, uncomfortable, and soon feel thirsty. You go get yourself a drink to quench your thirst, and think "It's too hot to sit by the pool today, I'm going back to my hotel room where it's cooler, to read for a while".

With "hot summer sun" as condition,

Sweat, thirst and discomfort arises.

With "cool hotel room" as condition,

Sweat, thirst and discomfort do not arise.

This draws attention to the constant flux of "Coming to be, and Ceasing to be" that is happening all the time. All phenomena are subject to this unending interaction. And since all phenomena are dependent on other phenomena, they are all transient and impermanent.

Applications

The general formulation has two very well known applications.

Four Noble Truths

The first application is to suffering, and is known as the Four Noble Truths:

1 *Dukkha:* There is suffering. Suffering is an intrinsic part of life also experienced as dissatisfaction, discontent, unhappiness, impermanence.

2. *Samudaya:* There is a cause of suffering, which is attachment or desire (tanha).

3. *Nirodha:* There is a way out of suffering, which is to eliminate attachment and desire.

4. *Marga:* The path that leads out of suffering is called the Noble Eightfold Path.

Twelve Nidanas

The other application is to the rebirth process and is known as the Twelve Nidanas or the Twelve Links of Conditioned Existence. In this application of pratitya-samutpada, each link is conditioned by the preceding one, and itself conditions the succeeding one. These cover three lives:

Former Life

- ignorance
- activities which produce karma

Current Life

- consciousness
- name and form (personality or identity)
- the twelve domains (5 physical senses + the mind + forms, sounds,..., thoughts)
- contact (between objects and the senses)
- sensation (registering the contact)
- desire (for continued contact)
- attachment

Future Life

- becoming (conceptior)f a new life)

- birth
- old age and death.

With respect to the destinies of human beings and animals, dependent origination has a more specific meaning as it describes the process by which such sentient beings incarnate into any given realm and pursue their various worldly projects and activities with all the concomitant suffering involved. Among these sufferings are ageing and death. Ageing and death are experienced by us because birth and youth have been experienced.

Without birth there is no death. One conditions the other in a mutually dependent relationship. Our becoming in the world, the process of what we call 'life', is conditioned by the attachment and clinging to certain ideas and projects such as having a family or making money. This attachment and clinging in turn cannot exist without craving as its condition.

The Buddha understood that craving comes into being because there is sensation in the body which we experience as pleasant, unpleasant or neutral. When we crave certain things such as alcohol, sex or sweet foods it is the sensation induced by contact with the desired object that we crave rather than the object itself. Sensation is caused by contact with such objects of the senses. The contact or impression made upon the senses (manifesting as sensation) is itself dependent upon the six sense organs which themselves are dependent upon a psycho-physical entity such that a human being is. The whole process is summarised by the Buddha as follows:

> *The thrust of the formula is such that when certain conditions are present, they give rise to subsequent conditions, which in turn give rise to other conditions and the cyclical nature of life in Samsara can be seen. This is graphically illustrated in the Bhavacakra (Wheel of life).*

There appears to be widespread misunderstanding of the formula in relation to time scales. Many references made to Prat+tyasamutpda are expressed over lifetimes. While this is true in the wider sense, more practically, this is to be seen as a daily cycle occurring from moment-to-moment throughout each day.

Its necessary to refer to the above in order to fully understand and make use of Pratitya-samutpada.

For example, Avidy the first condition, its necessary to refer to Three Signs of Being for a fuller explanation and a better understanding of its fit and function within Pratitya-samutpada. Its also necessary to understand the Three Fires and how they fit in the scheme of things.

A quick glance at the Bhavacakra, you will note that the Three Fires sit at the very center of the schemata, and drive the whole edifice.To understand this, it is necessary to study different sorts of conditions, because only one of them is called "causal condition". Example, ignorance can determine activities as an "object condition" if one... decide to reduce ignorance. And then because in this life one has been ignorant, and acted in such a way as to produce karma, the cycle continues round again.

Nibbana (Skt Nirvana) is often conceived of as stopping this cycle. By removing the causes for craving, craving ceases. So with the ceasing of birth, death ceases. With the ceasing of becoming, birth ceases... and so on until with the ceasing of ignorance no karma is produced, and the whole process of death and rebirth ceases. In fact the opportunity for change comes between the stages of sensation and desire, since as we saw above it is craving that drives the whole process. If one can simply experience sensations without desiring, then craving will not arise, and one can begin to be free from the cycle of birth and death.

Madhyamaka and Pratitya-samutpada

Though the formulations above appear might seem to imply that pratitya-samutpada is a straightforward causal model, in the hands of the Madhyamaka school, Pratitya-samutpada is used to demonstrate the very lack of inherent causality, in a manner that appears somewhat similar to the ideas of David Hume. The conclusion of the Mdhyamikas is that causation, like being, must be regarded as a merely conventional truth and that to take it as really (or essentially) existing would be both a logical error and a perceptual one, arising from ignorance and a lack of spiritual insight. According to the analysis of Ngrjuna, the most prominent Mdhyamika, true causality depends upon the intrinsic existence of the elements of the causal process (causes and effects), which would violate the principle of anatta, but prat+tya-samutpda does not imply that the apparent participants in arising are essentially real.

Because of the interdependence of causes and effects (*i.e.* causes depend on their effects in order to be causes, and effects likewise depend on their causes in order to be effects), it is quite meaningless to talk about them as existing separately. However, the strict identity of cause and effect is also refuted, since if the effect were the cause, the process of origination could not have occurred.

Thus both monistic and a dualistic accounts of causation are rejected. Therefore Ngrjuna explains that the anatta (or emptiness) of causality is demonstrated by the interdependence of cause and effect, and likewise that the interdependence (prat+tya-samutpda) of causality itself is demonstrated by its anatta.

In his Entry to the middle way, Candrakirti asserts, "If a cause produces its requisite effect, then, on that very account, it is a cause. If no effect is produced, then, in the absence of that, the cause does not exist."

Pratitya-samutpada in Dzogchen: In Dzogchen tradition the interdependent origination is considered illusory: '(One says), "all these (configurations of events and meanings) come about and disappear according to dependent origination." But, like a burnt seed, since a nonexistent (result) does not come about from a nonexistent (cause), cause and effect do not exist.

Being obsessed with entities, one's experiencing itself which discriminates each cause and effect, appears as if it were cause and condition.'

The Reversibility of Dependent Arising: Pratitya-samutpada is most commonly used to explain how suffering arises depending on certain conditions, the implication being that if one or more of the conditions are removed (if the "chain" is broken), suffering will cease.

There is also a text, the Upanisa Sutta in the Samyutta Nikaya, in which a discussion of the conditions not for suffering but for enlightenment are given. This is sometimes glossed as "transcendental" dependent arising. The chain in this case is:

- Suffering [of the rounds of rebirth]
- Faith
- Gladness
- Rapture
- Tranquillity
- Happiness
- Concentration
- Knowledge and vision of things as they really are
- Revulsion
- Dispassion
- Liberation
- Knowledge of destruction of the poisons

Karma in Buddhism

Karma (Sanskrit karman) or Kamma (Pli) means "action" or "doing"; whatever one does, says, or thinks is a karma. In Buddhism, the term karma is used specifically for those actions which spring from :

- mental intent
- mental obsessions

Which bring about a fruit or result (vipka), either within the present life, or in the context of a future rebirth. Karma is the engine which drives the wheel of samsara for each being. In a discourse (Anguttara Nikaya Nibbedhika Sutta) the Buddha said :

> *"Intention, monks, is kamma I say. Having willed, one acts through body, speech and mind".*

Karma is used as an ethical principle, rather than a cosmological explanation for the world. Buddhists believe that the actions of beings will affect their own future, and because of this there are no private actions: all actions have a consequence.

The emphasis of karma in Buddhism is on cause, not on effect: Buddhists do not say "it was due to her karma that it happened to her"-indeed the karmic consequences of one's actions are dependent on sufficient conditions.

Buddhism distinguishes saCsric happiness (birth in the high realms), from the final state of enlightenment: nirvana; so likewise there is saCsric good karma, which leads to the high realms (such as the human realm), and then there is liberating karma-which is supremely good.

Therefore the major dichotomy is saCsric karma and liberating karma, of which the former is typically divided into the three: good, neutral, and bad (in accordance with the degree of samsaric happiness or suffering that will mature as a consequence). Likewise, liberating karma is divided into three: according to whether it will mature the being as a [rvakabuddha, pratyekabuddha, or a samyaksambuddha.

In Buddhism, the term karma is often used to refer only to saCsric karma, as indicated by the twelve nidanas of dependent origination.

The differentiation between "good" karma and "liberating" karma has been used by some scholars to argue that the development of Tantra depended upon Buddhist ideas and philosophies.

Because of the inevitability of consequence, Karma entails the notion of Buddhist rebirth. However, karma is not the sole basis of rebirth. The rebirths of eighth stage (and above) Bodhisattvas in the Mahayana tradition refers to those liberated beings who consciously choose to be reborn in a future life in order to help others still trapped in samsara.

Some people have problems with the teaching on karma, often of what exactly the Buddha is asking them to believe in when asking them to have conviction in karma.

- First, action really is happening — it's not an illusion.
- Second, you really are responsible for your actions. There's no outside force like the stars or some good or evil being acting through you. When you're conscious, you're the one who decides what to do.
- Third, your actions have results — you're not just writing on the water — and those results can be good or bad depending on the quality of the intention behind the act.

Wrong Understandings of Karma: In Buddhism, Karma is not pre-determinism, fatalism or accidentalism, as all these ideas lead to inaction and destroy motivation and human effort that a human being can change for the better no matter what his or her past was and are designated as "wrong view" in Buddhism.

1. Pubbekatahetuvada: The belief that all happiness and suffering arise from previous kamma (Past-action determinism).
2. Issaranimmanahetuvada: The belief that all happiness and suffering are caused by the directives of a Supreme Being (Theistic determinism).
3. Ahetu-apaccayavada: The belief that all happiness and suffering are random, having no cause (Indeterminism or Accidentalism).

"Bhikkhus, adhering to previously done kamma as the essence, there are neither motivation nor effort with what should be done and what should not be done... Not upholding ardently what should be done, nor abandoning what should be abandoned, those ascetics and Brahmins are as if deluded, lacking a control, incapable of having any true teaching. (Buddha). In Buddhism, Karma is simply there as a guide and an indication of what your present is and how one's future can be made better by self effort, otherwise, fatalism and pre-determinism is the anti-thesis of the notion of perfection or self-conquest-which is the primary aim of Buddhism.

Buddhist Meditation: Buddhist meditation, meditation used in the practice of Buddhism, "includes any method of meditation that has Enlightenment as its ultimate aim". The closest word for meditation in the classical languages of Buddhism is bhavana or "mental development".

Methods of Meditation: The main methods of Buddhist meditation are divided into samatha (tranquility meditations) and vipassana (insight meditations).

The samatha meditations include anapana (mindfulness of breathing) and mett bhvan (development of loving kindness). The vipassana meditations includes contemplation on impermanence, the six element practice, and contemplation on conditionality. Samatha meditations usually precede and prepare for vipassana meditations.

Each of the five basic methods is an "antidote" to one of the five mental "poisons" :

Meditation type	*Method*	*Counteracts*	*Develops*
Samatha (tranquility meditations)	anapana	distraction	concentration
	metta bhavana	hatred [and sentimental attachment]	love
Vipassana (insight meditations)	contemplation of impermanence	craving	inner peace, freedom
	six element practice	conceit	clarity regarding nature of self
	contemplation of conditionality	ignorance	wisdom, compassion
Samatha (tranquility meditations)	karuna bhavana	cruelty, sentimental pity and horrified anxiety	compassion
	mudita bhavana	resentment, envy and vicarious enjoyment	sympathetic joy
	upekkha bhavana	fixed indifference and apathetic neutrality	equanimity

Not included under samatha in the above table are all the four brahma-viharas (lit. "sublime abodes") of which mett bhvan is the most often practiced one:

Anapanasati: Anpnasati, (Pali) meaning mindfulness of breathing ("sati" means mindfulness, "npna" refers to the breath moving in and out) is a basic form of meditation taught by the

Buddha. According to the Buddha's teaching in the Anpnasati Sutta, practicing mindfulness of breathing meditation as a part of the Noble Eightfold Path leads to the removal of all defilements (kilesa) and finally the attainment of Nibbna (Nirvana). The Buddha's teaching was based on his own experience in using anapanasati as part of his means of achieving his own enlightenment. Mindfulness of breath is often practiced along with mett bhvan to prevent withdrawal from the world and loss of compassion (Kamalashila 1996).

The Anpnasati Sutta is specifically about the mindfulness of in-and-out breathing. It recommends the practice of npnasati meditation as a means of cultivating the seven factors of awakening: sati (mindfulness), dhamma vicaya (analysis), viriya (persistence), which leads to piti (rapture), then to passaddhi (serenity), which in turn leads to samadhi (concentration) and then to upekkh (equanimity). Finally, the Buddha taught that with these factors developed in this progression, that the practice of npnasati would lead to release or Nibbna (Nirvana).

Anpnasati meditation is normally practiced either in conjunction with vipassan meditation, with zazen, or zen meditation in the soto Zen tradition (shikantaza). However, before the meditator can use vipassana, the meditator must first develop enough concentration using anapanasati meditation to be able to undertake vipassana meditation.

Practice: The practice of anpnasati varies. Typically, to begin, one needs to sit in a comfortable position, with the back and neck straight. It is also helpful if one can find a comfortable and peaceful environment. Breathe naturally, without attempting to change the length or the depth of the breath. If the breath is short, then observe that the breath is short. If the breath is long, then observe that the breath is long.

While breathing, the meditator trains the mind to be sensitive to or focused on various things, and calming or steadying various things. The meditator trains in breathing in sensitive to one or more of: the entire body, rapture, pleasure, the mind, or mental processes, and then breathing out sensitive to this thing. The meditator trains in breathing in focusing on one or more of inconstancy, dispassion, cessation and relinquishment, and then breathing out focusing on this thing. The meditator trains in breathing in steadying, satisfying or releasing the mind, and then breathing out steadying, satisfying or releasing the mind.

Tutors will explain that an untrained mind constantly has thoughts interrupting one's focus. Like the waves in the ocean, thoughts arise, and they slowly fall away. If one disregards the thoughts, they slowly wither and disappear. On the other hand, if one pays attention, then soon one is lost in a web of thoughts.

In this tradition there are two types of thoughts: thoughts from the past and thoughts about the future. It is said that when left unattended, the mind will flit from one thought to another, wandering aimlessly. There are thoughts which bring happiness, and there are thoughts which bring sadness.

Practitioners are tutored to avoid being disrupted by passing thoughts and to nudge themselves into concentrating on the breathing once again.

Practitioners may follow four stages:

1. Count the breath at the end of exhalation
2. Count the breath at the beginning of inhalation
3. Focus on the breath without counting
4. Focus only on the spot where breath enters and leaves the nostril/upper-lip area

Stages of Anpnasati: Formally, there are sixteen stages— or lessons — of npnasati which are divided into four tetrads. The first four steps involve focusing the mind on breathing, which is the body-conditioner (kya-sankhra in Pali). The second tetrad involves focusing on the feelings (vedan), which are the mind-conditioner (citta-sankhra). The third tetrad involves focusing on the mind itself (citta), and the fourth tetrad focuses on "the truth" (dhamma). (Compare right mindfulness.)

Any meditative session using anpnasati should start at the first stage, continue with the second state, and so on, in sequence. If the session ends at a given stage, then at the next meditative session one should start again at the first stage.

Arupajhana: In Buddhism, the arkpajhnas are four successive levels of meditation on non-material objects. These levels are higher than the rkpajhnas, and harder to attain. While rupajhanas differ considering their characteristics, arupajhanas differ as their object is determined by the level of the jhana:

- fifth jhna: infinite space,
- sixth jhna: infinite consciousness,
- seventh jhna: infinite nothingness,
- eighth jhna: neither perception nor non-perception.

This has to be understood. In the fourth rupajhana, there is already Upekkha, equanimity and Ekkagata, concentration, but the mind is still focused on a "material" object, as any color.

- In the fifth jhana, the meditator discovers that there is no object, but only an infinite space, which is empty. This perception motivates the interest of claiming arupajhanas.
- In the sixth jhana, it becomes obvious that space has no existence. There is only infinite consciousness.
- In the seventh jhana appears the feeling that there is no consciousness, but nothingness.
- The eighth jhana consists in the most discrete possible state of mind, which justifies the using of "neither perception nor non-perception".

These "explanations" obviously do not refer to any intellectual, philosophical comprehension, which disappear since the second jhana. They attempt to figure mental process. The arkpajhnas are part of the kammatthanas, and are referred to as the four "formless states".

The Two Elements of Arkpajhna

Some Tipitaka texts identify arkpajhnas as a part of the fourth rkpajhna, as they include two elements: upekkh (Sanskrit: upekc) and ekaggat (Skt: ekgrat).

Upekkha: Upekkh is a Pali word meaning equanimity. The opposition between comfortable sensations and uncomfortable ones disappears. More importantly, it is one of the fourth Jhna's factors, present only in this Jhna.

Ekaggat: Ekaggat or "singlepointedness", as a Jhna's factor, simply means a very deep concentration, which includes the ceasing of stimuli from the exterior world. It is the only jhnic factor present in each Jhna.

Dhyana: Dhyna in Sanskrit or Jhna in Pli refers to a type or aspect of meditation. It is a key concept in Hinduism and Buddhism. Equivalent terms are "Zen" in Japanese and "Chán" in modern Chinese.

Dhyana in Buddhism: In the Pali Canon the Buddha describes four progressive states of absorption meditation or Jhna. The Jhnas are said by the Buddha to be conducive to detachment but they must not be mistaken for the final goal of nibbana. The Jhnas are states of meditation where the mind is free from the five hindrances (craving, aversion, sloth, agitation, doubt) and incapable of discursive thinking. The deeper Jhnas can last for many hours. When a meditator emerges from Jhna, his/her mind is empowered and able to penetrate into the deepest truths of existence.

There are four deeper states of meditative absoption called the immaterial attainments. Sometimes these are also referred to as the "formless" Jhnas, or Arupajhana (distinguished from the first four Jhnas, Rupajhana). In the Buddhist canonical texts, the word Jhna is never explicitly used to denote them, but they are always mentioned in sequence after the first four Jhnas.

In East Asia, several schools of Buddhism were founded that focused on dhyna, under the names Chan, Zen, and Seon. According to tradition, Bodhidharma brought Dhyna to the Shaolin temple in China, where it came to be transliterated as "chan" ("seon" in Korea, and then "zen" in Japan).

Jhnas are normally described by the way of the mental factors which are present in these states:

1. Movement of the mind onto the object, Vitakka (Sanskrit: Vitarka)
2. Retention of the mind on the object, Vicra

3. Joy, Piti (Sanskrit: Priti)
4. Happiness, Sukha
5. One-pointedness, Ekaggat (Sanskrit: Ekgrat)
6. Equanimity, Upekkh (Sanskrit: Upekc)

First Jhna (Vitakka, Vicra)

The five hinderances have completely disappeared and intense unified bliss remains. Only the subtlest of mental movement remains-perceiveable only by those who have entered the second Jhna.

Second Jhna (Sukha, Ekaggat)

All mental movement utterly ceases. There is only bliss.

Third Jhna (Sukha, Ekaggat)

One half of bliss disappears (joy).

Fourth Jhna (Upekkh, Ekaggat)

The other half of bliss (happiness) disappears, leading to a state with neither pleasure nor pain, which the Buddha said is actually a subtle form of happiness (more sublime than piti and sukha). The Buddha described the Jhnas as "the footsteps of the tathgata". Traditionally, this fourth Jhna is seen as the beginning of attaining psychic powers.

Kasina

In Buddhism, kasina are a class of basic visual objects of meditation. There are ten kasina:

1. earth (pathavi kasina),
2. water (apo kasina),
3. air, wind (vayo kasina),
4. fire (tejo kasina),
5. blue, green (nila kasina),
6. yellow (pita kasina),
7. red (lohita kasina),
8. white (odata kasina),

9. enclosed space, hole, aperture (akasa kasina),
10. bright light (aloka kasina).

The kasina are typically described as a colored disk, with the particular color, properties, dimensions and medium often specified according to the type of kasina. The earth kasina, for instance, is a disk in a red-brown color formed by spreading earth or clay (or another medium producing similar color and texture) on a screen of canvas or another backing material.

Kasina meditation is a concentration meditation (variously known in different traditions as samatha, dhyana, or jnana meditations), intended to settle the mind of the practitioner and create a foundation for further practices of meditation. In the early stages of kasina meditation, a physical object is used as the object of meditation, being focused upon by the practitioner until an eidetic image of the object forms in the practitioners mind.

In more advanced levels of kasina meditation, only a mental image of the kasina is used as an object of meditation. Unlike the breath, Buddhist tradition indicates that the kasina are not appropriate objects for certain higher levels of meditation, nor for meditation of the vipassana (insight) type. The ten kasina are part of the forty kammatthana: objects of meditation. They are described in detail by Buddhaghosa in the meditation section of the Visuddhimagga. Unlike breathing meditation, kasina meditation is rarely taught or practiced in the West.

Lotus Position

The Lotus position (Sanskrit: Padmasanam—"lotus posture") is a painful cross-legged sitting posture which originated in representations and meditative practices of Hinduism. It is an established part of the Hindu Yoga tradition, Zen and other meditative disciplines. The position is said to resemble a lotus, encourage "proper" breathing and foster physical stability.

It is perhaps the marquee image of the Eastern religious figure. Famous depictions of the lotus-posture include Shiva, the meditating ascetic god of Hinduism, and Buddha, the founder of Buddhism. The first pictorial representation of padmasana is seen in the ancient Indian depiction of Shiva as Pashupati, Lord of Beasts, in Harrapa.

In this position the right foot is placed on the left thigh and the left foot on the right thigh with the soles of the feet turned up, the spine is straight (note the difference in the position of the feet between this and the "Indian" or "Tailor" style sitting position). In Hinduism the hands are placed on the knees whereas in zazen the hands form the cosmic mudra hand position.

Instructions: "Padmasana (lotus pose)

Sit with the legs straight in front of the body. Slowly and carefully bend one leg and place the foot on top of the opposite thigh. The sole should face upward and the heel should be close to the pubic bone. When this feels comfortable, bend the other leg and place the foot on to top of the opposite thigh. Both knees should ideally touch the ground in the final position. The head and spine should be held upright and the shoulders relaxed. Place the hands on the knees in chin or jnana mudra. Relax the arms with the elbows slightly bent and check to make sure the shoulders are not raised or hunched. Close the eyes and relax the whole body. Observe the total posture of the body. Make the necessary adjustements by moving forward or backward until balance and alignment are experienced. Perfect alignement indicates the correct posture of padmasana.

Mett

Mett (Pli) or Maitr+ (Sanskrit) means unconditional and unattached loving kindness. It is one of the ten pramits of the Theravda school of Buddhism, and the first of the four Brahmavihras. The mett bhvan (cultivation of mett) is a popular form of meditation in Buddhism, practiced with mindfulness of breath, which provides concentration, so as to prevent the loss of compassion.

The object of mett meditation is to cultivate loving kindness (love without attachment, non-exclusive love) towards all sentient beings. The practice usually begins with the meditator cultivating loving kindness towards themselves (though this is not specifically recommended by the Buddha himself in the relevant suttas/sutras), then their loved ones, friends, teachers, strangers and finally their enemies. It is a good way to calm down a distraught mind because it is an antidote to anger. Someone who has cultivated mett will not be easily angered and can quickly subdue anger that arises. They will be more caring, more loving, and more likely to love unconditionally.

Buddhists believe that those who cultivate mett will be at ease because they see no need to harbour ill will or hostility. Buddhist teachers may even recommend meditation on mett as an antidote to insomnia and nightmares. It is generally felt that those around a mettful person will feel more comfortable and happy too. Radiating mett contributes to a world of love, peace and happiness.

Mett Meditation: The Practice of Loving-kindness

Mett signifies friendship and non-violence as well as "a strong wish for the happiness of others", but also less obvious or direct qualities such as showing patience, receptivity, and appreciation. Though it refers to many seemingly disparate ideas, Mett is in fact a very specific form of love – a caring for another independent of all self-interest – and thus is likened to one's love for one's child or parent. Understandably, this energy is often difficult to describe in words; however, in the practice of Mett meditation, one recites specific words and phrases in order to evoke this "boundless warm-hearted feeling." The strength of this feeling is not limited to or by family, religion, or social class. Indeed, Mett is a tool that permits one's generosity and kindness to be applied to all beings and, as a consequence, one finds true happiness in another person's happiness, no matter who the individual is.

Six Stages

The full instructions for the theory and practice of mett bhvan is available in the Visuddhimagga ("The path to purity"), Chapter IX, of the Buddhist scriptures.

The six stages of mett bhvan meditation which are most commonly found involves cultivating loving-kindness towards:

1. Yourself
2. A good friend
3. A 'neutral' person
4. A difficult person
5. All four
6. and then gradually the entire universe

For 2 avoid choosing someone that you feel sexually attracted to, or that is much younger or much older than yourself, or who is dead. For #3 choose someone that you might come in contact with every day, but who does not give rise to strong positive nor strong negative emotions. For #4 traditionally choose "an enemy", but avoid choosing a person who has just wrecked your life, unless you are very well grounded in awareness. For #5 treat them as equals, equally deserving of loving-kindness.

The Metta Meditation is attributed as words of the Buddha (Karaniya Metta Sutta):

This is what should be done
By one who is skilled in goodness,
And who knows the path of peace:
Let them be able and upright,
Straightforward and gentle in speech,
Humble and not conceited,
Contented and easily satisfied,
Unburdened with duties and frugal in their ways.
Peaceful and calm and wise and skillful,
Not proud or demanding in nature.
Let them not do the slightest thing
That the wise would later reprove.
Wishing: In gladness and in safety,
May all beings be at ease.
Whatever living beings there may be;
Whether they are weak or strong, omitting none,

The great or the mighty, medium, short or small,
The seen and the unseen,
Those living near and far away,
Those born and to-be-born—
May all beings be at ease!
Let none deceive another,
Or despise any being in any state.
Let none through anger or ill-will
Wish harm upon another.
Even as a mother protects with her life
Her child, her only child,
So with a boundless heart
Should one cherish all living beings;
Radiating kindness over the entire world.
Spreading upwards to the skies,
And downwards to the depths;
Outwards and unbounded,
Freed from hatred and ill-will.
Whether standing or walking, seated or lying down
Free from drowsiness,
One should sustain this recollection.
This is said to be the sublime abiding.
By not holding to fixed views,
The pure-hearted one, having clarity of vision,
Being freed from all sense desires,
Is not born again into this world

Mindfulness: Mindfulness is the practice whereby a person is intentionally aware of his or her thoughts and actions in the present moment, non-judgmentally. Mindfulness is applied to both bodily actions and the mind's own thoughts and feelings. In Buddhism, the second kind of mindfulness is considered a prerequisite for developing insight and wisdom. Right Mindfulness is the seventh path from the Noble Eightfold Path, which is in its turn the fourth of the Four Noble Truths.

Examples from Meditation and Daily Life: Right mindfulness is also known as Right Meditation. There are many, many forms of mindfulness and meditation. One example of mindfulness is to mentally give a verbal label to each inbreath and outbreath during sitting meditation. So, each time one breathes in, one thinks (*e.g.*) "rising", and each time one breathes out, one thinks "falling".

In this type of meditation, the breath serves as a tether that the practitioner uses to bring his or her awareness back to the present moment. By residing more frequently in the present moment, practitioners begin to see both the inner and outer aspects of reality. As one more closely observes inner reality, one finds that happiness is not a quality brought about by a change in outer circumstances, but rather by realizing unhappiness starts with one's own "mindless", and therefore automatic, reactions toward pleasant and unpleasant situations or feelings.

Mindfulness is an activity that can be done at any time. It does not require sitting, or even focusing on the breath, but rather is done by bringing the mind to focus on what is happening in the present moment, while simply noticing the mind's usual "commentary". One can be mindful of the sensations in one's feet while walking, of the sound of the wind in the trees, or the feeling of soapy water while doing dishes. One can also be mindful of the mind's commentary: "I wish I didn't have to walk any further, I like the sound of the leaves rustling, I wish washing dishes wasn't so boring and the soap wasn't drying out my skin", etc. Any activity done mindfully is a form of meditation.

Research and Writing

Largely associated with Buddhism, the practice of mindfulness is also advocated by such people as medical researcher and author Dr. Jon Kabat-Zinn who developed the Mindfulness-Based Stress Reduction (MBSR) program. MBSR is a form of complementary medicine offered in over 200 U.S.

hospitals and is currently the focus of a number of research studies funded by The National Center for Complementary and Alternative Medicine.

Mindfulness is a core exercise used in Dialectical behavior therapy, a psychosocial treatment Marsha M. Linehan developed for treating people with Borderline Personality Disorder, and is also used in some other newer psychotherapeutical methods, such as Acceptance and Commitment Therapy and Mindfulness-based Cognitive Therapy, which is based on the Mindfulness-Based Stress Reduction program.

Psychologist Ellen J. Langer has written several books on what she calls "Mindfulness," (including a book with that title), which popularize the experimental work she has done on the topic. Langer acknowledges that what she calls "Mindfulness" is similar to, but distinct from, "Mindfulness" as understood by Buddhism and related traditions.

In addition to various forms of meditation, there are mindfulness training exercises that develop awareness using designated environmental cues. Those who find it difficult to practice sitting meditation may consider trying an approach based on Multiple Intelligences, such as Real-World Mindfulness Training

Rupajhana: In Buddhism, rkpajhnas (Sanskrit: rkpadhyna "form meditation") are successive levels of meditation in which the mind is focused on a material object: it is a word used in Pli scriptures. Each higher level is harder to reach than the previous one. It is distinguised from arkpajhna (Skt: arkpadhyna "formless meditation") which is meditation focused on immaterial objects.

There are eight jhnas in total, out of which the first four are rkpajhnas. All four rkpajhnas are characterized by ekaggat (Skt: ekgrat) which means one-pointedness, *i.e.* the mind focuses singularly on the material object during meditation.

The four rkpajhnas are:

1. pamhama-jhna (Skt: prathamadhyna)
2. ḍutiya-jhna (Skt: dvitiyadhyna),

3. tatiya-jhna (Skt: tetiyadhyna)
4. catuttha-jhna (Skt: caturthadhyna)

These first four jhnas can be characterized by certain factors called jhnaEga (Skt: dhynega) whose presence or absence in each rkpajhna is summarized in the following table:

jhna	*vitakka & vicra*	*piti*	*sukha*	*ekaggat*	*upekkh*
pamhama-jhna	*	*	*	*	
dutiya-jhna		*	*	*	
tatiya-jhna			*	*	
catuttha-jhna				*	*

The jhnaEga have the following meanings: vitakka means the noticing of the object of meditation, vicra means the experiencing of the object, piti means rapture, sukha means joy, ekaggat means one-pointedness of concentration, upekkh means equanimity.

Samadhi

Samadhi (Sanskrit, lit. "establish, make firm") is a Hindu and Buddhist term that describes a non-dualistic state of consciousness in which the consciousness of the experiencing subject becomes one with the experienced object, and in which the mind becomes still (one-pointed or concentrated) but the person remains conscious. Sahaj samadhi is the effortless and continual state of perfection of a satguru.

Samadhi is also the Hindi word for a cenotaph, a structure commemorating the dead (akin to a tomb, but without remains).

Etymology: Samadhi IPA: sadmdhi is a Sanskrit term for the state of consciousness induced by complete meditation. Its etymology comes from sam (together or integrated), a (towards), and dha (to get, to hold). Thus the result might be seen to be to acquire integration or wholeness, or truth (samapatti).

Samadhi in Hinduism: Samadhi is the main subject of the first part of the Yoga Sutras called Samadhi-pada. According to Vyasa, a major figure in Hinduism and one of the traditional authors of the Mahabharata, " yoga is samadhi." This is generally interpreted to mean that Samadhi is a state of complete control (samadhana) over the functions and distractions of consciousness.

In practice Samadhi is said to be the state of being aware of one's Existence without thinking, in a state of undifferentiated "Beingness." Three intensities (depths) of Samadhi are usually understood in Hinduism.

1. Laja Samadhi
2. Savikalpa Samadhi
3. Nirvikalpa Samadhi (or Sahaja Samadhi)

Laja Samadhi is a latent ("laja"), potential level of samadhi. It begins in deep meditation or trance-even with movement such as dancing. This kind of samadhi is a state of joy, deep and general well-being, and peaceful meditation.

Savikalpa Samadhi refers to the initial temporary state of full-valued samadhi. The conscious mind is still active, as is the kalpa, meaning imagination. One should compare this meaning to that of sankalpa, which is 'wish.' Kalpa takes on a different, but related, meaning to sankalpa because one must use imagination or consciousness (kalpa) to envision a wish or desire (sankalpa). Conversely, vikalpa means "against imagination." At this final level of samadhi, the mind has become quiet and given up its desires and attendant. Vikalpa leads to the Truth, releasing one from any binds of mind (which are mostly imaginations). In Savikalpa Samadhi, we get the taste of Bliss and Beingness, but are still attached to our erroneous identification with the body as well as to our numerous worldly attractions.

Nirvikalpa Samadhi is the end result. There are no more kalpas (imaginings, wishes or other products from work of the mind), because the mind is finally under control. Upon entering Nirvikalpa Samadhi, the differences we saw before have faded and we can see everything as one. In this condition nothing but pure Awareness remains and nothing is missing to take away from Wholeness and Perfection.

Entering samadhi in the beginning takes effort and holding on to a state of samadhi takes even more effort. The beginning stages of samadhi (Laja and Savikalpa Samadhi) are only temporary. By "effort" it is not meant that the mind has to work more. Instead, it means work to control the mind and release the self. Note that normal levels of meditation (mostly the lower levels) can be held automatically, as in "being in the state of meditation" rather than overtly "meditating." The ability to obtain positive results from meditation is much more difficult than simply meditating.

It is recommended to find a qualified spiritual master (guru or yogi) who can teach a meditator about the workings of the mind. Samadhi is the only stable unchanging reality; all else is ever changing and does not bring everlasting peace or happiness.

Staying in Nirvikalpa Samadhi is effortless but even from this condition one must eventually return to ego-consciousness. Otherwise, this highest level of Samadhi leads to Nirvana, which means total Unity and the logical end of individual identity (and also death of the body). However, it is entirely possible to stay in Nirvikalpa Samadhi and yet be fully functional in this world. This condition is known as Sahaja Nirvikalpa Samadhi or Sahaj Samadhi (sahaja means "spontaneous" in Sanskrti). Only the truly Enlightened (Satguru) can be and remain spontaneously free.

In Nirvikalpa Samadhi, all attachment to the material world and all karma is dissolved. All awareness is withdrawn step by step from the physical, astral and causal bodies until self-realization or oneness with the soul is achieved.

During this process, breathing ceases and the heart stops beating. Aware and fully conscious oneness with soul is then achieved in a most loving way and all cells of physical body are flooded with the Ocean of Divine Love and Divine Bliss for any period of duration-hours, days, weeks until the individual shifts his awareness from the soul back to the physical body. Being fully functional in this world, his awareness stays in connection with the Divine.

But some "strange" conditions accompany this state-better health (the body is sustained by Divine Grace), better feelings (even for other people who may contact the body which the enlightened soul has reidentified with) and various miraculous happenings may occur in connection with the Enlightened one.

Maha Samadhi (literally great samadhi) is the Hindi term for a realized yogi's conscious departure from the physical body at death. Which is also known as Nirvana (see above).

Maha Samadhi is the final conscious exit from the physical body. Every infinitesimal piece of attachment or karma is completely surrendered unto God and dissolved into the Divine Ocean of Love. The individual transcends to worlds beyond karma and returns to God, merging into transcendental Bliss.

Samadhi in Bhakti: The Vaishnava Bhakti Schools of Yoga define Samadhi as 'complete absorption into the object of one's love (Krishna)'. Rather than thinking of 'nothing', true samadhi is said to be achieved only when one has pure, unmotivated love of God. Thus even while performing daily activities a practitioner can strive for full samadhi.

Samadhi, a Description: In his book "Autobiography of a Yogi", Paramahansa Yogananda, a reputed, modern day spiritual saint of India and teacher of Kriya Yoga, gives this stirring description of Samadhi consciousness:

> *My body became immovably rooted; breath was drawn out of my lungs as if by some huge magnet. Soul and mind instantly lost their physical bondage, and streamed out like a fluid piercing light from my every pore. The flesh was as though dead, yet in my intense awareness I knew that never before had I been fully alive. My sense of identity was no longer narrowly confined to a body, but embraced the circumambient atoms. People on distant streets seemed to be moving gently over my own remote periphery. The roots of plants and trees appeared through a dim transparency of the soil; I discerned the inward flow of their sap.*

The whole vicinity lay bare before me. My ordinary frontal vision was now changed to a vast spherical sight, simultaneously all perceptive. Through the back of my head I saw men strolling far down Rai Ghat Road, and noticed also a white cow who was leisurely approaching. When she reached the space in front of the open ashram gate, I observed her with my two physical eyes. As she passed by, behind the brick wall, I saw her clearly still.

All objects within my panoramic gaze trembled and vibrated like quick motion pictures. My body, Master's, the pillared courtyard, the furniture and floor, the trees and sunshine, occasionally became violently agitated, until all melted into a luminescent sea; even as sugar crystals, thrown into a glass of water, dissolve after being shaken. The unifying light alternated with materialisations of form, the metamorphoses revealing the law of cause and effect in creation.

An oceanic joy broke upon calm endless shores of my soul. The Spirit of God, I realized, is exhaustless Bliss; His body is countless tissues of light. A swelling glory within me began to envelop towns, continents, the earth, solar and stellar systems, tenuous nebulae, and floating universes.

The entire cosmos, gently luminous, like a city seen afar at night, glimmered within the infinitude of my being. The sharply etched global outlines faded somewhat at the farthest edges; there I could see a mellow radiance, ever undiminished. It was indescribably subtle; the planetary pictures were formed of a grosser light.

The divine dispersion of rays poured from an Eternal Source, blazing into galaxies, transfigured with ineffable auras. Again and again I saw the creative beams condense into constellations, then resolve into sheets of transparent flame. By rhythmic reversion, sextillion worlds passed into diaphanous luster; fire became firmament. I cognized the center of the empyrean as a point of intuitive perception in my heart. Irradiating splendor issued from my nucleus to every part of the universal structure. Blissful amrita, the nectar of immortality, pulsed through me with a quicksilver-like fluidity. The creative voice of God I heard resounding as Aum, the vibration of the Cosmic Motor.

Suddenly the breath returned to my lungs. With a disappointment almost unbearable, I realized that my infinite immensity was lost. Once more I was limited to the humiliating cage of a body, not easily accommodative to the Spirit. Like a prodigal child, I had run away from my macrocosmic home and imprisoned myself in a narrow microcosm.

Samadhi as Leaving the Body: Advanced yogis have been said to consciously leave (or disidentify with) their bodies as a vital step in the attainment of this final samadhi, or soul-liberation. It is at this time that the soul knows a complete and unbroken union with the Heavenly Godhead, and, being free from the limitations of the body, merges effortlessly into the transcendent amrita of Divine Bliss. It is said that sometimes the yogi leaves the body and returns. According to Meher Baba, Jesus entered into nirvikalp samadhi at the time of his crucifiction.

Samadhi in Buddhism: Samadhi, or concentration of the mind, is the third part of the Eightfold Path of the Buddha's teaching: panna(wisdom), sila (conduct), samadhi or samatha (concentration).

It has been taught by the Buddha using 40 different objects of meditation, such as mindfulness of breathing (anapanasati) and loving kindness (metta). Upon development of samadhi, one's mind becomes purified of defilement, calm, tranquil, and luminous. Once the meditator achieves a strong and powerful concentration, his mind is ready to penetrate and see into the ultimate nature of reality, eventually obtaining release from all suffering. In the language of the eight-fold path, samatha is "right concentration".

Important components of Buddhist meditation, frequently discussed (1, 2) by the Buddha, are the successively higher meditative states known as the four jhanas. The Buddhist suttas mention that samadhi practitioners may develop supernormal powers (called siddhis), and list several that the Buddha developed, but warn that these should not be allowed to distract the practitioner from the larger goal of complete freedom from suffering.

Samatha Meditation

Budhism somewhat considers meditation in general to be an act of concentration on a particular object and/or idea.

Therefore, meditation from other religious traditions are soetimes referred to as a variation of samatha meditation that differ in the focus of concentration; such as breathing, scriptural passage, mantra, religious picture, a rock, body (as arepresentation of death), and so on. In this sense, samatha is not a strictly Buddhist meditation.

For Buddhists, it is commonly practiced as a prelude to and in conjunction with vipassan meditation (insight meditation) which focus on Buddhist dharma. Traditionally, there are 40 objects of meditation, although the breath as an object of meditation has always enjoyed the widest popularity. Mindfulness of breathing or npna meditation which accompany Buddhist doctrine of rising and falling can be used for both Samatha and Vipassan Meditation.

Samatha lead to states of meditative absorption or concentration called jhna (Sanskrit: dhyna) which is often translated as state of tranquility or bliss. Thus, it furthers the right concentration aspect of the Noble Eightfold Path.

Zamatha is also used in Tibetan Buddhism.

Satipammhana: It is often called the Four Foundations of Mindfulness, namely, mindfulness of the body, of thoughts or the mind, of feelings and of mental objects or qualities. These are also known as the "four frames of reference" or Satipammhna-saCyutta. Satipammhna can also be thought of as "establishing mindfulness" or sati-upammhna.

Satipammhna is a way of implementing the right mindfulness and, less directly, the right concentration parts of the Noble Eightfold Path. Satipammhna meditation goes hand-in-hand with vipassana, samatha or calming meditation, and anapana meditation. Satipammhna is practiced with the aims of vipassana and most often in the context of Theravada Buddhism although the principles are also practiced in most traditions of Buddhism which emphasize meditation such as the Zen or Sot Zen tradition. There is also a Satipammhna Sutta or sutra which is also known as the Discourse on the Foundations of Mindfulness. This sutta explains how to systematically cultivate mindful awareness or sati.

Shikantaza: Shikantaza is literally translated as "only focused on doing sitting". More often it is called: "just sitting" or "silent illumination". It is the main meditation technique of the Soto school of Zen Buddhism. The "just" in "just sitting" has two connotations: Firstly, one should do nothing but the sitting. Secondly, one should sit in the right "mindful" way. The Shobogenzo, an ancient document by the zen master Dogen Zenji (1200-1253), is the most important description of shikantaza.

Meditation Method: Shikantaza is often referred to as the method of no method. While other forms of meditation often have quite clear instructions-such as focusing on the breathing process-shikantaza is held to make use of pure consciousness or mindfulness. The basic idea is that one has to transcend, go beyond, the thinking mind. While sitting one should not think about the sitting, but "really" sit, being one with the sitting. The moment one stops thinking about methods or other things, the correct way suddenly appears. From the viewpoint of Zen, thoughts are a fundamental problem. Most of the time we don't really do things, but rather think about them. That's why zen-masters often stress the point that enlightenment is to be found in things like dish-washing, soaking in a bathtub, and going to the toilet.

There's a famous distinction by Dogen: not-thinking versus non-thinking. One could imagine what it would be like to be "without thoughts", yet a completely blank mind is absolutely not the goal of shikantaza. The thinking has to be transcended altogether. One needs to discover individually what lies behind all these thoughts.

Empirical Explanation of Central Buddhist Concepts: Meditative practice stands in close relationship with central Buddhist concepts. Some people actually "see" them work. The three marks of conditioned existence, a central Buddhist doctrine (see Buddhism), will be explained from the viewpoint of the meditator.

Anicca (impermanence): This first aspect points at the continuous flux of life. Everything is always in motion. Nothing is stable and permanent. Shikantaza is practiced from this point of view. The meditator doesn't discriminate between experiences. Everything is accepted exactly as it is, because ultimately nothing lasts. Knowing there's no real foundation one could hold onto, the actual practice also is of this nature. There's no focusing on any specific experience or thought (as is usual in most meditative practices, for example anapana sati). Because of this the meditation is experienced as a mental state of openness and acceptation.

Dukkha (suffering): This is perhaps one of the most difficult concepts to understand from the perspective of practice. Gautama Buddha says the fundamental problem of life are our desires (see Four Noble Truths). These create attachments. This implicates that we like some, but dislike other experiences. The meditator learns to be fully aware of the experience as it is. It isn't possible to add or subtract anything any more. In this way no new attachment is created and older ones slowly fade away. Over a period of time (some teachers say it takes approximately four years of intensive practice) it is held to be possible to transcend all attachments, thereby acquiring the original and natural state of mind (see enlightenment) in which all experiences reveal themselves as emptiness (sunyata).

Anatta (no self): Buddhism teaches the concept of Anatta. Although every human has the idea of a soul, or a deep feeling of "me" or "self", Buddhism claims there's no stable essence in a human. This can be explained as follows. When incorporating shikantaza in one's life, gradually experiences are welcomed more and more.

A great awareness develops itself, which makes it possible to look very carefully at every experience. Which reveals itself as emptiness-as explained before. Then it turns out that even the idea, or this deep "feeling" of a soul every human has, is merely an idea. A thought. Even this idea reveals itself as empty. Which means that the complete identification with this idea no longer holds. Then at once all boundaries break; suddenly there's no difference between the thought of "me" and the sound of a singing bird.

Theoretical Context: For an experienced practitioner Shikantaza is straightforward and simple. Yet, for a beginner this strange "method" is almost impossible to understand. It demands literature study (and/or teaching) and actual practice to understand it thoroughly. Its primary elucidation is in Dogen's Shobogenzo, which is an infamously difficult work of immense philosophical, linguistic, and hermeneutic complexity.

He makes extensive use of paradoxical logic, subversive quotation strategies, imagery, and a rich literary education, and it is impossible to imagine how someone without significant general education and specialized training in the Buddhist textual tradition could begin to access most of the work. Contemporary teaching is often relatively easy to understand, as well as a good introduction to the classic works. Nowadays, many zen-masters have a typical, very "down-to-earth" way of speaking about the practice. Also they try to explain the whole idea of meditation and the connection to this specific practice very lucidly.

Singing Bowl: A singing bowl, also known as a Himalayan bowl or cup gong, is a musical instrument used in Buddhist meditation, dating back many centuries. They are traditionally played in Tibet, Nepal, India, China, Japan, and Korea, mostly by Buddhist monks and in monasteries.

The instrument is made of metal, often including precious metals such as silver and gold. Many other metals, including copper, tin, zinc, lead, iron, and, nickel also feature in many bowls' metallic makeup. Generally, singing bowls can be made of many different metals. Singing bowls are played by hitting, striking, or slowly rubbing/stirring a wooden striker/mallet within or on the top outer surface of the bowl. When done correctly, the bowl will produce a continuous harmonic sound, said to be relaxing and good for the chakra. Some claim that many bowls are "tuned" to a specific chakra. Currently, these bowls are used for meditation, yoga, healing, sound massage, sound therapy, and chakra balancing.

Singing bowls can be found in a variety of shapes, sizes, designs, colors, carvings and craftings. They may be found with various religious themes and symbols, like Tibetan mantra chant om mani padme hum, dragon carvings, mandala carvings, asta mangal (eight auspicious good luck symbols), Buddhist religious symbols and many more. The making of traditional bowls is now considered a lost art. Most old bowls contain very little, if any, ornamentation.

Most bowls are handmade, apart from some tools used for shining and polishing, and fall into two categories. The first is the hand-hammered (beaten) singing bowl, most of which come from Nepal and India, and are manufactured using traditional processes. Hand-hammered bowls are very much more popular for meditation, healing and sound therapy. The second type is the colored, carved and crafted bowl. These are popular for gifts, decorations and souvenir items, and are mostly from Nepal, the Himalayan Country.

Six Yogas of Naropa: The Six Yogas of Naropa describe a set of advanced Tibetan Buddhist tantric meditation practices compiled in and around the time of the Indian monk and mystic Naropa (1016-1100 CE), and conveyed to his student Marpa the translator. The Six Yogas were intended in part to help in the attainment of enlightenment in an accelerated manner.

As Naropa is a Kagyu lineage holder, the six meditative practices are strongly associated with the Kagyu lineage of Tibetan Buddhism. The teachings of Tilopa (988-1069 CE) are the earliest known work on the Six Yogas. Naropa learned the techniques from Tilopa. Naropa's student Marpa taught the Tibetan Milarepa, renowned for his yogic skills. Milarepa in turn taught Gampopa. Gampopa's student, the future first Karmapa, Düsum Khyenpa, attained enlightenment while practicing the Six Yogas.

The Karmapa, the first figure in Tibetan Buddhism to reincarnate, has been strongly associated in certain reincarnations with particular yogic attributes. Many Gelukpa practitioners, including the Dalai Lama, are expert in the Six Yogas of Naropa.

The Path to Nirvana In the religion Buddhism, Meditations carry a higher weight in One's practice to attain Nirvana. But, Dana, giving Alms and Shila, observing at least the basic five disciplines (Panchasheela, in Pali) are also vital for One's practice.

In the Maha Satipattana Sutta in Digha Nikaya, the Buddha describes Success of Four Pattana Meditations as: "One who is honest to himself and practice this four Pattana Meditations without a delay, he should be willing to achieve Arahat or Anagami level, in seven days to seven years in time which would ultimately direct to Nirvana". The Buddha always said: "One who is willing to attain Nirvana, has to understand Four Noble Truth. These Noble Truth is the key to attain Nirvana, without proper understanding of Suffering, Cause of Suffering, Relief of Suffering and the way to end Suffering, These are the four Noble Truth."

Dana, Sila, Samadhi, Pagngna

Steps to Nirvana: Dana & Sila practices generate thoughts, (Punya Karma, in Pali), that would create well-being within Samsara. One to give away things, which oneself earned through hard effort might know an easy task. In order to complete Dana Punya Karma, one has to give Alms without a thought of any return.

Observing Sila, or Shiksha, requires much more effort than Dana. Sila is also a Punya Karma, however, basic discipline in oneself would create a powerful platform for such person to attain Nirvana.

The Buddha said: "One who knows that oneself is not breaking these five root disciplines, shall not fear to live anywhere"

Four Sathipattana Meditation: The most important Meditation practices laid by the Buddha are Four Sathipattana Meditations. These four different meditations guide one's mind to understand reality behind the connection between the Mind and the Body. It is increases the Wisdom of dividing Nma and Rkpa, Nmarkpa Paricceda Gnna. By word meaning, Sathipattana means being in Mindfulness.

- Kayanupassana (Contemplation on the Body)
- Vedananupassana (Contemplation on Feelings)
- Cittanupassana (Contemplation on Thoughts)
- Dhammanupassana (Contemplation on Dhammas)

Pattana and Anupassana carries the same meaning. All beings associate some kind of a body, Kya in Pali, and humen associate or link up with a body which is made up with Patawi (Feeling of Hardness), po (Feeling of Liquidity), Thejo (Feeling of hot or mild temperature) and Vayo (Feeling of Air). Kayanupassana meditation starts from understanding the true nature of body. The body is the beginning of all sarrow, anger, unwise, likeness, and ultimately Suffering. The Buddha always said:

- "Pagncha Upadanaskadha Dhukkha"
- "One's birth, sickness, death and all affairs along life is suffering. Whatsoever feeling, or thought generated by mind during One's interaction with world or mind through these six bases is Suffering"

Vedana

Vedan is a word in Sanskrit and Pli meaning "feeling" or "sensation".

Synonyms: One of the five aggregates (skandhas). Described by the Buddha as having both mental and physical aspects; therefore vedan offers a means to examine the totality of the mental-physical phenomenon. In the Chain of Conditioned Arising (Prat+tyasamutpda / Pamiccasamuppda), the Buddha explained that t[cG (taGh), the cause of suffering, arises as a reaction to vedan. By learning to observe vedan objectively one can avoid any new reactions, and can experience directly within oneself the reality of impermanence (anicca). This experience is essential for understanding the nature of attachment, leading to liberation of the mind.

Vipassana

Vipassan (Pli) or vipasyan (Sanskrit) means "insight". While it is often referred to as Buddhist meditation, the practice taught by the Buddha was non-sectarian, and has universal application. It does not require conversion to Buddhism. While the meditation practices themselves vary from school to school, the underlying principle is the investigation of phenomena as they manifest in the five aggregates (skandhas) namely, matter or form (rkpa), sensation or feelings (vedan), perception (saCjn, Pli sann), mental formations (saCskra, Pli saEkhra) and consciousness (vijnna, Pli vinnGa). This process leads to direct experiential perception, vipassan.

In a broader sense, vipassan has been used as one of two poles for the categorization of types of Buddhist meditation, the other being samatha (Pli) or [amatha (Sanskrit). Samatha is a focusing, pacifying and calming meditation, common to many traditions in the world, notably yoga. It is used as a preparation for vipassan, pacifying the mind and strengthening the concentration in order to allow the work of insight. This dichotomy is also sometimes discussed as "stopping and seeing." In Buddhist practice, it is said that while samatha can calm the mind, only insight can reveal how the mind was disturbed to start with, which leads to prajn (Pli: pann, knowledge) and jnna (Pli: nGa, pure wisdom) and thus can lead to preventing it from being disturbed again.

The term is also used to refer to a religious movement modelled after Theravda Buddhism which employs Vipassan and npna meditation as its primary techniques and places emphasis on the teachings of the Satipammhna Sutta. Vedan (sensation/feeling) is the primary initial subject of investigation.

Etymology: Vipassan is a Pali word from the Sanskrit prefix "vi-" and verbal root dr[. It is often translated as "insight" or "clear-seeing," though, the "in-" prefix may be misleading; "vi" in Indo-Aryan languages is cognate to our "dis." The "vi" in vipassan may then mean to see apart, or discern. Alternatively, the "vi" can function as an intensive, and thus vipassan may mean "seeing deeply". In any case, this is used metaphorically for a particularly powerful mental self-perception. A synonym for "Vipassan" is paccakkha (Pli; Sanskrit: pratyakca), "before the eyes," which refers to direct experiential perception. Thus, the type of seeing denoted by "vipassan" is that of direct perception, as opposed to knowledge derived from reasoning or argument.

Practice of Vipassan: Vipassan meditation is a very simple, logical technique which depends on direct experience and observation. It can be related to the three trainings taught by the Buddha as the basis of a spiritual path-adherence to (abstinence from killing, stealing, lying, sexual misconduct and intoxication), which is not an end in itself but a requirement for the second part, concentration of the mind (samdhi). With this concentrated mind, the third training, in the context of this technique (pann, Sanskrit prajn), is detached observation of the reality of the mind and body from moment to moment. This practice both develops a deep, experiential understanding of the impermanence of reality and also brings to the surface and dissolves deep-seated complexes and tensions. Put another way, Vipassan meditation consists of the experiential observation of mind and matter (nma and rkpa) in their aspects of impermanence, unsatisfactoriness and lack of an inherent, independent essence or self.

To see through the mode of impermanence means to examine things as to whether they are permanent. To see through the mode of unsatisfactoriness means to examine things as to whether they are satisfactory or are imbued with suffering. To see through the mode of non-self means to examine the phenomena that are the objects of the meditation to see if they have a permanent, isolated, and enduring entity. In other words, to see through non-self relates to having a sense of non-doership and a sense of non-possessorship while examining things. In Vipassan meditation, the meditation object is one's own consciousness, although it can be further refined to be one's consciousness while observing, say, the breath, as in npna meditation. In this context, the modes of seeing refers to focusing on those aspects of consciousness which appear to have (or not have) these characteristics. Some steps are described as vipassan jhnas, or simply as knowledges. A major 19th century vipassan instructor in Burma was Ledi Sayadaw.

Vipassan Today: Today, the term "Vipassan" also refers to a series of meditation techniques used by many branches of modern Theravda Buddhism, for example in modern Sri Lanka, Burma, Laos and Thailand, and to a specific branch of Buddhism popularized by the Indian businessman S.N. Goenka and his mentor U Ba Khin as a nonsectarian form of Buddhism, and also by Americans Joseph Goldstein, Sharon Salzberg, and

Jack Kornfield (who were inspired by the monks Mahasi Sayadaw and Ajahn Chah) under the rubric "insight meditation." The vipassan centres supported by S.N. Goenka are present around the world in more than 100 countries. Here locals and visitors can have vipassan training, always given free of charge including accommodation and meals.

Vipassan in the Theravda, Mahyna and Vajrayna

In the Theravda: Vipassan as practiced in the Theravda is the understanding of the Four Noble Truths that were taught by the Buddha. It is understanding the transitory nature of phenomena and the selflessness of persons, that the conceptual consciousness, "I" does not exist. Most of Theravda's teachers refer to knowledges evolving during practice. The meditator gradually improve his perception of the three marks of existence until he reaches the step sensations constantly disappear, which is called bhaEgnupassan nGa (Sanskrit: bhaEgnupa[yanjnna), knowledge of dissolution. The yogi will then experience fear and ceasing of attachment, and eventually will reach the step of knowledge of equanimity of formations. This step leads to the attainment of nirva. In practise one can use various methods to do Vipassan Meditation. For example one method is that there are 40 topics that can be concentrated by the meditator such as anitya (Pli anicca, impermanence), dukha (Pli dukkha, suffering), roga (illness), and so on. The meditator can meditate on one of these until he sees the truth in everything in the universe.

In the Mahyna: Mahyna Vipaayan consists of meditating on the two truths: conventional truth and absolute truth. One realizes that phenomena likewise have a lack of inherent existence, and have the nature of emptiness (knyat). This is determined by the inferential path of reasoning and direct observation through meditation. Gradualism or subitism and the realisation is a debate in the Mahyna. Nevertheless, Huineng, sixth patriarch of the Chan, considered the practice cannot be described as gradualistic nor subitist, but implies people with more or less clear minds.

In the Vajrayna: Mahmudr and Dzogchen use Vipa[yana extensively, though in a different manner than in the Theravda.

In the Vajrayna (tantric) path, the true nature of mind is pointed out by the guru, and the practitioner takes the path of direct experience.

"In the Sktra path (Theravda) one proceeds by examining and analyzing phenomena, using reasoning. One recognizes that all phenomena lack any true existence and that all appearances are merely interdependently related and are without any inherent nature. They are empty yet apparent, apparent yet empty. The path of Mahmudr is different in that one proceeds using the instructions concerning the nature of mind that are given by one's guru. This is called taking direct perception or direct experiences as the path. The fruition of [amatha is purity of mind, a mind undisturbed by false conception or emotional afflictions. The fruition of vipa[yan is knowledge (prajn) and pure wisdom (jnna). Jnna is called the wisdom of nature of phenomena and it comes about through the realization of the true nature of phenomena."

Thrangu Rinpoche, Looking Directly at Mind : The Moonlight of Mahmudr

Vipassan in Prisons: In 1993, Kiran Bedi, a reformist Inspector General of India's prison learned of the success of using Vipassan in a jail in Jainpur, Rajasthan. This 10 day course involved officials and inmates alike. In India's largest prison, Tihar Jail, near New Delhi, another attempt was made. This program was said to have dramatically changed the behavior of inmates and jailers alike.

It was actually found that inmates who completed the 10 day course were less violent and had a lower recidivism rate than other inmates. This project was documented in the television documentary, Doing Time, Doing Vipassana. So successful was this program that it was adopted by correctional facilities in the United States and other countries as well.

Vipassana Jhanas: Vipassana jhanas are steps that describe the evolution of Vipassana's practice. They contrast with samatha's jhanas. The usual description opposes the concentration attained by practicing samatha : the jhanas, and concentration used in vipassana : neighborhood concentration (upacara samadhi). Nevertheless, Sayadaw U Pandita, a disciple of Mahasi Sayadaw, describes four vipassana jhanas.

- The meditator first explores his body, then his mind, discovering the three characteristics. The first jhana consist in seeing these points and in the presence of vitakka and vicara. Phenomena reveal themselves as appearing and ceasing.
- In the second Jhana, the practice seems quite automatic. Vitaka and vicara both disappear.
- In the third Jhana, piti, the joy, disappears too: there is only happiness (sukha) and concentration.
- Then the practice leads to knowledge. The comfort disappears because the disparition seems the only phenomenon; this step is known as bhanga nupassana. The practice will become very difficult, showing every phenomenon as terrible, dangerous, disenchanting. The desire of freedom will take place. Upekkha, equanimity, will emerge, as the state of mind of an arahant.

The only further steps are the knowledge of attaining Nirvana.

Vipassana Knowledges: This unusual description of Vipassana's practice does not replace vipassana knowledge. Bhanga nupassana is one example of traditional step on the way of wisdom. The steps to nirvana were also described by Buddhaghosa as five purities following purity of discipline (sila) and purity of mind (samadhi), in his famous Visuddhimagga.

Vitakka: Vitakka or Vitarka both in hinduist yoga and Buddhist meditation, means the action of taking care of any object : God, one's body, the Self, a color, any sensation... It refers to attention in a different way than cognitive neuroscience, implying a very strong leading of attention, as it leads to more mental process : sukha and ekaggat. Vitakka is the first element to appear in meditation's process, still present in the first Jhana, but absent of any further Jhana.

7

JAINISM

Jainism was born in India about the same period as Buddhism. It was established by Mahavira in about 500 B. C. Mahavira like Buddha belonged to the warrior caste. Mahavira was called 'Jina' meaning the big winner and from this name was derived the name of the religion.

In many senses Jainism is similar to Buddhism. Jainism like Buddhism, developed as a dissention to the Brahmanic philosophy that was dominant during that period in north-east India. Mahavira just like Buddha isn't the first prophet of his religion. In Jainism like Buddhism there is a belief in reincarnation which eventually leads to liberation. Both these religions don't center in religious philosophy around Almighty worship. But Jainism is different than Buddhism in its ascetic beliefs. Both these religions emphasis on non-violence, but in Jainism non-violence is its main core.

Jains believe that every thing has life and this also includes stones, sand, trees and every other thing. The fact that trees breath came to be known to the science world only from the 20th century. Mahavira who believed that every thing has life and also believed in non-violence practically didn't eat anything causing his self-starvation to death. Mahavira was also extremely ascetic and walked around completely naked because of his renouncement of life.

Mahavira's religion followers are less extreme than him in diets. They are vegetarians. But the religious Jains will do everything possible to prevent hurting any being. They won't walk in fields where there are insects to prevent the possibility of stepping on them. They also cover their mouth to prevent the possibility of swallowing small invisible microbes. They mostly do not work in professions where there is a possibility of killing any living being like in agriculture instead professions like banking and business. But it is not clear what came first, businessmen who adopted Jain philosophy because it was easy for them to follow or Jainish philosophy which convinced the Jains to adopt non violent professions.

There are two Jain philosophies. Shvetember and Digamber. Digamber monks like Mahavira don't wear any clothes, but normally they don't walk like that outside their temples. The Digambers include among them only men. The Shvetembers monks wear white clothes and they include women.

Gave us Non-Violence as an Ethical Outlook

Parallel to Buddhism another religion has flourished in India since ancient times. This is the Jaina religion or Jainism. The term Jaina or Jain implies follower of Jina which means 'the victorious one'. Jina is the formal title of the 24 spiritual teachers (Tirthankaras) of the Jaina religion. In this sense the term 'Jina' is similar to the term 'Buddha. Popularly, Mahavira who was the last Jaina Tirthankara is confounded to be the founder of this faith. But as per Jaina records, 23 Tirthankaras preceded him. He was only the last and incidentally the most famous Tirthankara.

Jainism like Buddhism arose us a protest against the ritualism of the Hindu religion. It's origin is traced to Vedic times. The first Jaina Tirthankara was Rishabha. After his appearance, 23 Tirthankaras made their appearance at successive intervals of decreasing length of time. Details about their lives are given in the Jaina treatise Kalpa-Sutra. The 23rd Tirthankara was Parshwanath who though not as famous as Mahavira is still widely remembered among the Jains. Parshwanath is said to have lived 250 years before Mahavira.

The Life Story of Mahavira

Mahavira lived in the 6th century B.C.E. and was a contemporary of Gautama Buddha. There are close parallels not only the teaching of Buddha and Mahavira but also in the story of their lives. Mahavira, like Gautama Buddha was born in a kshatriya family. His father whose name incidentally was Siddhartha, belonged to the Kashyapa clan and was ruler of Kundagrama located near the powerful kingdom of Vaishali, Mahavira's mother Trishala was the sister of the reigning king of Vaishali. That Mahavira himself is referred to at times as Vaishilika is an evident proof of Mahavira's close connection with this powerful kingdom located in eastern India.

According to Jaina legend, Mahavira was to be borne by a Brahmin woman but his embryo was transferred to that of a Kshatriya woman, for it was impossible for a person so great to be born "in low families, mean families, degraded families, beggar's families or Brahmin families". This statement in the Kalpa-Sutra is an indication of ill-feeling that existed in ancient times between the practitioners of Vedic rituals and the Jainas.

The name given to Mahavira at birth was Vardhamana or 'increaser'. But later on he acquired fame as Mahavira or the 'Great Hero' which we are told was a name bestowed to him by the Gods. When he was thirty years old his parents died and in fulfillment of a promise, he decided to renounce material pleasures and meditate in solitude Like the Buddha, he subjected himself to severe penances, he had stripped himself naked observed fast and neglected his body. After revelation he spread his gospel among the people. At his death his following was considerable.

Similarities and Differences with Buddhism

Unlike Buddhism, the Jaina faith does not seem to have received considerable royal patronage in Northern India. The only great pan-Indian monarch said to have embraced Jainism was Chandragupta Maurya and he seems to have embraced it at the end of his reign. On embracing Jainism he is said to have renounced his throne in favour of his son Bindusara and migrated to the Jain spiritual centre at Shranvanabelgola in Karnataka (South India). In South India though, many local kings did give generous grants to Jains to build beautiful temples and monoliths of Bahubali.

At Khajuraho in central India, the Chandellas in the 10th century did build some temples dedicated to Parshwanath. But despite the absence of considerable royal patronage, Jainism has kept itself alive through the ages although its following has always been a modest one. Unlike Buddhism, Jainism has remained limited to India and never spread overseas. In India also its followers are concentrated in North Gujarat, South Rajasthan, around Agra region in Uttar Pradesh and Sammed Shikhar in North India. Jains are also found in parts of Karnataka in the South.

Two Sects-Shwetambara and Digambara

The followers of Jainism are divided into two sects, *viz.*, the Digambars or 'sky-clad' who theoretically accept the principle of a living person being shorn of garments. The second sect is that of the Shwetambars who clothe themselves with unstitched white cloth. The Shwetambars split from the main body of the Jaina religion some 200 years after Mahavira but today they account for a majority among the Jains. The Shwetambar Jains are concentrated in Gujarat and Rajasthan. The Digambars are mostly found in Karnataka.

The Central Principal of Jivadaya-Respect for all Living Forms

The principle that is central to the Jaina religion is that of Jivadaya (Respect for all Living Forms) and Ahimsa (non-violence). Although Ahimsa is recognised even by the Buddhists and the Hindus, it is practised ritually, only amongst the Jains. Under this obligation they abstain entirely from meat, fruit and wine and may drink only that water which has been used earlier by someone else for cooking.

The logic behind this is that if by drinking such water if a Jain causes harm to any living organisms in the water, the guilt for that rests not on the Jain who drinks it but on the person who first used it for cooking. For the same reason a Jain monk does not bathe lest he should inadvertently destroy life, nor is he allowed to move about except on foot, he is prohibited from lighting a fire or to breath openly for which a piece of white cloth is tied loosely around his mouth so as to prevent the inadvertent killing of living organisms in the air by inhaling them. All this would appear ridiculous to a non-Jain or even to a modern-day Jain.

Despite these strictures against harming or killing any living creature, remarkably this logic is not applied by the Jains to themselves.

When certain conditions have been fulfilled, a Jain ascetic may undertake Samadhi (defined in theological literature as a state of 'Super-consciousness' and is considered by lay people to be a suicide for religious reasons). This act is not only innocent, but is an act of merit or even a duty. The concept of Samadhi is not peculiar among the Jains. It exists amongst the Hindus too.

An Order of Jaina Monks (Munis) and Nuns (Sadhvis)

Like the Buddhists, the Jains have an order of Monks. In addition to Monks, the Shwetambars also have an order of Nuns called Sadhvis. In addition to the alms bowl, a Jain monk is supposed to carry a broom to sweep the ground before them as they walk on it so as to clear away whatever living creatures that may be there. The institution of monks no doubt is derived from the Hindu concept of Sanyasa. During the four months (Chatur-masa) of the monsoon, a Jaina monk is required to stay indoors so as to avoid treading on the many creatures that run around during the rains. This observance, during the four months of the monsoon is shared by the Jains with the Buddhists and is perhaps derived from the Hindu concept of Chatur-masa during which indoor spiritual activity is recommended probably due to the physical difficulty of journeying during the rainy season

KAIVALYA—THE JAINA CONCEPT OF SALVATION

Like the Buddhists, the Jains have a concept of *Kaivalya* which is similar to the Buddhist concept of Nirvana but the connotation differs from that in Buddhism. The Jaina connotation of Nirvana is derived from their interpretation of the universe. According to Jains, all things in existence are divided into two parts Jiva (*i.e.* living beings having a soul) and

Ajiva (non-living things having no soul). The entanglement of living beings (Jiva) with things not having souls (Ajiva) is a source of all misery. Kaivalya is a result of a living beings becoming free of this entanglement. In this concept of Kaivalya, the Hindu attitude of not expecting the fruits of labour as preached by Srikrishna in the Geeta is reflected. As in the Hindu concept of Moksha, Kaivalya is attained in Jainism as a 'release from the cycle of rebirth' when the soul is free of attachment to all material things. Till the soul is so entangled, it has to continue to be reborn.

Affinity of Jainism with Hinduism

Like the Hindus, the Jains also believe in ages that are defined in terms of morality. Unlike the four ages that are recognised in Hinduism, the Jains recognise only two *viz.* the Utsarpini or Ascending and the Avasarpini or descending. This connotation of these two ages have a close parallel in the Satyuga and Kaliyuga of the Hindus. Over the ages the Jains have in practice drawn so near to Hinduism as to present outwardly little difference in modes of worship and ritual. The Jains reject the authority of the Vedas but recognize the caste System.

Jainism's Contribution to Hinduism

The Jains like the Hindus (today) practice *Moorti Puja* (Image Worship). In fact, Moorti Puja is a gift of the Jains to Hinduism. In the Vedic age, Hindus did not practice Moorti Puja. The Gods were the forces of nature who were not personified and they were propitiated through the yagnas. Later on came the first break in Hinduism, when a section of the Hindus declared that the performing a Yagna sacrifice-where many animals were originally offerred-was an act of apostasy and that the Vedas were not the true embodiment of knowledge.

These breakaway Hindus later became the Jains, who for the first time in India (after perhaps the Indus or Saraswati valley civilization) introduced the worship of Images. One instance of such worship is that of the image of the Bahubali who was the son of Rishabha Deva, the first tirthankara. Such

Jain shrines with images are found at many places all over India, some of these places are Shravanabelagola, Palitana and Sammed Shikhar.

This practice of Moorti Puja was absorbed by the rest of the Hindus as their mode of worhip too and later on came the first personified Gods of the Hindus like Brahma-Vishnu-Mahesh and then Sri Rama, Sri Krishna, Shakti, etc. Thus Moorti Poja which was pioneered by the Jain sect, became the most important and far-reaching contribution that the Jains made to Hinduism. This contribution was only second to their other contribution of the concept of Ahimsa and Jivadaya which also the Hindus borrowed from Jainism and Buddhism.

However, though the Jains were the first to split from the Hindu mainstream, nowadays there is observed among the Jains, a sub-conscious tendency to move into Hinduism. Many Jains allow themselves, whether by indifference or set purpose, to be described as Hindus. Though Jainism, like Buddhism arose as a reform movement directed at the then prevailing form of worship that made up Hinduism. It has in modern times shown a stronger tendency for being reabsorbed into the mother faith from which it sprang.

Before, we move ahead, we need to mention here that the difference between the collection of modes of worship termed Hinduism with that of the sects which broke away from the Hindu mainstream was that while within Hinduism, the different Hindu sects recognised all the dieties of the Hindu pantheon, when selecting one deity as its patron deity (Ista-Devata), the sects that broke away, withdrew recognition to the other deities of the Hindu pantheon. This was the only difference between the various sects within Hinduism and the sects that broke away from the Hindu mainstream.

8

Other Religions of India

ZOROASTRIANISM

A small religious community, which exists mostly in Mumbai, is Zoroastrianism. The follower is called Parsi because the religion arrived in India from Persia. This religion was established by Zarathustra in 6th or 7th century BC. The followers of this religion exiled from Iran in the 7th century AD. because of religious persecutions by the Muslims. They arrived in Gujarat region of India.

The Parsis believe in the existence of one invisible God. They believe that there is a continuous war between the good forces (forces of light) and the evil forces (forces of darkness). The good forces will win if people will do good deeds think good and speak well. God is represented in their temples through fire, which symbolizes light. The holiest place for them is the village of Udvada in Gujarat, India. The holy language of the Parsis is an ancient language spoken in Iran, Avesta. The Parsis believe that fire, water, air and earth are pure element to be preserved and therefore they do not cremate or bury their dead ones but leave them on high towers, specially built for this purpose, to be eaten by hawks and crows.

The Parsis are less then 0.02% of India's population but their contribution to India is much more than their proportion in India's population. Some Parsis were main figures in establishing the Indian Nationalist movement. They were the pioneers in establishing the modern Indian industry. The rich Parsi families contributed enormously to establish institutions of all kinds in India. Even today some of the bigger finance houses in India belong to followers of this religion.

A community in whose religious ceremonies the invocation of fire occupies the central place, who wear the sacred thread, whose ancestors worshipped gods named Mitra Vayu, Veretraghna, whose society was traditionally divided into various orders of priests, warriors and peasants, who consider themselves descendants of the Aryans-a race which originally lived in the sub-Artic regions near the North Pole-this obviously is a description of the Aryan settlers of India. Yes, but it applies equally well to the ancestors of the inhabitants of Iran and the Zoroastrian Parsis who migrated from Iran and settled in India around 900 C.E.

In talking about the ancient history of the Parsis, we have to begin at the same point as we would when we talk of the history of the Vedic Aryan immigrants of India. Racially Zoroaster was of the Indo-European stock which about 2000 B.C.E. had divided into two great sections. One was spreading west to settle in Europe. This is also called the Cetum group by historians from the Latin word Centum meaning, a hundred. The other group of Aryans moved east and further divided itself into two groups. This eastward bound group is called by historians the Shatem group from the Sanskrit Shatam for 100. Of these east bound Aryans one group settled in what is now India and the other in the land we now call Iran.

The word Iran is itself a corruption of the original word Airyana meaning land of the Aryans'. **India** was referred as Aryavarta which also means 'land of the Aryans'. Many root-words and racial customs from the original people still survive in these communities. The words for mother, father, brother, etc., are practically the same in the language of the Avesta (holy book of the Zoroastrians) and that of the Veda, they are also similar in Latin, Greek, English, German, Russian and other Indo-European languages.

An Indian especially can find many familiar root words in the text of the Zoroastrian Scriptures. The word Zarathustra which in the Avestan language means 'Loving the camel' (Zarath means to love and Ustra means camel) is exactly identical with the Sanskrit word for camel which also is Ushtra. The Zoroastrian term Vohu Manah meaning 'Good Thoughts' also has a very Similar Sanskrit word 'mana' for mind. Other similarities include 'Kshtra' which means power in both Sanskrit and Avestan Pahlavi.

Amertat which means immortality in Avestan comes close to the Sanskrit word Amara for Immortality, the word Asha, which means righteousness 'in Avestan means hope' in Sanskrit, though not identical the connotations are close, the Avestan word Gatha which means a holy book is same as in Sanskrit.

Here is a rock edict at Naqsh-i-Rustam in Iran engraved at the orders of Darius (Darayavayush) the Persian Emperor of the 5th Century B.C.E. which says:

"Adam Darayavaush Khshaayathiya vaazraka,

Khshaayathiya Khshaayathiyaanaam,

Parsyha Parshya Puthra Arya, Arya Chitra.

This is translated as:

"I Daries, the great King, The King of Kings, A Parsi, the son of a Parsi, an Aryan of Aryan family". This comes quite close to Sanskrit and to a person unfamiliar with languages could be confusingly similar.

Zoroaster's Life Story

Zoroaster was born in 660 B.C.E. He was born into the Spitama family. Zoroaster's mother Dughdova was said to be a virgin since she conceived after she had been visited by a shaft of light. The parallel with Jesus Christ Who came later in evident. It is also interesting to note that Zoroaster's lineage is traced to Gayomart (the Persian Adam) through his father just as that of Jesus is traced by Luke to Adam through Joseph.

Both his father's name Pourushapa and his mother's name Dughdova bear striking resemblance with the Sanskrit words having the; same meaning. This a combination of the two words Pourushapa or Purusha in Sanskrit which means man and Aspa, which becomes Ashva in Sanskrit which means a horse. The term Dughda in Duagdova means milk in Sanskrit and Avestan. This is underlines the striking Similarity between the two Indo-Aryan languages in the 7th century B.C.E.

The boy Zarathustra whose name means 'Lover of Camels' lived up to his name by feeding other peoples' cattle from his father's barn. Once he is reported to have brought bread to feed a dying dog. Between the ages of fifteen and thirty we hear little about him. Tradition asserts that in the interval there was a long period of wilderness meditation.

During his meditations the story goes that one day at daybreak when Zoroaster stood upon the bank of the third channel of the sacred river Daiti, the Gods appeared before him. As he lifted some of the holy Water he suddenly saw a figure coming to him from the south bearing a shinning staff. It was the archangel Vohu Manah nine times as large as man. He bade the enrapt Zoroaster to lay aside his body and follow him to the audience-room of the great Ahura-mazda.

Here Zoroaster was taught the cardinal principles of the true religion. After this experience, Zoroaster returned to the earth, assumed his body, and following the instructions from Ahura-mazda Preached for two years to the religious leaders of his country. His sermon had four points :

Worship Ahura-mazda

Magnify the archangels

Damn the demons

Marry you nearest relative.

But this preaching fell on cold ears, he was scorned and ridiculed. The disappointed prophet turned homewards: and for some years wandered preaching without success. : In fact there were ten long years between the revelation and the first convert. And this convert was his own cousin Metyomah. For two years following the conversion of Metyomah, Zoroaster spent his energies trying to convert the King Vishtaspa to the new faith. Now Vishtaspa was a mighty monarch in eastern Iran whose realm was especially devoted to those aspects of the old religion which was most distasteful to Zoroaster.

Superstition and dark magic was practiced by the Kais (chief Priests) and Karaps (scribes). His duel of wits with the chief priests and scribes of Vishtaspa's court are referred to by his later followers as the 'terrible conflict'. Thirty Three questions were put to Zoroaster by the magicians of the court. The debate lasted for three days and Zoroaster passed the test.

The beaten priests then bribed Zoroaster's new servant and planted incriminating evidence of witchcraft in his room. When this was discovered, Zoroaster was imprisoned. But in a few days, King Vishtaspa's favourite horse fell ill and none of the courts physicians could restore it to health. The horse's feet had been drawn into the belly due to the sickness. Thereupon, Zoroaster promised to cure the horse on certain conditions. Zoroaster demanded four rewards, one for curing each leg. The king agreed to do this. And when Zoroaster cured the horse, he also won his four fold fee. Zoroasters four fold fee, included that the king accept the new religion the king's son Isfendiar become a crusader for the new faith, the Queen be converted; and the plotting priests be put to death. Thus it was almost a kingdom for a horse.

In the crusading which followed king conversion Zoroaster passed the happiest days of his life. He was ever a crusader for twenty five years, until his violent death at the age of seventy seven. The episode of his death is also intriguing.

In the great war with Arjasp, (who incidentally is supposed to have been mentioned as Rijra-ashva in ancient Sanskrit slokas) the infidel Turanian King, Zoroaster was much occupied. Whether or not the ageing prophet actually used the sword, we do not know. Tradition says he died at the hands of an invading Turanian, but that in the moment of death, the prophet hurled his rosary and killed his murderer.

The Great Achemenian (Hakkamanishiya) Empire

After his death, Zoroastrianism spread throughout Persia. The Achemenian (Hakkamanishiya) emperors who ruled Iran from 550 B.C.E. to 330 B.C.E. were ardent Zoroastrians, though they were also tolerant towards other faiths. The Achemenian empire was founded by Cyrus (Kurush) the Great. It had its capital at Pasargade and later at Persepolis. Persepolis was a grand city in those days. Cambyses (Kambastha), Darius

(Darayavayush), Xerses (Ksharaya), were its leading emperors and the empire stretched from the Danube to the Indus during its heyday.

The Greek Invasion and the Parthians

The last ruler of this line was Darius Condomannus who was defeated by Alexander the Great in 330 B.C.E. After a brief spell of Macedonian (Greek) rule, the Parthians became rulers of Iran.

The Parthians were a native Iranian race and were Zoroastrians, but the intervening Greek rule had made a deep impact on them and the early Parthian emperors were culturally Hellenised. But in late Parthian times, a nationalist revival was seen.

The Sassanians-Zoroastrainism at its Zenith

The Parthians were followed by the Sassanians who ruled Iran from 211 C.E. to 641 C.E. The Sassanians were ardent Zoroastrians and this brought them in conflict with their Armenian subjects who originally were Zoroastrians but had subsequently embraced Christianity. The 405 years of Sassanians rule saw a running struggle between the Persians and the Romans.

The Arab Onslaught

In the early 7th Century, Islam was growing out of: Arabia but the Sassanian and Roman empires were still at each others necks. As late as 628 C.E. the Roman and Persians were engaged in active hostilities. Only six years after that in 634 C.E. the Arabs sent an ultimatum to the Persian Emperor Hormazd and to the then reigning Roman (Byzantine) emperor to embrace Islam or face war. Both empires decided on war. In the year 634 C.E. the Arabs decided first to attack the Persians (Sassanian) in a large way and gave them a shattering blow at the Battle of Cadesia (Quadisiyyah) and captured the Sassanian capital of Ctesiphon (modern Baghdad).

Had the Persians held the Arab hordes at Cadesia, not only would have Persia remained Zoroastrian, but the history of South-Asia would have changed.

The Romans (Byzantines) fared no better. At the battle of Yarmuk only a few days before the battle of Cadesia, the Roman army was defeated by the Arabs and the boundaries of the Roman empire shrank from the Red sea to the Cilician Gates in Turkey. The local Arab population was converted to Islam But the many of the Christian Arabs retreated to the hills of Lebanon.

The conflict of the Maronite Christians in Lebanon with the Muslims which we saw in the 1970s owes its ultimate origin to the Islamic-Arab conquest of the 7th century. Meanwhile, the Romans (Byzantines) held the Arabs at the Cilician Gates (A narrow pass in the Taurus mountains in Southern Turkey) for nearly 700 years till the Uthman (Ottoman) Turks bypassed this mountain range to occupy the whole of Turkey and capture the Byzantine capital of Constantinople (Istanbul) in around 1453. The Turks reached Vienna two centuries later but were driven back into Yugoslavia. The Bosnian Muslims are a result of this Muslim-Turkish rule in Europe.

The Coming of Islam

The Zoroastrian Sassanians of Persia fared extremely badly against the Arabs. After their initial defeat at Cadesia, the Arabs gave a second and mortal blow to the Sassanian Empire in 641 C.E. at the battle of Nehavand.

Yazdgard, the last Sassanian emperor died as a refugee ten years later in 651 A.D. The defeat of the Iranians at the hands of the Arabs has been described by an Iranian historian in the following words, "In 636, in Ghadasi, located on the southern parts of Mesopotamia, Rostam-e-Farrokhzaad, chief commander of Iranian armies faced the new power coming from the south: Muslim Arabs.

Headed by their greatest army genius, Sa'ad ebn Vaghas, and powered by their new faith, Arabs defeated the Iranian Army. Rostam was killed, and Arabs were walking toward Tispoon, the capital of Iran on the banks of Tigris. Yazdgerd flew Tispoon and went to eastern Iran. Arab invaders captured the glorious capital of Sasanids, and plundered the city's treasures. Yazdgerd was killed by the hands of a miller in

Marv. Arabs conquered the rest of the frightened country, and established their rule over the vast empire of Khosro and Shahpour.

"End of Sasanid Era and beginning of the Islamic rule

"There is about 1200 hundred years that people talk about this amazing incident. The defeat of Sasanid Empire from bare-foot Arabs was unbelievable. The same country that hold back in front of the well organized Roman legionaries for over 700 years, could not stop the Arabs."

The subsequent history of Iran is that of Islamization and Arabisation. After the Arabs overran the whole of Iran, a small group of Zoroastrians left that country and came to India to seek asylum. they landed at Sanjan, a place in Gujarat around 900 C.E. and have lived in India ever since.

The Parsis in India

As mentioned at the inception, the Zoroastrian religion and the Parsi Community have many common with the inhabitants of India and much of this similarity is due to the fact that deep in the past, the ancestors of these two peoples sprang from a common Indo-Aryan stock. But this apart the stay of the Parsis in India for many centuries has led to their adopting many Indian customs and attitudes. Their language is Gujarati, the traditional dress of the womenfolk is the Indian saree. During their baptism ceremony (Navjyot) they apply red ochre powder on their foreheads as the Hindu custom of tilaka.

These are some of the cultural traits picked up by the Parsi community from the Hindus. But there are innumerable other similarities which are due to the common origin from one racial stock in pre-historic times. For instance. The Parsi ritual invocation of the Fire is called Yasna (Jashn) which corresponds to the Hindu ritual of Yagna.

The Parsis wear a Kusti (a holy thread around their waist) which corresponds to the 'Hindu Yagnopavit or Janeu worn around the shoulder and the waist. The Parsis also use coconuts and. grains of rice during their Navjyot and wedding ceremonies like the Hindus. There are many other similarities in their cuisine, manners and mannerisms, attitudes, etc., Some of which are due to their common Indo-Aryan origin and some others due to a cultural interchange due. to the residence of the Parsis in India for 1300 years.

JEWS IN INDIA

The Jews of India aren't one singular community. Among themselves they are divided into different communities. Each community has its own different culture, background and origin. Each community claims its arrival in India in different ways and it is not always clear how they really came to India. The three main Jewish communities of India are: Bene Israel, Cochini and Baghdadi. Besides there were Ashkenazi Jews and a community in east India which claim Israeli origin and call themselves Bne Menashe. The first three communities had some social religious connections with each other but most of the social religious connections of each community were within their own community and they regarded the other as 'outsiders'.

Jews have been present in India since the 1st century of our era. Most of the Jews were concentrated in Kerala in South India. Cochin was their main centre of settlement. Even today we have some ancient synagoges at Cochin. They also lived in Western India mainly in Mumbai and Pune.

In Mumbai, Jews from West Asia called Bagdadi Jews immigrated in the 19th century. They were mainly industrialists and traders. Sir David Sasson is the most illustrious name of this community of Jews. In Mumbai, the Jewish community was concentrated in the Jacob Circle (now renamed Gadge Maharaj Chowk) area in Central Bombay. They have a synagogue there.

The Jews in India were a microscopic community of around a few thousands. They had totally integrated themselves with the society around them. Their dress is traditionally Indian. Their womenfolk wear saree; and bangles. Their surnames and family names like those of other Indians. Their culinary habits are totally Indian. (Charles F. Potter-The Story of Religion, Geroge Harrap, London, 1930 PP 111,112)

Their Indian character is so pronounced that even after many of them have migrated to Israel, they are known their as Bene-Israelis. While Israel is their original homeland and it is natural for them to migrate to Israel, the fact that have completely absorbed Indian culture is evident from the fact that the first generation of Indian Jews settling in Israel find it difficult to adjust to their new surroundings. But this too is natural as Israelis are composed of the immigrant Jews who for thousands of years had been living in different foreign countries. As Israel is the original homeland of all Jews, a time may come when there are no more Jews in India, even today they are not more than a few thousands. Though this emigration is a natural one for the Jews to realise their own national and cultural aspirations, we in India do stand to lose a microscopic but dynamic element of ourselves. to the emergent sovereign state of Israel.

JUDAISM

The Lost Tribes Found a Safe Haven in India

We now turn our attention towards a much misunderstood and much maligned religion which was in fact the mother of Christianity. Judaism, the religion of the Jews has many features common with Hinduism.

Commonality with Hinduism

These common features are not a result of cultural interchange alone but owe their a similarity in conditions in which the came into being. The common factor in both these religions is that they have preserved a continuous link with antiquity, in the sense that they were not established by any one person or a group of persons at any identifiable time in history. They had evolved out of the religious attitudes that were nurtured since pre-historic times by humankind. No doubt both the religions have undergone changes with the passage of time but their links with antiquity remained unbroken. Judaism has had a very traumatic and tragic history for the past two thousand five hundred years since the destruction of their first temple up to the establishment of the state of Israel in 1948.

A Diaspora of 2,500 Years

Apart from having been tyrannized, right from Babylonian and Assyrian times 2500 years back when their first temple at Jerusalem was destroyed, the Jews have been oppressed by many subsequent rulers like the Persians, Greeks, Romans and non-Jewish Semitic people (after Islam) in their home-land of Israel. A large part of the history of the Jews was enacted in exile. After the beginning of their diaspora due to Roman persecution about 2000 years back, the Jews have been living in various countries as exiles.

In Europe they were generally looked down And most of the reasons for this were a result of the arbitrary hatred of the community by their hosts. The Spanish inquisition let loose a reign of terror on the Jews living in Spain, when many Jews were burnt at the stake. The latest wholesale organised slaughter the Jews, ' the Holocaust', was the result of a sick Teutonic mind. The Jewish community today still bears the scars of this Hitlerite nightmare. But the Hitlerite legacy is not yet a thing of the past, it exists today in the jaundiced attitude of those who continue to treat the Jewish state as an outcaste with the aim of appeasing the theocratic states around it.

Recent History of the Jews back in their Homeland

The recent history of the Jews is associated with their original homeland called Palestine which was part of the Turkish empire till 1917. Following Germany' s defeat in the First World War, the empire of its ally Turkey was dismembered. The British took a large part of it-Palestine as the spoils of their victory. As a reward for helping them in defeating the Turks, they carved off Palestine and gave away the larger part to a Bedouin Arab, named Abdullah, who became the first Hashemite King of Transjordan (now Jordan) by which the 70% of Palestine was called. his grandson Hussein now rules Jordan. The remainder of Palestine was mandated by the British. In 1947 Britain had to give up control over this part of Palestine which was divided into Israeli and Arab Zones.

The Arab Zone went to Jordan. This division was accepted by the Jews but not by the Arabs. The Arabs went to war in

1948, they lost. They went to war four times after that and lost. They chose to live in refugee camps and did not settle in the other half of Palestine which was now Jordan. Their efforts were concentrated on destruction of the State of Israel and expulsion of the Jews who had returned there after living in exile for more than 2500 years. The Arab states and the Arabs living in what is now Israel could not bring themselves to accept the fact that Israel had been created by dividing Palestine into two parts, with Israel being a homeland for the Jews and the other half of Palestine *i.e.* Jordan, being the country of the Arabs previously residing in Israel.

Today there are many Arabs living in Israel, but most Arabs whether living in Israel or outside it have never reconciled themselves in their heart of hearts to the fact of Israel's existence, unlike the way Indians have accepted Pakistan. Pakistan which too was created after partitioning a formerly united ~ country. Israel is today like a fishbone stuck in the Arab throat and try as they can the Arabs have not so far been able to spit it out. But due to international pressures and Israel's conciliatory approach, we see today a state of Palestine which occupies parts of territory which had formed a part of Israel since 1967.

The establishment of the state of Israel in 1948 was the only ray of light in the history of the Jewish community. The remarkable progress achieved by the state of Israel amidst oppressive conditions of the mid-east, is a 20th century miracle. Any other community would have easily withered away in the face of the challenges that Israel faces. The ancient history of the virile community is as glorious as its present. It has given us Solomon, Abraham, Moses not to mention Jesus Christ, Karl Marx, Albert Einstien and many others.

The origins of Judaism are lost in thc misty realms of the past. The Old Testament like the Rig Veda of the Hindus, cannot be dated. One of the composers of the Old Testament is Moses. Even to talk about him we have to go thirteen centuries before Jesus Christ *i.e.* 3,300 years behind our age. The Jewish religion is even older than Moses.

The pre-mosaic religion of the Jews is considered to have been a mixture of animism and fetishism. Certain places and objects were worshipped as sacred. The natural feeling of awe which came upon the Hebrew speaking nomads of pre-biblical times, when they viewed a mountain a majestic tree or the starry host of heavens, it grew into a superstitious recognition of the powers supposed to be resident there. These powers were called elohim. The singular of which is Eloha or el, meaning 'lord'. (The Arabic term "Allah" is quite close to the hebrew "Eloha")

The transformation from the plural elohim to the singular eloha was perhaps due to the Mosaic injunction according to which Yahweh (Jehovah) says ' Though shalt have no other Gods, but me'. (This finds reflection in the Islamic dictum "There is no God, but Allah".) Some scholars maintain that Yahweh himself was a local god of the Kenites or Cannanites, a Hebrew tribe, and that Moses' father-in-law was a priest of that tribe who initiated Moses into Yahweh worship. Thus Yahweh may well have been originally a local god, but Moses made Yahweh the universal God of all Hebrews. The word Yahweh means 'he who causes to be', has been interpreted variously as 'the creator', the 'fulfiller of promises' and more recently as 'the God of Procreation'.

The word Moses is in the original Hebrew, Mosheh and might have been derived from the Hebrew verb mashah, ' to draw out. Thus the word Moses may mean Deliverer or saviour. It is possible that he was named, or rather re-named 'Deliverer after he delivered the Jews from their bondage in Egypt

From the biblical legends about Moses we learn that he spent his youth in Egypt. He is supposed to have married f a women called Zipporah. The first meeting of Moses with Zipporah was at the usual place where pastoral men and maidens met and their courtship began when Moses helped Zipporah to water her flock of sheep. The first child of Moses and Zipporah was given the the name Gershom which means stranger and the second one was named Eliezer which means 'God help me'.

The names Moses gave his children indicated the discontent in Moses' mind. The name ' stranger' seems to reflect the slavery of Jews in Egypt and the second name is an invocation for divine assistance As Moses was a shepherd he had plenty of time to think and every great-religions leader has come forth with a message after a long period of meditation in a lonely g place. We are told that during his meditations God appeared before Moses like a flame of light. Describing his experience Moses said that, as he walked along leading the flock of sheep to the back of the wilderness near the Mountain of God (Horeb-Sinai) he saw a burst of flame with an angel in its midst.

Then he noticed that the f lame came from a bush which burned but was not consumed, and from the bush, God spoke saying that He had long been the God of the Hebrews, even in the days of the fathers, that He knew about the oppression of His people (in Egypt). Then came the divine commission "Come now and I will send thee unto Pharoah, that thou may bring forth my people the children of Israel out of Egypt Inspired by his new found religion and anxious to inform his people that Yahweh would bring them out of bondage, Moses started for Egypt taking his wife Zipporah and his two infant sons with him.

After impressing the Egyptian Pharoah with magic tricks, Moses acquired liberty for the Jews in Egypt. Now it was Moses' task to lead the Jews out of Egypt to the holy land of Israel. Another of his problems was to make wise laws to maintain proper relations among the anatagonistic groups and tribes. With this aim he formulated or rather gave the Jews the following "Ten Commandments" which he had received from Yahweh.

Bibliography

Aiyar, R. Krishnaswami: *Outlines of Vedaanta*, Chetana, Bombay, 1978.

Anwarullah : *The Islamic Law of Evidence,* Kitab Bhavan, New Delhi, 2000.

Arnold, Sir Thomas W.: *Painting in Islam: A Study of the Place of Pictorial Art in Muslim Culture*, New York, 1965.

Auboyer, Jeannine: *Buddha: A Pictorial History of His Life and Legacy,* Crossroad, New York, 1983.

Behl, Benoy K.: *The Ajanta Caves: Artistic Wonder of Ancient Buddhist India,* Harry N. Abrams, New York, 1998.

Bhattacharji, Sukumari: *Literature in the Vedic Age*, Kali Ram Press, Calcutta, 1984.

Chaturvedi, M.D.,: *Hinduism, The Eternal Religion,* Bharatiya Vidya Bhavan, Bombay, 1992.

Datta, M. R.: *The Secret Serpent,* Kali Ram Press, Calcutta, 1913.

DeLamotte, Roy C.: *Jalaluddin Rumi, Songbird of Sufism,* Lanham, Md., University Press of America, 1980.

Dimock, Edward C.: *In Praise of Krishna*, University of Chicago Press, Chicago, 1998.

Edward, Mortimer : *Faith and Power, the Politics of Islam,* Oxford, New York, 2002.

Goetz, Hermann: *The Art of India*, MacMillan, New York, 1964.

Grisenold, H.D.: *Insights into Modern Hinduism*, Oxford, New York, 1934.

Harman, William: *The Sacred Marriage of a Hindu Goddess,* Indiana University Press, Bloomington, 1989.

Hassan, M. : *Hadrat Abu Bakr Siddique (R.A.A.),* Kitab Bhavan, New Delhi, 2004.

Hopkins, Thomas J.: *The Hindu Religious Tradition*, Dickenson, California, 1971.

Horner, I. B.: *The Living Thoughts of Gautama the Buddha,* Cassell, London, 1948.

Jafar, Sharif : *Islam in India,* Oxford, New Delhi, 1972.

Keith, Arthur Berriedale: *The Religion and Philosophy of the Veda and Upanishads*, MacMillan, Delhi, 1925.

Kottackal, Jacob: *Religion and Ethics in Advaita*, C.M.S. Press, Kottayam, 1982.

Mahendranath, S.: *Comparative Studies in Vedaantism*, Humphrey Milford, Bombay, 1927.

McDermott, James P.: *Karma and Rebirth in Classical Indian Traditions,* University of California Press, Berkeley, 1980.

Prime, Ranchor: *Hinduism and Ecology*, Motilal Banarsidass, Delhi 1994.

Schmitz Barbara: *Islamic Manuscripts in the New York Public Library*, New York, 1992.

Schwartz, H.: *Reimaging the Bible: The Storytelling of the Rabbis,* Oxford University Press, New York, 1998.

Seneviratna, Anuradha: *King Ashoka and Buddhism,* Buddhist Publication Society, Kandy, 1994.

Sergeant : *Constitution of Madina,* Feroz Pub., Lahore, 1992.

Sivaramamurti, C.: *Sri Lakshmi in Indian Art and Thought*, Kanak, New Delhi, 1982.

Tejomayananda, Swami: *Hindu Culture: An Introduction,* Chinmaya Publications, Piercy, 1993.

Vable, D.: *The Arya Samaj. Hindu without Hinduism.* Vikas Publ., Delhi, 1983.

Vidya, D.: *Yogini Cult and Temples: A Tantric Tradition*, National Museum, New Delhi, 1985.

Wagle, Narendra: *Society at the Time of Buddha,* Humanities Press, New York, 1967.

Welch, S. C., and Welch, Anthony: *Arts of the Islamic Book: The Collection of Prince Sadruddin Aga Khan*, Ithaca, 1982.

Yusuf, S.M. : *Economic Justice in Islam,* Kitab Bhavan, New Delhi, 1988.

INDEX

□□□